BORN TO SCORE

DWIGHT YORKE

BORN TO SCORE

MACMILLAN

First published in Great Britain 2009 by Macmillan
an imprint of Pan Macmillan Ltd
Pan Macmillan, 20 New Wharf Road, London N1 9RR
Basingstoke and Oxford
Associated companies throughout the world
www.panmacmillan.com

ISBN 978-0-230-74203-1 HB
ISBN 978-0-230-74457-8 TPB

1 3 5 7 9 8 6 4 2

A CIP catalogue record for this book is available from
the British Library.

Typeset by Ellipsis Books Limited, Glasgow
Printed and bound in the UK by
CPI Mackays, Chatham, ME5 8TD

For Harvey, so that he may know the truth,
and for Orlando, who already does.

PICTURE ACKNOWLEDGEMENTS

All photographs are from the author's personal collection apart from the following:

Big Pictures: page 14 bottom, page 15 top

Debbie Bragg: page 16

Getty: page 4 bottom, page 5 top, page 8 top, page 9 middle & bottom, page 11, page 13 top

Mirrorpix: page 5 bottom, page 6, page 7 bottom, page 10 bottom, page 14 top

Press Association: page 2, page 3 bottom, page 4 top, page 7 top, page 8 middle & bottom, page 9 top, page 10 top

Offside: page 3 top, page 13 bottom

CONTENTS

FOREWORD

When I was in London there was always a good chance that you'd find me in the Funky Buddha nightclub in Mayfair. It's the perfect weekend spot and *the* place to hang out with celebrities, actors and actresses. As a successful footballer with more than my fair share of headlines on and off the pitch, I valued discretion. That frequently meant sneaking in and out of the club through the back to avoid the constant attentions of the paparazzi out the front. Over time I became very good friends with Eddie, the owner, who would always look after me. He made sure his staff afforded me special attention.

A Tuesday night in June 2004 found me at my favourite London venue killing a few hours before going on holiday to Dubai the following day. The season was over – thank God because it had been a bad one – and I was leaving my copious troubles behind and flying off to catch up on some well-needed R & R. But before that, I was enjoying some downtime. Or so I thought. One of the mates I was hanging out with back then was Lennox Lewis and I could have done with him that night.

It was getting very, very late. I had had a few drinks and was feeling nice and loose. I went to the men's room where, strangely, the normal attendant was nowhere to be seen. There were just a couple of other guys there, strangers. I heard one of them speak to me but I didn't take much notice. Slowly his words began to cut through my thoughts.

'Give me your watch,' he said bluntly.

You're having a laugh, mate, I thought to myself. Outwardly, I took no notice.

'I'm being serious. Give me your watch!'

'You got the wrong guy,' I said. They hadn't of course. I was wearing a Franck Muller watch worth £45,000.

He repeated it a third time, this time putting his hand in his jacket, making the outline of a gun and prodding me in the side. Now I wasn't quite sure what he had in there – a gun, a knife or just his hand. It was at that moment that the alarm bells started going off.

Sure I was scared but not beyond thinking. I looked at his pal who was standing guard at the door and ushering away anyone trying to get into the toilets. They were located at the bottom of maybe thirty or forty steps which I knew this pair would have to climb rapidly to reach the exit. Then they would have to get past the bouncers and leap over the barriers where, I figured, paparazzi would be waiting. They were going to have to be very fit to do that – especially as I was planning on chasing them. I'd had a few drinks, but with my running speed, I had every chance of catching them. I just had to get out into the open and away from this isolated setting.

So he took my watch – and immediately starting running

with his accomplice just as I predicted. I was right behind them. They were a couple of young dudes but I still knew I could make ground on them.

Up the stairs they bolted, knocking people out of the way, as I gave chase behind them shouting, 'He stole my watch, he stole my watch!' But when I made it to the exit they were already jumping over the barriers to startled looks from everyone outside. When I came sprinting out of the club seconds later and shouted, 'He's got my watch!' everyone quickly worked out what was going down.

It's amazing what you do when you are wired.

The two robbers split, one runs left one runs right. I am only interested in the guy who has got my watch and that's the guy I'm going to track. Hot on my heels were the security guards from the club, wanting to lend a hand, and the paparazzi guys sensing a scoop.

The guy must have run for five, maybe ten minutes but there was no way he was going to shake me off. Eventually, I recall him running into a dead end where some workmen had closed off the entrance to a Tube station because of maintenance work. With nowhere to go, everyone just pounced on him and I walked up to him saying, 'He's got my watch. I just want my watch back.'

The security men, who were now acting as arresting officers, recovered it and handed it to me. But man, I was angry. So angry. All these years, I have worked my butt off to buy that watch with money earned through my own hard graft. Who do you think you are? Do you think you can just walk up to me and take it? Without doing anything? All of that was rushing through my head.

And suddenly I found myself running up to him and drop-kicking this guy Cantona-style full in the chest. Everybody moved in to pull me away. 'Come on, man, that's enough, take it easy,' I hear them saying to me. And I told them, 'It's OK, it's OK. I've finished. I just needed to do that.'

And so they let go their grip of me. I was lying. I turned and smacked this kid a perfect right-hander on the jaw.

If I had been in a dodgy area, falling down drunk and wearing that watch . . . well, I would almost deserve to be mugged for arrogant stupidity. But I wasn't. I was in a very respectable place, minding my own business. It seemed to me that this guy, who had stolen something I had worked so hard for, represented all those people who did not understand what I had been through to make it to a position where I could buy a Franck Muller watch. This kid had shown complete contempt and disrespect for all I had done with my life – and at that time it seemed there were many people treating me that way – and it brought out in me a rage I did not think I possessed.

All the pain and frustration from recent times welled up in me. I had lost my shine, my trademark smile had downturned like my career and my personal life was in tatters. And now they wanted to take my watch too?! All these feelings were fixed on this one kid who dared to take the little I had left: my self-respect and my hard-earned belongings.

I was surprised, shocked even, at the strength of my reaction. Anyone who knows me personally, or who only knows the happy, smiley side of the public Dwight Yorke, would have been equally surprised. I really am a placid guy. I believe in the joy of life, of not getting wound up over the provocations that come your way. I have a high tolerance level for most things. And yet here I was hitting this guy not once but twice even after he had been caught and was clearly going nowhere else that night but the police cells.

I can honestly say that when I eventually walked away from that melee, it was with tears in my eyes. I realized that my life was in freefall and I needed to get it back on track.

1

THE SECOND CHANCE

Close your eyes, conjure the perfect image of a Caribbean island, the kind of snapshot they will show you in adverts to sell dream holidays, and you've got the Tobago of my childhood. White, palm-treed beaches, turquoise seas hiding coral reefs, tropical vegetation, long, long days for a happy-go-lucky people soaking up the endless sunshine. That's my memory anyway. Idyllic.

Tobago today is much more developed. It has things that I could not imagine in my youth – traffic, motorways, office buildings, even a McDonald's. I go home now and I don't recognize it. I accept that times change and it had to develop but the paradise I remember as my playground back then will always be with me.

Canaan was little more than a hotch-potch collection of brick or wooden houses, home to a few hundred villagers on dirt-track roads leading off the one main highway which led to our capital, Scarborough. And down one of those dirt tracks you would find the Yorke family – my mum, Grace, father, Fulton, and their nine children. I grew up the second youngest of five brothers and three sisters brought into the world by my darling mum over eighteen years of child-bearing. That may seem strange through the eyes of modern-day Britain but it was nothing unusual in my culture at that time. Large families were the norm; mum herself had eight sisters and four brothers.

Juliet, her first, arrived in September 1955, a second girl, Verlaine, followed three years later, after which along came Keith, Clint, Deborah, Gary and Garth at regular intervals until I was born on 3 November 1971. The last of this clan, Brent, appeared nearly two years later.

I've now got a garage at my house bigger than the two-bedroomed, brick bungalow into which we all squeezed so you can imagine the congestion and chaos. If privacy and a bit of space is what you wanted, our house was not the place to be. I am still not quite sure how we all managed to find anywhere to sleep or how we managed to get along with each other as well as we did. My first memory is of little Brent and myself having to bunk down together. in the same bedroom as Mum and Dad. The other seven must have shared the other bedroom at some stage with the help of bunk beds although some left to find their own way and accommodation.

The facilities were basic and simple. Water had to be fetched from a standpipe at the end of the road while our tiny outside 'bathroom' amounted to a toilet and another standpipe under which you could shower. Cold water, mind. We had no concept of hot water in Canaan; it wasn't until much later in my teenage years that I experienced my first hot shower.

Mum found work as a cleaner at the nearby Crown Reef

Hotel; my dad I recall having a variety of jobs although mostly I remember him working as a garbage collector. It was a gruelling routine for Mum – clean the house, work all day at the nearby hotel, come home, clean again, cook – but she never complained no matter how hard she struggled. We were poor and sometimes there would not be enough food to go round, especially with so many of us. To this day, my mum can conjure a meal from the simplest of ingredients and no wonder. She would rustle up whatever meals she could in an outside baked-earth kitchen, two big stones acting as stoves.

Despite all of this, we never went hungry. Never. The island was full of fruits: mangos, bananas and coconuts. We'd climb trees and pick the fruit before finding a nice quiet corner to sit down and eat as much as we could. Every household had its own little dirt garden with tomatoes or whatever else we could grow. And the surrounding sea was full of fish and crabs. All we needed was some wood for burning, a little flour for dumplings, two hot stones to cook on and we had dinner. Wonderful.

We were surrounded by beaches in whichever direction we walked. Beautiful beaches. The larger island of Trinidad was pretty industrial even then, but little Tobago, which has around 5 per cent of the population, has relied on tourism for its trade. But in those days, there were just a few American tourists and on Sundays all the locals would head for the sands. My country gave the world steel pan, calypso and the dance called *soca* so we knew how to party! Yep, Sunday was beach day and Kiligwyn was my favourite; we'd play football all day, and where it would be jumpers for goalposts for the British kids it was two sticks in the sand for us. Keep-ups and five-a-side games that would end up with numbers of goals like cricket scores.

The other focal point of Canaan was Block 22 – the name we gave to the crop of buildings which featured the nearest bar, Popo, where the men sat outside playing cards as they drank their beers. One shop, Sheila's, provided all our groceries while nearby the post office, which was really little more than the back of someone's house, was the source of all worldly knowledge. A chalkboard outside would provide our news bulletins, telling us everything from football scores to what was going on in the village. And if a letter came for you, it was like gold dust, something to be treasured.

I remember my first school vividly – a kindergarten called Baby-Jo Nursery just 150 yards from our house and run by a local woman. A wonderful little set-up, which my elder siblings would take me to (although it wasn't unusual in our relaxed world for me to walk home by myself).

In these early years, I had to make do with one battered pair of all-purpose trainers which served for everything – especially football. Sometimes, we used a breadfruit for a football which would eventually be kicked out of shape but all I can remember is laughing until I could laugh no more.

My background is humble, but I would not change it for the world. I have always been grateful for my upbringing. It is so far removed from the life I eventually led and yes, I could – and frequently did – go out and spend thousands of pounds on clothes I might never wear in a single shopping spree. I could – and did – stockpile a mini-fleet of high-performance, luxury cars outside a swanky million-pound pad in one of England's super chic suburbs. But I never forgot where I came from. I'm sure in the years that followed when I was a famous footballer receiving enormous attention there were times when I came across as arrogant and perhaps aloof. If I did, I apologize to anyone who may have been offended. This was just my guard going up in self-defence. But I don't think I ever abandoned the simple courtesy and respect I was taught to show everyone during those early years. There were no airs and graces in Canaan.

Those principles were not the only lessons of my childhood. But others are a little more difficult to talk about. Grace, my mother, is the rock of my life. Strange really. In our culture, we do not easily express our emotions. I can say to my mum at the end of a phone call 'I love you' and although she will return the expression, I can almost sense her awkwardness in doing so. But she loves me all right. She loves us all. She is a most remarkable woman who I can still see laughing and smiling even amid the gruelling schedule, always cleaning if she wasn't cooking, always hurrying off to work while my elder brothers and sisters saw me off to school.

My father is a much more difficult character to talk about. If my mum was typical of her time and culture then so, I regret to say, was my dad. He was king of the household, a reign never to be questioned. And often this was enforced quite brutally. He would hit my mum. He would hit my sisters. He would hit my brothers. He would hit me. Sometimes with fists, sometimes with whipping branches snapped off what we called a 'whistle tree' just outside our house. But if things were not 'just so', if someone stepped out of line, or if he was just plain drunk and angry and came home to find some food he wanted not available or something missing, then he would fly into a rage which led to violence.

I can see him now hitting my poor mum. I have long since realized that she would put herself in the firing line to try to make sure none of her children were hurt. If Dad had been out drinking or was late coming home, then we would all get to bed early to avoid the prospect of encountering him in one of these ugly moods. He was a big athletic man and when we saw one of those rages coming on we used to run for our lives. But he would catch us if he wanted to. There was no opposing him, at least not until my brothers were much, much older and could stand up to him.

He was a difficult man to approach. There was none of this 'new-man' parenting where my father came from. No cuddles, no 'I love you's'. His message, his upbringing, was telling us that life was tough, you had to stand up for yourself and make the best of things.

In all of this, I can only think of one moment of tenderness and that was when he used to ask Brent and myself to take the tweezers to the grey hairs on his head and pull them out. You might think that uncomfortable but Dad used to love nothing more than to drop off to sleep as his youngest boys attended to his grooming.

I would later learn that most men on the island were

what you might call 'womanizers' and I'm sure my dad was no different. It's just the way it was. I think my father had other women; in fact I know he did. It was almost like an unwritten rule, I reckon. The wife brought up the children while the husband provided for them and conducted affairs.

I can even look back and smile at some of the images now. Like the time we were messing about in the house and I was being chased by my brothers – just youngsters messing around. But we knocked his telly over and broke it. His beloved black-and-white telly. That was dad's pride and joy in those days and you could understand why. There were not that many TVs in our neighbourhood.

He went absolutely berserk and the scenes that followed as we all tried to run away from his rage were bedlam. The neighbours must have heard but were probably too scared to intervene; it must have appeared comical, though, as a succession of Yorke children came flying out of whatever window or door we could reach to escape.

Was this abuse? In today's terms, yes, of course. Transport this scenario forward forty years and place it in modern-day Britain and I imagine welfare officials would soon intervene. But I don't look back on it in those terms. My dad is my dad, not my ideal father but a man in his seventies now and what can I say? He is my father and I love him. A heavy drinker and smoker who I can recall going off 'liming' or 'on the block' – 'out with the lads' we would call it in England – after which we might not see him for days. I can picture him now all cleaned up and decked out in his best suit as he left the house. In our community and culture that was very important; to men like my dad, the head of the household, you had to look the top dollar. You had to be 'the man'. And on the streets, outside the bars, men just like him would sit there, drinking their rum all night and talking.

In later years I challenged him about how he behaved and spoke at length to my brothers. I think we were all affected by it; I know I was. To this day, he has not apologized but he never would. Oh, he knows he did wrong. He realizes it was not the way to behave or bring up children. But he's too much of a man's man to say 'sorry'. I think it was very much the behaviour of his generation and our culture. In short, he didn't know any better.

He was never a loving, supporting dad, taking you to school or watching you play. I wish he could have done more to help out but, at that time, he was behaving as he thought he had to. We can share a drink now and talk about old times. But he has never been to England to visit and never will. I sense it's all too far away from his life and what he knows.

I realize now that he at least gave me an object lesson in how not to be a parent. He's my blood but I knew that was not the way I wanted to be. From an early age, I vowed to myself I would never behave that way. I would never beat a woman. I would never beat my kids. And I never will. But he also made me stronger and tougher and that would be of great use to me in the years ahead.

Mum and Dad stayed together for a long, long time before going their separate ways later in life and then, more recently, getting back together. That is typical of my mother's sense of family and generosity of spirit. She withstood all of his violence with a mixture of courage and laughter I have never stopped admiring, simply getting on with making the lives of her children her priority. And always, always, with laughter. She had laughter for everybody. And she wanted what all mothers want – for her children to do well, be happy and healthy.

The greater miracle to my family is that I am still with them, that I lived long enough to enjoy the life I have had so far. But for luck and a guardian angel, I wouldn't have a story to tell. My life would have been over on 28 July 1974, a little more than three months before my third birthday.

It was early evening, about 6.30 p.m., and it was getting dark. I was walking with one of my brothers, Clint, who was then twelve, to the shop, Sheila's, about five hundred yards from our home when I spied one of my older sisters, Verlaine, then sixteen, on the other side of Canaan's one main road.

I have no memory of the incident but it has passed into legend, among family, friends and the folk who witnessed me dash across the road. My brothers and sisters tell me I wrenched my hand free of Clint's grip and shot off to run to Verlaine straight into the path of an oncoming car. You know the way these stories grow in the telling. According to Clint, the vehicle was going as fast as 60 mph. I find that impossible to believe because I don't see how I could have survived a collision with a car travelling at that speed. (Besides, there was little speeding possible on the pot-holed surfaces.)

Apparently, I bounced off the front bumper and was then dragged beneath the car for a hundred yards or more before the driver could stop. I was a slightly built child and this may well have been another key factor in my survival because the undercarriage of the car did not touch me. But the exhaust pipe scraped along my back burning me. Fortunately, I did not land under the wheels.

The driver was known to us all, a man who lived nearby. He died not too long ago but at that time only lived three or four streets away. He was a cabby with a big left-hand-drive car which was distinctive at the time. (Over the years I would see him when I arrived at the airport for visits home and he would always acknowledge me and offer me a lift. It was good to be sitting in his taxi rather than rolling underneath it!) On that day, my brothers and sisters screamed at him but he told them it was my fault and eventually just drove away.

That should have been it. Over and out. No more Dwight Yorke. But then suddenly a second car appeared and a man got out. He was of Asian descent and he has since been referred to as 'the Chinaman'. To this day no one knows his name or where he came from. Clearly possessing medical training, he attended to my injuries while an ambulance was called. Then he disappeared as quickly as he arrived and was never seen again. I have absolutely no recollection of the event. But that's how the story goes.

I was all busted up and needed three months in hospital. Two broken feet and burns all down my back. Medical care back then wasn't what it is now but somehow I survived it. My brothers and sisters, who watched the whole thing unfold, are convinced the stranger saved my life. The story has lived with me ever since and probably assumed even more elements as it has been retold. God knows how it will end up.

But it has left its legacy. Although I have no recall of the accident, my memory does stretch just far enough back to leaving hospital where my father was waiting to take me home in his garbage truck. By then, the only sign of my brush with death was on my back – a tell-tale scar, courtesy of that red-hot exhaust. As the years rolled by, my family watched it change shape and form a perfect replica of the island of Tobago. It is still there to this day and, I must admit, does offer an uncanny resemblance to my homeland. All of which has only added to the sense of mystery.

As for the Chinese guy . . . well, wherever he is today, if he still out there alive, I can only thank him. An aura has grown around him, a mystery. What was he doing there? As I have mentioned, there were so few tourists on the island, let alone visitors from the Orient, that no one can understand why no trace of him was ever found. But he became my guardian angel. As I gradually came to understand what happened to me, how fate had placed this mysterious Chinaman with medical skills in the car behind and how I had somehow survived . . . well, even by the age of seven or eight, I was thinking to myself: 'This has got to be a second chance. Whatever I do, I must make the best of it.' I believe that I was spared for a reason; that some mysterious force was at work, deciding that the world should hear more from me.

2

BRIAN LARA
CAUGHT BEHIND

To this day, I remain convinced the world of sport should have heard from the Yorke family long before I began making headlines. Within such a large family group, you will always develop special bonds with one or two of your siblings. Verlaine, particularly, was always special to me. Maybe we bonded from the moment of that accident. Whenever anything was wrong, whenever I needed comforting, it was Verlaine I went to. There was something different about her. She was a peacemaker and a protector, and after the accident she was always there for me. Perhaps in some way she felt responsible because I running towards her.

My oldest sister, Juliet, was another with whom I also developed a close bond. A bit later when I was in my teens she moved to Trinidad to work at the island's Hilton Hotel and when I was over there for football she looked out for me.

Keith and I have remained in constant touch, too, down the years. He worked in the police force back home, a fingerprint expert, and spent time studying and working in

America. We often talk on the phone. My 'favourite' brother – I guess that means the one I have a soft spot for – is little Brent. He had real ambition and drive and went to America to pursue work as a computer engineer, got all his qualifications and has made a successful career for himself. And I think maybe he looked up to me as a role model.

My sister Deborah was seven years older than me but was the first goalkeeper I scored against in our Sunday games on the beach while both Garth and Gary remain close to my life; they all are really. But the family member I have always believed the world should have heard about is Clint. He was an immensely talented batsman who played for Trinidad and Tobago at the top level. I swear he should have gone on to play for the West Indies (even allowing for the raft of great batsmen in 1980s teams). But Clint always seemed to fluff his lines when the big moment came. I don't know why he could not make it count on the day but I always felt he should have made it.

And that's why it fell to me to be the one in the family to make it.

I don't know if I can place a moment when it dawned on me that I was gifted at football. From about the age of six all I lived for was sport; that was when I began to realize that I was quite good at games. It's just luck, I think, having that sort of skill or learning. But it was my good fortune to be blessed that way. I did it all – cricket, marathon running, basketball. But football was my favourite. I was small for my age but with stocky thighs, which gave me a strength which would surprise opponents.

Football came naturally to me. I don't recall any great

moment of dawning when I thought to myself I was better than my pals. Seriously. I was just having fun. From the moment I came out of school, the only thing I could think of was to play football. There were no great footballing role models in those days. This was the era of the all-conquering West Indian cricket team: Clive Lloyd and Viv Richards were the icons that had us glued to TV sets. All the kids wanted to emulate them and cricket, which I also enjoyed, was seen as the only way to sporting fame. Football never carried that impact in my early years.

But within the village, I guess they began to talk about 'little Dwight'. The games that were organized were local affairs which all the villagers would come to watch as a community event and at the age of eight or so I can remember playing against much older boys and teasing them a little. I would flick the ball between their legs or just dribble round them. And I would score goals, not one or two but six or seven. But I just saw it as fun.

That began to change when my playing came to the attention of Bertille St Clair, who even then was one of the most recognizable football coaches on the island. He would go on to have a huge impact on my life. Bertille was then a small, slight unremarkable-looking man in his late thirties but his reputation was huge. Forget all the scouting, coaching, organizations and qualified coaches we now take for granted. This was a small, isolated Caribbean community thirty-odd years ago and football was a far more ramshackle, haphazard experience. But we all knew this man Bertille had experience of coaching overseas and if he thought you were worthy of attention, then it meant something. He was the one man who put together organized sessions for Tobago's youngsters.

He used to drive round the villages looking for players to attend his sessions. He had heard about this kid in Canaan from someone who had happened to see me play. It was such a small community, I wasn't hard to find. Would I like to join his Saturday morning coaching clinics in Scarborough, a bus ride, or a hitchhike, away from my home?

My eyes widened at the invitation but it wasn't that simple. This was 1980, I was eight years old and I didn't have the five T&T dollars I needed to go. That's about 50p in today's money but it was 50p which we could not spare from the family budget. The fact it was staged on Saturdays was another problem – my mum was a devout Seventh Day Adventist who reserved that day for services. She was not happy that I would have to forgo them. But I really wanted to go and somehow we found a way. It was nothing fancy. We probably 'loaned' some cones from the roads for goalposts and Bertille would drill about fifty of us in the game's basics. That's all it was.

But it was a valuable lesson in growing up quickly, especially as I had to find the five dollars to pay my way. I used to do what I could to help with the family finances by then with my constant companion and great mate, Rama. His real name is Bert Benjamin but don't ask me how he got the name Rama. He was distinctive-looking having fallen on a stick when he was young, which had left one of his eyes crooked. He is probably one of the most famous people on the island, partly because of our friendship but also because he has done his own thing. I guarantee if you land on Tobago and ask a cab driver to take you to Rama he will know where to go. He's been to England once but it is not for him; too cold and too far away. But he is a great friend.

We were inseparable back then, my best buddy and me. I could climb coconut trees or catch the crabs like Rama but not as elegantly or as cleverly. And catching crabs could earn you money – the equivalent of a couple of pounds for two dozen back then. At night-time in the rainy season, what we called 'dark rain', we would creep to this little ravine by the beach and out would come the crabs. We would have the time of our lives snaring them, take them home and keep them alive for sale; some boys even got to take their catches over to Trinidad because Tobagonian crabs were such a delicacy.

Rama has remained a lifelong friend. A few years ago, I got the opportunity to set him up with a boat to take tourists scuba-diving in Tobago from which he makes a living. If our lives were exchanged, would we be the same? Rama and I have spent long hours sinking a beer over this discussion and have never been less than convinced that we would have always remained friends. I have looked after him if and when he has needed it down the years; I would not want it any other way. I know he would have done the same for me.

Somehow I managed to scrape the money together to get to Bertille's sessions., I had no boots of course. We couldn't afford them. So I went in my school shoes – which Mum was not very impressed about – but I loved every minute of it. For the first time I was being told what to do, how to improve. I listened to every word Bertille told me and practised everything when I got home.

So that's how it all started. There are so many folk who seemed to step in and help me in those early days. I have no recollection of my father paying much heed to this potential but I knew that funding these trips would be a terrible strain on the family budget; simply trying to reach Trinidad, very much the big brother of the two islands, was a problem for me. So I will always be grateful to a neighbour, Selwyn Archer, who knew of my family's financial struggles and helped fund the cross-island ventures. On one occasion, he took me to see the Brazilian team Flamingo play a friendly against Trinidad and all the way through I kept jumping up and pointing out the player I wanted to copy.

'Him, I want to be like him,' I apparently kept saying. I didn't know his name but Selwyn told me it was somebody called Zico.

But at a young age, it was difficult for me to see where my dreams of playing professional football could take me. A cricketer's path was firmly established but no one from our islands had ever carved out a big-time football career for themselves.

I was not long into my coaching under Bertille when I was selected for trials for the Under 12 Trinidad and Tobago team. I was young for the team, as I would be from then on – I was ten when I was in the Under 14s and fourteen when I played for the Under 16s. However, even though I was not yet ten, I was selected to play for the national team in a tournament being staged in Puerto Rico involving seven other Caribbean and American nations. A lot of people were saying that I was too young and too slight for the Under 12s but Bertille was the coach and had great faith in me. We reached the final, where we were beaten by the USA, but I recall scoring plenty of goals just as much as I remember my first sight of an electronic scoreboard which flashed up 'Goal!' every time someone scored. It was mesmerizing and all very exciting for a youngster. It was also a key point in my early life, a moment when I realized the limitations – as sunny as they were – of a life in Tobago were not for me. I wanted more.

I kept on practising and training hard over the next couple of years. Playing for the junior national side meant I was something of a local celebrity, and one day I was hanging out on a street corner with my pals feeling pretty pleased with myself. I had a reputation, even at that tender age, and naturally I thought I knew it all. But that day would prove to be one of the defining moments of my life.

A slow-moving car approached us and before I could react, there was Bertille, leaping out to confront me. I tried to hide behind my back the beer I was drinking.

Too late. He saw it, slapped me across the face and ordered me to do twenty press-ups in the street, right there, right then, in front of my pals. Bertille was being what we called a 'mamma guy' – trying to put me back on course. I had seen him like this with other young players once or twice and they had blown his words back in his face (and most probably ended up working at the airport). Now I was faced with the same conflict as Bertille delivered the lecture of all lectures.

'So this is what you are going to do, eh?' Bertille began

raging at me. 'Throw it all away? Hang around on street corners? End up a drunk or a druggie? Do you really want that? Or do you want to make something of yourself?

'Don't be stupid. You have talent, Dwight. You can be special. Don't throw it all away just to act big with your mates.' And so on.

I could have said, as others before me, 'Oh fuck all this . . . I'm having a beer. What's the harm in that, man? Leave me alone.'

But yet again that voice was back in my head, reminding me of the significance of that scar on my back and whispering: 'This is a second chance don't forget – don't mess it up.' I knew what the answer must be. I dropped to the dirt and did those twenty press-ups. In front of my pals. Drinking, even at that age, was a perfectly normal thing where I came from; we like to drink in the Caribbean. And drugs too. I knew every dope dealer in and around the island. The smell of a spliff was ever present in my youth. I have never smoked it in my life, never done drugs. But it was a road I might have strayed down.

At that moment, as I was listening to Bertille's fury and doing those press-ups, I promised myself that I would not touch alcohol (and I didn't again until I was twenty-one). Bertille, I realized, was so angry with me because he wanted me to avoid the fate of so many others, especially as he clearly felt I had the ability to go further than any other footballer from the island before.

Down the years, my great mentor has done so many things for me. He would be my only form of transport to games at times, often shutting me in the boot of his car to take me the five-minute drive back to the village after games or training. He has coached me, advised me and always been a wise voice when I have needed one.

But nothing he did for me was ever more valuable than the twenty press-ups he demanded in the dirt of my home village that evening.

This period in my life would see the start of some life-long friendships with some remarkable characters. The last time I checked, our homeland's population was somewhere between 1.2 and 1.3 million but a generation of sports talent emerged during my time that makes you wonder if they were putting something in the water. For a start there were greater football talents than me. The real 'star' of the island was the Little Magician, Russell Latapy, who was three years older than me and a player I have always looked up to. As my trips to Trinidad for these trials and matches became a regular feature in my life, Russell and I developed a friendship that would eventually see me stay with his family when necessary. He became the idol of Trinidad because of the way he played the game. He would not go on to have the kind of top-level club career that would come my way, although he is highly thought of in Scottish football, but as far as our island is concerned, Russell is the man, not Dwight Yorke.

And there was another young footballer who impressed me. Again, a couple of years older than me but clearly someone with ability. It turned out his name was Brian Lara. I first came across him when he was a right midfield player and we were in trials for the national schools team, the final 48 out of 1,000 kids. It was 1987 and I was playing for my then high school, Signal Hill. Yes, this lad Lara could play all right.

Our sporting choices then were very simple. In Trinidad and Tobago, we only have two seasons – wet and dry. When it was wet you played football, and when it was dry, out came the cricket bats. And if you didn't play either of those sports, it was presumed you were gay – it was that brutal a judgement I'm afraid.

I was a handy cricketer and began to become aware of this same Lara fella scoring a ridiculous amount of runs; while others were getting 30s and 40s, this guy was scoring 100s. I finally got the chance to see for myself when Trinidad played Tobago in a match. As the smaller island, we were always the underdogs but relished the chance to have a go at the boys from the bigger island.

Lara, as I came to know him and have always called him, came out to open the batting; I was the wicketkeeper-batsman for my team, intrigued to see just how good my footballing acquaintance was. Remember, this is the 1980s, every young West Indian boy wanted to bowl like an express train in those days and we had a group of fairly power-ful lads capable even then of hurling down 70, 80 mph deliveries.

I was fifteen at the time but will always feel what hap-pened next was one of the privileges of my life, standing behind the stumps and watching a seventeen-year-old Lara smash this ball wherever he wanted. He made it look ridiculously easy. Wow, I thought, this is something else. I think he had scored about 60 when he decided to give his pal behind the stumps a little test by deliberately 'nicking' one. I caught it and danced around like an idiot in celebration. As football became my overriding passion, that would be my final game of cricket but you won't be surprised to know it is not the final time Lara has been reminded of that dismissal.

A young goalkeeper was also making a name for himself, Shaka Hislop, who would go on to establish a Premier League career as well. His younger brother, Kona, was another talented footballer who would briefly play at Hartlepool, and he went on to become one of my closest friends.

We were a little magic circle of sportsmen reaching out from our tiny island home.

3

RHONDA

I left home when I was fourteen. Sound crazy? Maybe it does in the world we know today. But it made perfect sense then. I went to live with my friend Sherwin Patrick, the goalkeeper in our school team who lived just a stone's throw away from our family home, simply because his family had more space in their house.

We shared bunk beds and I flitted between his house and mine in a move that was intended to help me with my school studies; give me a little peace and quiet to concentrate on homework. It was all very relaxed and easy-going, typical, I suppose, of the Caribbean nature. All I could really concentrate on, however, was football. Yes, I was fourteen and enjoying the kudos of being a bright young talent of football in Trinidad and Tobago. And yet I still did not own a real pair of football boots. Clearly that had to change. But how?

One day, I found myself staring longingly into the window of a sports shop in Tobago run by Gary Sobers – same name as the cricketing legend but a different fella – marvelling at the shiny leather and flash branding of the boots on display. An idea came to mind.

I stepped inside to make my challenge to the shop owner. 'You see those boots,' I said, 'if I can stand in this bin, throw a ball up in the air and keep it up on my head a hundred times, how about you give them to me. If I fail, I'll buy them.' Which, of course, I knew I didn't have the money to do.

I had to make it something that would seem impossible or he would never go for it and the owner looked at me as if I was mad. 'You'll never do that,' Gary said.

I wasn't sure that I could. I hadn't planned it. I hadn't tried to do anything like it before. I hadn't even practised it. My feet could barely fit flat in that bin and I would struggle for balance. But I wanted those boots so badly and juggling a football with either feet or head was second nature to me.

I asked him if I could have more than one attempt but he wasn't going for that one. He wanted this cheeky little kid out of his shop as soon as possible I imagine. But he accepted. I stepped into the bin and threw the ball up in the air only to realize it was a bad throw and I would probably struggle to get past two. So I caught it and covered up the mistake by saying, 'You sure?'

Yes, he was sure. 'It's a hundred, and nothing short of a hundred and you've got to pay for them if you fail,' he said. There were six or seven people in the shop amused by all this and acting as witnesses. I couldn't back out now. And off I went a second time.

This time the throw was OK but I was all over the place with the first few before I settled into the rhythm of it. Reaching fifty was the benchmark. When I got there, I knew it would be plain sailing. I did and it was. Everyone in the shop counted down the last ten. I even threw in an extra ten just to make sure. And for showboating I suppose. Gary was true to his word and gave me my boots.

After going through all that to get the darn boots, I honestly can't remember what happened to them once I outgrew them. But I have seen Gary many times since and our friendship has endured. He always reminds me of the cheeky little kid who tricked him into handing over a treasured pair of boots for nothing. But I needed them badly because my football was beginning to attract more and more attention, the word having spread across the water to the larger island of Trinidad, where this precocious young kid was starring in the national age group teams despite being so much younger than his teammates.

Football's popularity really began to blossom in the 1980s as the colour TVs arrived and we began to see highlights from the English and Italian leagues. For the first time, I found myself staring at these faraway players in their huge stadiums packed with thousands of fans and wondering: 'Could I do that? Could I be that good?' The Spurs team of this era was the one that caught my imagination. I loved Ardiles and Villa, the two Argentinians, but my hero was the Englishman Glenn Hoddle. He was unlike any other English player; he played with such grace and style and he had a legendary passing ability. Like Zico before him, I had another role model for my game.

By the time I was fifteen, Jack Warner, the president of the Trinidad and Tobago FA, had decided that my talent was worth cultivating and came to my parents' home to discuss the prospect of moving to the main island to live with his family. By now, I was training with the national team but the relentless travelling from Tobago was a problem. I don't think my mum was impressed with the idea of my leaving Tobago and I can't say I was. But sacrifices had to be made. This was now 1988, and there was a World Cup qualifying campaign for the Italia 90 tournament approaching – and nothing captured the excitement and enthusiasm of our islands more. Could this young lad Yorke, even at this early age, make a difference? So Jack wanted me in Trinidad to take a more active role in the team.

We had to sort out my schooling, though. I had failed my eleven-plus at Bon Accord Junior School. In Tobago, that meant missing out on one of the better secondary schools available but fortunately by then my football prowess was such that I was offered a scholarship for Scarborough Secondary School. It had never been done before and it was nothing to do with money. It was all about being offered a place at the school, despite failing the exam, purely on my sporting merit. After Scarborough, I had switched to Signal Hill in Tobago when I was fourteen. I would have to move again to Arouca School in Trinidad, which was a shame as I'd enjoyed Signal Hill. There I had been a star after we won the national schools football final one year. As the word about me spread, I was beginning to enjoy the benefits which came with this first taste of a little 'fame'. By which I mean girls.

Ah yes, the girls.

I don't know when I was first aware of the opposite sex

but it would have been difficult not to notice them. We lived in a very easy-going place and it would be no surprise to be walking along the dirt tracks or the beaches near Canaan and suddenly stumble over a couple doing what came naturally. You could not blame them. They were probably from large families crammed into small homes short of privacy like me. You would mind your own business and let them get on with it. It was no big deal.

That's how I lost my virginity, at the age of about twelve, to a girl from the neighbourhood on the beach one night. She was older than me and, well, let's say wiser. But it was extremely enjoyable and represented the start of many such adventures even at that age. I realized that my football had given me a name and with that name came an interest from the girls. Even though I had older brothers, I was the one grabbing the attention through my deeds on the football pitch.

By the time I got to Signal Hill, I was a minor celebrity and the bonuses kept coming. It would be no surprise for two or three girls to offer to do my homework while I went off to play sport. I wasn't a pupil who struggled but I can't recall doing any homework. I was off playing football or cricket or competing in athletics or playing basketball, table tennis, running cross-country . . . it was relentless.

Playing sport was always sustained by a level of natural fitness which at times surprised even me. I remember being picked to run a marathon due to start at 8.30 a.m. I mistakenly thought it began at 9 a.m. I got there to find the runners had set off but changed quickly and raced away in pursuit, half an hour after the rest of the field. I caught them up and beat them. I finished exhausted and retching and unable to move. But I beat them. Don't ask me how – but I will always remember that raising yet more eyebrows.

In order to accommodate me, my teachers would organize extra lessons to help me catch up with my studies while other perks also came my way. I was given the privilege of borrowing my teachers' cars even though I did not have a proper licence. Another guy became such a fan of mine that he gave me the freedom of his mango trees. 'Anytime you want to pick the fruit, Dwight, just go ahead,' he told me.

And then there was Rhonda. Oh yes, I should tell you about Rhonda. Because while that collision with a neighbour's car left a scar on my back, it was my collision with the lovely Rhonda which first scarred my heart. In fact, she possibly marked me more than she ever realized.

I was the big guy in the school at Signal Hill by this time, the star sportsman who needed the best-looking girlfriend. That was how it worked. And the best-looking girl was Rhonda. We were like a Tobagonian version of the classic American jock dating the prettiest cheerleader. But it was Rhonda who dealt me a blow I wasn't expecting – public humiliation.

I can't be precise on dates here but I think we were fifteen, perhaps sixteen, and had become an established item when I asked Rhonda one day if she would be coming to a dance with me at the school that night. She said no, she had too much work to do, or something like that. Would I still go? No, I didn't think so, not without 'my girl'. But later that evening, chatting with my pals, they persuaded me to tag along because they were going. And there, to my horror, I found Rhonda in the arms of another boy.

I don't know if she ever realized how much that affected me. Honestly, it felt like it ripped me apart inside. Yes, I know – it was a long time ago and I really should move on. But I can't deny what I felt and what I still feel. Ever since then, I have found it difficult to put myself right out there. She is the girl who broke my heart and may well be the reason why, even to this day, I have found it difficult to fully, openly commit to one woman. Is that too much to place at the door of a childhood sweetheart? Maybe. But do not underestimate how much 'face' is at stake for young males from my culture in that social setting. Someone had finally tripped up the great Dwight Yorke. That was how it felt and I crumpled.

I called her a couple of times in the years that followed. She was delighted to take my calls. It was never going to be a nasty conversation but I wanted her to know what she had passed up and how much she had hurt me that night. I don't think it ever really registered with Rhonda like it did with me. The last I heard, she emigrated to the United States or Canada and I think has a couple of children now. We have never seen each other since. But that rejection so got to me.

Looking back now, I know my reaction was a strong one because it was the first time someone dared to prick my bubble. A girl as well. I thought I had that field covered. Until then, I had been the boy the girls wanted, the star in the team, the guy everyone did favours for. I was in the limelight and who wouldn't enjoy that? Everyone wanted to be my friend. It was all I had ever known – until Rhonda. Along came Rhonda and did it to me. I was never going to let anyone else get close enough to do that again.

4

THE TRIAL

It was big, big news of course, made even more momen-
tous by its timing. The year 1989 was a vital one for
Trinidad and Tobago's hopes of qualifying for the 1990
World Cup, and to help with the preparations, a famous
English First Division team, Aston Villa, were coming on
tour.

I thought no more of it than that, to be honest. March
1989. But I was breaking into the full national team by
then and this would be an opportunity to try my hand
against some serious players. There were names in their
team that I recognized from TV and news bulletins, players
who had forged big careers for themselves in the far-off
English league. Allan Evans, Derek Mountfield, Nigel
Spink, Gordon Cowans, Alan McInally. And I had much
to thank Vinnie Jones and the infamous Wimbledon Crazy
Gang for at this point. They had knocked Villa out of the
FA Cup in January 1989 leaving their manager, Graham
Taylor, looking for a break to fill in a blank fortnight in
his team's schedule. Without that, who knows where I
would be now?

In our part of the world, a typical English team then would have meant powerful in the air, hard running and lots of long balls. All I wanted to do, in contrast, was have fun and express myself on the pitch. The forthcoming match with Villa was the talk of the islands but the last thing on my mind was hitching a lift to the English professional scene.

Timing was again on my side. Aston Villa's arrival coincided with a call on the island for me to play more for the full senior team. But no one from our part of the world had ever broken into the game in a big way, not in the serious leagues around the world; there was simply no precedent for what was about to happen.

At this point, you might expect me to recall every minute detail of this life-changing experience. But the truth is I can't. It was a fairly ordinary game that Villa won with a single goal. What stood out for me was the physical condition of the opposition. They were so fit, hard and strong; I could not believe how much running they did. We played a game where we liked to slow things down; these boys were hurtling around at 100 mph in comparison. I could see how well-drilled and organized they were. There was also a kind of togetherness I had not seen before.

I finished the match with a clearer understanding of what you had to do to make it in England. But as soon as I came off the pitch, I thought little about it and went off back to my routine. It really wasn't that remarkable a game.

The following day I was due to play Villa again for a Tobagonian XI in what would be little more than an exhibition match before our guests were let off the leash for some serious R & R. It was a token gesture on Villa's part; they wanted the game out of the way so they could hit the beaches.

I shared the flight over with them from Trinidad but they had no idea who I was. I wasn't yet seventeen and they probably didn't realize I had just played against them. Anyway, I was sitting in the dressing room at half-time with our team already two or three goals down when I heard an announcement over the tannoy. Aston Villa wanted Dwight Yorke to play for them in the second half. I knew absolutely nothing about it but the request caused uproar. 'You can come and swim in our ocean, lie on our beaches and drink our beer – but you're not stealing our best players' – it was that kind of attitude. I think some fairly urgent half-time conversations took place during which that proposal was abandoned. But that was the first time it was suggested that I should go to England for a trial.

By now, one of Tobago's most prominent businessmen, Neil Wilson, was helping to look after my interests. It was Bertille who had introduced me to him a few years earlier when, at the coach's encouragement, he had whipped a fifty US dollar note out of his wallet to give me some pocket money for another international tournament with the Under 14s. He actually first came to see me play in that national schools final in 1987 and was bowled over. Whenever Neil asked me what I wanted from life the answer was always the same: 'To be a professional footballer.' He had different businesses to attend to, including a travel agency and a jewellery shop, but he saw my determination and began to part sponsor me, part look after my welfare.

I finished the match, showered and began to pick up the vibe that Neil and Graham Taylor were discussing the possibility of flying me over at some stage for a trial. The word swept around the island in no time; the reality followed a few months later. I was to go to England for a five-week trial with Neil and another player, a lad I had always rated in the Tobagonian team named Colvin Hutchinson who was a couple of years older than me. Before we left I had bought my first ever suit. I bought it especially for the trip – a minging grey striped affair. Naturally I thought I looked pretty devastating in it. I begged and borrowed everything else I needed, relying on hand-me-downs and favours from neighbours.

All I remember of the flight was that it was so long and that I spent the time gorging on the airline food and chocolate. Colvin and I stepped out of the plane to be greeted by cold, dark, September clouds the like of which I had never seen before. It was so damp, so cold. Surely people didn't live in this climate?

The length of the flight had been expected but the length of the drive, after being met by Villa's kit man Jim Paul, from Heathrow to Birmingham amazed me. I kept thinking: 'Where can they be taking us?' The answer was Villa's training ground at Bodymoor Heath just outside Birmingham, which was another awesome experience for two boys who had never seen so many pitches, so many goalposts, balls and footballers in the same place at the same time before. The pictures on the wall of Villa's old players and old triumphs was another source of wonder as was the kit they promptly handed us. Our own kit?

And a 'tracky' top? What sort of miracle land had we come to?

We were in awe of everything but there was no time to get too scared. We were thrown straight into training the next day, immediately aware of how much fitter and stronger the English boys were. But I was never in doubt of my actual ability; I felt that would stand up against the best of them. I realized quickly, however, that the big challenge for me would be to match their physical strengths.

The trial settled into a luxurious routine. We went to the training ground in the morning, got fed, trained, got fed again, rice pudding and beans on toast until we wanted for no more. They had young lads cleaning our boots, guys of my age, a little more than sixteen; I would have been happy to oblige but I guess as trialists we were exempt from this duty. Then it was back to the digs we were given under Jim Paul's roof, talking, talking, talking and dreaming. One contract, if we could just get one contract of the type some of these young players were on, we would be made for life back home.

I thought we would stick out in training but there were already quite a few black players at Villa and we blended in naturally. The only problem was in conversation afterwards – they couldn't understand a word we were saying and we could not make any sense of them! We were not used to going into communal showers and baths either. I thought: 'What them doing? Them can't go in a bath with another guy!' We kept our shorts on while the rest of the guys were naked; it was quite a culture shock. That was just our upbringing, having to hide or keep yourself covered with so many sisters around. They must have thought we were equally strange.

But the football went well. We were quite confident, Colvin and I, that we were both going to be taken right up to the big day itself, when Graham Taylor pronounced his judgement. He called me into his office and told me the good news – Villa would be offering me a contract. I was ecstatic! This was beyond my wildest dreams. But then he told me that because of Colvin's age they would not be offering him one.

I was devastated for him. Colvin is always the man I feel for most in this story. I don't know whether Villa brought him over to keep me company or whether they thought that giving a trial to two was as cheap as one. I knew how much of a difference this would make to our lives. And I could think of nothing to say to him, nothing from the moment I was in Graham's office, nothing as we packed our bags and got ready to return, nothing all the way back home. I had no idea how to cope with his disappointment; God knows how he coped himself.

He went back home, tried his best for a breakthrough elsewhere, but never got anywhere. I think at one stage he ended up working at the airport before emigrating to America where I once saw him briefly. He must have looked at where I ended up and tortured himself with endless 'if onlys'. I don't know if I would have been able to cope with that rejection, not having been given a glimpse in those five weeks of what the opportunity could offer. Wherever you are, Colvin, I will always feel you deserved better.

But then things got complicated for me. Trinidad and

Tobago were in the middle of this World Cup campaign and didn't want me flying off to England just yet. Jack Warner didn't want me to sign, Bertille and Neil were cautious too. What if this goes wrong? You will be left with nothing. As it turned out, the eventual heartbreak we all felt when we failed to qualify for the World Cup that November took some of the heat out of the decision. The nation was devastated – we were beaten to the last spot by the United States – and I was inconsolable; I cried my eyes out.

But when the tears dried, I knew I had another chance calling to me. I was leaving behind the sun, the beaches, catching crabs, my family, friends, all the things which had been the anchors of my life. It was time to step into the unknown with that voice in my head telling me: 'You've been given a second chance for a reason. Don't waste it.'

5

FOOTBALL, FOOTBALL, FOOTBALL

Snow. The worst snow England had seen in an age and it was there to greet me in my first weeks in Birmingham in winter 1989 as I settled into life as an Aston Villa player. I had never seen it before of course and it took some getting used to. I thought it had been cold three months earlier but now this was a whole new definition. It was absolutely freezing and I had just left blistering sunshine. What on earth had I done?

This time, I was very much on my own. No fellow-trialist in Colvin, no adviser or older head from home like Neil to help me. Now, with only Villa to support me, it was up to me. But aside from the apprehension, I had spent the long plane journey over dreaming about making it as a footballer in England. I still couldn't believe how much I was going to get paid. The contract I had signed offered me 200 English pounds a week which, if I should ever make the first team, would have another £50 added. I had just turned eighteen and that was an unimaginable fortune. I would have enough to live on in England, I calculated, and still send plenty back to Mum. Incredible.

Graham Taylor had decided that as I was a young guy arriving from the Caribbean it would make sense to find me digs with the family of the club's exciting young winger Tony Daley, who lived just a short distance from the stadium. It was a reasonable assumption on Graham's part but Tony's family heritage is Jamaican and while we might have had some things in common there were plenty we did not. I just could not settle there at all. I couldn't take to the area, such a concrete contrast to everything I had known in my homeland and even a little scary in its strangeness, although there were no problems with Tony. He was everything I wanted to be at that time, the rising star of Villa with the look and the car to match. He was now living away from his parents but every time he visited, he was a reminder of how far I had to go.

Graham must have been surprised when I soon asked to change digs but it would be a vital decision in helping me settle into the English way of life. I was eventually introduced to the folk who would become my substitute parents, Sheila and Bryn Dudley, who put up Villa trialists and youth players in their typical English cottage in Shustoke. Much quieter, much more peaceful.

I was glad to be out of the city – quite a culture shock to a boy from Tobago – and right from the beginning I loved it at Sheila and Bryn's. There I shared a room with another Villa hopeful, Andy Comyn, an intelligent lad with an eye for a career away from football; lots of O levels and A levels as I recall. But he became an immediate pal as he showed me the ropes of my new life. We shared our club car, a battered old red Montego. I had passed my test in Tobago and Andy and I took turns with the driving duties.

I loved my new digs immediately. Loved it. This village life was how I imagined England to be and I have so much to thank my 'adoptive' parents for. Sheila was very much a mother figure, so much so that after a while I began calling her Mum. She had never had children of her own and so I think she liked me calling her that. Bryn was around less because of his work as a long-distance lorry driver but as he watched his wife happily adopt the role of mother to this youngster from the other side of the world, he was comfortable with it too. Sheila and my mum eventually met some time later and they got on brilliantly. My English 'family' would provide a vital anchor for me to grow and develop as a footballer and a man.

And these were still strange days, so different to anything I had ever known before. That snow for a start. I once missed training because I presumed no one would be mad enough to train in heavy snow. How wrong I was!

Months later, when my first spring finally came, I can recall making my way from Sheila's to our local shop and passing an old guy on the street. It was a lovely sunny afternoon and I was going to buy myself an ice cream and it seemed the most natural thing in the world to buy one for the man I had just walked by. So I did. The look on his face when I caught him up on the return journey and offered him this ice cream was amazement; and yet to me it was how I had been brought up, to respect and help my elders.

Sheila and Bryn were very 'normal' folk and all I thought about in these early days was football, football, football.

Eat, sleep, train and play football whether at Bodymoor or in Sheila's back garden.

My welcome among the group of Villa youngsters was a little cagier than it had been during the trial. We were all chasing the same goal and while I never ran into any racism, I had it in my head that if it came down to a decision on who would be kept on and who would be sent back, I would have to be so much better than a white, locally reared rival. I don't know whether that was the right conclusion on my part but I just thought that was naturally how an outsider such as myself should have looked at the challenge. So I worked as hard as I could.

I struck up good friendships with other guys sharing the same dream. Andy was soon joined in my circle by a young defender named Bryan Small, who would go on to enjoy a brief first-team career ahead of me before moving off to other clubs. But Smally and I remain great friends to this day, bonded I think, by our shared experience of these early years.

We were all young and naive, me probably more than the others because of my different background, and it was a daunting task to try to establish myself. Did I say naive? By the end of March of that first half-season at Villa, Graham felt it was time to give me my first taste of senior action when he brought me on as a substitute. Every player dreams of coming on and scoring in their debut but the game ended in a 1–0 victory to Crystal Palace. It was still an amazing feeling going on to the pitch that first time. Imagine the excitement and anticipation I felt on that day and it seemed only natural to take a call from a local press guy who wanted to speak to me about the opportunity. I was halfway through the answer to his first question when I heard howls of laughter coming down the other end of the line. It was not a reporter of course but two of my teammates, Stuart Gray and David Platt, who had pulled off the hoax. And they didn't let me forget it.

The laughs at my expense continued when, for a change, Graham decided we would play a little cricket by way of relaxation before another match. 'Come on, Dwight, you're supposed to be quite good at this, take the bat and be first in,' said Graham. I walked to a wall at the training ground on which the stumps were drawn only to see the entire first-team squad lined up at the other end.

'Come on then, lads, let him have it,' barked Graham – and dozens of balls came hurtling at my head and body from players who were in hysterics as I tried to dodge them.

'Have a taste of your own medicine,' laughed Graham, in reference, of course, to the battering the England batsmen regularly received from the fearsome West Indian pace bowlers of that era.

You either shy away from that kind of thing or overcome your shyness and insecurities and come through the other side. With Graham there to provide support, I was not worried. Not even when my full debut against Manchester United a couple of weeks later – another defeat I'm afraid – was followed by a stinging and famous attack from Tommy Docherty in a column in a local newspaper. Docherty, having managed both United and Villa, wrote: 'If that lad makes a First Division [Premier League] footballer, my name's Mao-Tse-Tung.' I like to think that it's become famous for all the wrong reasons as far as the author is concerned.

Undoubtedly, the most important figure in my career throughout these first months was Graham, whose faith in me had brought me this far but when the summer of 1990 arrived I got a huge shock.

Graham was leaving. He was departing to take the England job, a departure which left me isolated and worried about what would happen next. I was there solely because Graham had seen something in my game he felt was valuable. I had no idea what would happen to me now. I felt alone and empty inside and hurried back to Tobago that summer wondering if my English dream was already over. I had been there barely five months after all and while I'd broken into the first team at such a young age and had worked damned hard, I knew I still had to prove myself. I was also homesick, even with the support of my adopted mum. The endless supply of beans on toast I had got used to but the culture, the people, the climate . . . it was still a little strange and disorientating, despite the laughs with my teammates. When the club then appointed Dr Jozef Vengloš as Graham's successor (who I found out later was the first non-British or Irish manager to run a top-flight club), I did not have a clue who he was or whether he would have any interest in me.

Again I have to thank Sheila and Bryn for so much at this stage. They loved Villa and loved their football; they were the ones who helped me persevere and come to terms with what had happened when I returned in July to begin pre-season training and met the new manager.

I wanted it to work. I wanted it to work so much and the fact that I had nothing to concentrate on other than my football – no social life, certainly no drinking or going out at nights – would prove a big help. And I was surrounded by some great role models at Villa. David Platt had been a sensation with England at the World Cup in Italy that summer when he'd played a crucial part in the team reaching the semi-finals and was making huge strides; Gordon Cowans had been and would once more become an England player, a wonderful footballer. Despite their success, they would be the guys who would go back and do endless hours of extra work on finishing or dribbling skills or passing or whatever else was required to take them to the top and keep them there. I was in awe of them and so I watched and followed. Their dedication was inspirational and, I realized, it what was needed to reach the peak of the profession. Villa was my education.

In a way, Docherty was right. He didn't think I would ever be strong enough to withstand the rigours of the English game and those early matches told me I had to add power to my physique if I was to prove him wrong. My strength and stamina needed building up. Again, I sought out the right help and advice from the senior players and the physios and got to work. Hour after hour. Day after day. Week after week. Work, work, work. On the pitches, in the gym.

I had plenty of natural talent but it was my work rate and my work ethic that would make me a great player. I would stay behind after training, take a bag of balls, and work on my scoring, heading and kicking. Heading perhaps didn't come as naturally to me, but with extra practice it was no longer a problem. I would do a goal kick up to the sky and then bring it down on my chest, kick it up, control the ball, make it stick to my feet, do little tricks. I'd get the coach to fire balls at me from different angles so I could learn to control it from every direction. Even when things were going well I was still working hard behind the scenes. You couldn't get me off a football pitch.

The trouble with a new manager coming in, especially a stranger to our game in Dr Vengloš, was that he was going to stick with experienced, proven players where possible. He was a much-travelled former coach of the old Czechoslovakia as well as working in Australia and Portugal but he had no previous experience of the English game – and he did not have much use for this young kid brought over from the Caribbean on a hunch of his predecessor. I had to fight for my survival and I did.

I would stay with Sheila and Bryn for the best part of my first two years at Villa; Vengloš's stay was short and not particularly sweet. The team went from ending the 1989–90 season second only to Liverpool to fighting against relegation. Happily, we survived the drop to the second division, but Vengloš left in May having not got to grips with the English game at all.

For me, my second year had been a positive experience. I had seen some game time, my confidence was growing along with my physical condition – and there was absolutely no doubt about my determination. And as I matured on the pitch, then so I matured off it.

I began to venture out a little more, with Smally and

then another newcomer to the camp, Ugo Ehiogu. A circle of friends was developing which would stay firm through the years to come. Ugo, a powerful defender who reached the England team, was signed from West Brom that summer and we immediately hit it off – the same age, the same ambitions, the same challenges, training together. He remains a big pal to this day and someone with whom I would share many an adventure.

We even share the same birthday although I think that represents a mark against those who believe in astrological charts – you could not imagine two more different personalities. He is so fussy, entirely the opposite to me. I dread going out for dinner with him because he takes an age to order with his constant queries about the menu and methods of food preparation. And he's a big smoker too. Seriously. Yes, I know that's surprising in this day and age but he would put away a packet a day when we were out of season. Ugo ribs me about the amount of salt I like in my food – a legacy of my Tobago upbringing – but I can always respond about his puffing away on the ciggies. And at least his dress sense has got a little better with age.

Ugo and Smally became constant companions as I slowly came out of my shell and found other interests away from football. This included my first English girlfriend – quite a moment for a young man coming to terms with this new, predominately white culture. Going out with Rachel, who was from nearby Nuneaton, was a whole new experience for me. And a good one. Being taken back to her house to meet her mum and dad was something I had not encountered before; very formal, very English, very proper. A long way from lazy dates on the local beach in Tobago! I got on fine with her family and I felt very comfortable as I think they did with me. I can't recall what went wrong between us – other than we were both very young – but she was a good person who was there at an important time in my life.

I dated another local girl, Lisa Matthews, for a year or so after Rachel; it was another steady relationship that helped me feel more mature and calm. It was just normal stuff. Drinks, the movies, meals. But it helped provide a steady routine that made me feel more settled in England.

Back in training, the club had welcome its new manager, Ron Atkinson, who arrived in July 1991 from Sheffield Wednesday. Big Ron was a giant personality in the English game during the 1980s and 1990s and proved to be a manager who helped me to bring my game on further. He was a very different managerial force from what I'd experienced before. He was big, colourful, funny, known to be a lover of attacking, exciting football. He was also a crazy, raging bull when the mood took him.

Until then, the management styles I had encountered had taught me to expect a 'Well done' if I had played well and a 'Don't worry, but you can do better' if I had not. Now here was this crazy guy, a big name, a big man, looking to wind up players to get the reaction he wanted. Ugo once confessed to me that he had been approached by Atkinson with the orders to 'launch' into me in training – give me a kick or two. Ron was convinced I needed toughening up. Ugo said he didn't do it because he didn't have the heart to kick his mate. My version is that he couldn't do it because he was never quick enough to catch me. Where Graham had been supportive but firm and straight and Venglos had been quiet and introspective, Ron was a raging bull. If we won, great; if not, then look out, here comes the raging bull.

For the first time in my career, I saw some monumental bust-ups behind the scenes, most famously a showdown with one of his signings, the striker Dalian Atkinson, after one defeat at Chelsea a couple of years into his reign. I was right in the middle of it all, staring almost open-mouthed at the intensity of their confrontation. There was Dalian, a player the manager always thought was capable of more, calling Ron 'a fat twat' and Ron screaming back at him, 'Come on you c— let's see how fucking hard you are!' And then everybody jumping in trying to pull them apart. Amazing. I was only a kid, watching this unfold, not wanting to get involved but wondering: is this how it really is?

We all know the problems Ron ran into in the latter stages of his career and it did not surprise me in a way. I would hear him express the kind of language that got him into trouble in that unguarded moment on the TV gantry. But at the time? I just took it as the sort of thing men of Ron's era said and it never carried any malice. It was the language of his generation and I didn't take any great offence at it.

And his methods were always unusual. He even gave me a shot of brandy before one mid-winter match. 'Come on, son, take a nip of this, it's freezing out there,' he said. Imagine that these days. Not very Arsène Wenger, is it? But it was normal enough back then. His arrival coincided with the birth of the Premier League which, although we didn't realize it at first, would send the game hurtling into a different universe. But Ron was 'old school'.

I think he had a regard for my talent but doubted whether I would be strong enough for him. He brought in top strikers in Dean Saunders and Dalian and they were always going to delay my breakthrough into the first team. But, OK, that was his call and it was up to me to do something about it. Nobody said it was going to be easy. And it didn't help that I ruptured a thigh muscle in my first year under him anyway, which took me out of the game for six months.

But a career-shaping moment arrived in the 1993–94 season when our team fought its way through to the League Cup final. It should have been a highlight but it became one of the worst experiences of my career. I had figured in the team, now largely playing as a wide midfielder, all the way through the route to the final and felt I had done well. I remember all the build-up so clearly, the excitement, and my thinking 'I'm going to play.' And then I remember settling in at the hotel team meeting, everyone but the established guys on a knife-edge about whether they will be playing. Deep down I was confident of selection . . . but suddenly, the team is read out and my name is missing.

I was stunned. It hurt so much. I was never exactly sure why he left me out. But he's the gaffer, he picks the team. Villa won the game against Manchester United 3–1 – a result against the odds I must add as United had won the double the year before. Nobody predicted that scoreline and for Ron that's all that matters. But it left me feeling badly hurt.

I had come to England because I wanted to be a somebody. I had worked hard, so I thought; I trained hard, took on board lessons from the older lads and I'd led a clean life off the pitch. But it obviously wasn't enough. I was so disheartened I felt like packing it all in and going back to Tobago. But then I reasoned that if I went back now, it would be as a failure. What was there for me except a dull local job and a lifetime of regrets?

And Big Ron's decision made me even more determined to improve. He would leave Villa before the following season was halfway through but I was a tougher and even more determined player for his presence.

6

HIGH JINKS

Stuart Pearce scared me and I don't mind admitting it. When I used to play out wide he would frighten the living daylights out of me. I think Stuart knew about his stature in the game – this hard-nosed, hard-tackling proven international famous for those surging runs from left back.

On several occasions, I found myself playing out wide directly against the Nottingham Forest and England left back and was supposed to contain him. But I think he knew where he stood in the food chain and used that to intimidate those he felt would be threatened by it. I was one of them. He used the fear he saw in me as a young boy still coming to grips with the ferocious physical demands of top-flight football in England. It was all in his face really. That cold-eyed, fiercely determined, emotionless expression. After coming in to tackle you he would get up and grunt, as if to send a message of 'Don't tangle with me, boy.' And it worked. I never enjoyed a game against Stuart Pearce.

There was only one other guy who intimidated me as I made my way up the ladder. At Blackburn, Colin Hendry was a horrible centre half to play against. I used to call him 'the leech' because I could never get him off me. He used to put anything in the way to make a challenge, his head, legs everywhere ... he was a nightmare to play against.

But then one night that changed, a freezing cold February night in 1996, and it was a big moment for me. I was starting to come into my own when Hendry and I clashed on the halfway line – and I 'rag-dolled' him. Just barged him over and got the better of him. And from that moment onwards, I never feared another opponent. I was surprised by my physical strength as much as anything. Here was a player who had always given me a hard, tough time and suddenly I had been too strong for him. That was quite a moment, a realization that I could match these guys, no matter how big and tough they were.

Looking back at the records, it is no surprise to me that this should happen when Villa were under the management of Ron's successor Brian Little – and I was locked into one of the happiest and most fruitful periods of my career.

I had learned much under Ron without ever feeling he truly trusted in me. When things got tough for him, he reverted to his tried and trusted players. By the time he left I was nursing a deep sense of grievance that I should be in the team. From the moment Brian arrived, I realized that things would change. He had been a hugely popular striker at Villa in his playing days, a forward who perhaps recognized in my game elements of his own. He had been recruited from Leicester City, a quietly spoken but clearly intelligent football man.

'I want you to be my main man,' he began telling me

from the moment he arrived. 'I've watched you for a while now and I want you to be the number one striker.' It was music to my ears and inspired me to play great football. You ask any player and he will tell you there is nothing better than the 100 per cent backing and faith of your manager. I'd always known I was capable and now I felt invincible with Brian. And not just in training or on the pitch. I was also becoming a key part of the Villa team off the pitch, and was in demand for sponsorship promotions and personal appearances.

It was around this time that I got my nickname. The fans often referred to me throughout my career as Yorkie, which I think came from the Yorkie bar! But in fact my nickname was something else entirely. I was partnered at Villa with Savo Milošević, who played with us for three years from 1995. Playing alongside him, I thought it would be funny to be called Yorkovič. 'He's Milošević,' I told the boys, 'and I'm going to be Yorkovič.' I thought this was hilarious, and in the end the name sort of stuck. Even now all my friends in football know me as Yorkovič.

Although I enjoyed socializing, first with Smally and Andy but then with a gradually growing group of teammates, I stuck to my pledge of not drinking all the way up to the age of twenty-one. This made me extremely popular with the senior professionals when their chance came to unwind. Who were they going to get to chauffeur them around? None other than the teetotaller up front! I didn't mind it for a moment because this gave me more opportunity to get to know some of the big, big players who flooded into the Villa dressing room in these years – Steve

Staunton, Andy Townsend, Ray Houghton, and of course Paul McGrath. I loved Paul, absolutely loved him. A legendary figure in the game, one of the finest footballers I ever had the pleasure to play alongside. And yet, as we all know, a gentle soul cursed by demons which gave him a serious drinking problem.

He produced some of the finest football of his career at Villa but reckons he did so through the bottom of a glass. I went to pick him up on three occasions as I recall; I would get calls at night from his drinking companions to come and fetch him because he was legless. And I'd be driving him home with an empty bottle of vodka rolling around the back seat and Paul barely conscious next to me. But there was nothing a young man such as myself would say in criticism – especially when you then saw this very same footballer go out on the pitch and play like a king.

He started taking me to Dublin occasionally after Saturday matches and introduced me to his city. It was like walking around with that nation's reigning monarch. Towns, villages, hotels ... everywhere we went he was feted. He would go missing for a few hours and then ring up again and tell me where to find him.

Did Paul introduce me to the partying side of football? Maybe a little. But that was always in me and I always felt I had it under control. But in the mad, mad world of Paul McGrath, he could get anything he wanted and he could get it in minutes.

Why did he drink so much? I don't think I ever saw Paul sober enough to ask him the question! That's not being disrespectful and don't forget he was an older guy unlikely to confide in me. But he would never pour his heart out. All I knew was that the drink brought him some kind of comfort and, for a guy I admired so much and one who would always try to help me in my football, that was good enough.

My growing up continued under the influence of some heavyweight figures during these formative years in the early 1990s at Villa. But they taught me so much about living and enjoying this great career. It was Dean Saunders, the Welsh international and former Liverpool striker, who introduced me to golf. I never thought it would be for me. Never. The first shot I played, I shanked a tee-shot into the rough nearby. Naturally, I went to the spot, took out another tee to place the ball on for my second shot. 'What are you doing?' said Deano. 'You can't do that!' I was that naive.

But what a character. He had the worst dress sense of any player I have encountered and when we pulled him up on it, he would reply, 'Yeah – but have you seen the label?' And he was the last pick in training. Always the last pick. He would be telling us, 'Feeling sharp today, boys, I'm feeling sharp,' but still nobody wanted him on their team. Even so, come match day he was invariably on the button. He wasn't interested in any tricks. Didn't want to know about any of them. We would take the mickey out of him but Deano would say, 'Ah, but can you do this?' And smash one into the top corner from twenty-five yards. Every time. That's all he wanted to do.

'The Beak' – Andy Townsend – was another fantastic professional who was a great storyteller away from the battlefield and a wonderful teammate on it. He might be more familiar to younger folk now as a radio broadcaster but, let me tell you, The Beak could party when he wanted to.

Then there was 'Fash the Bash' – John Fashanu, who briefly played for Villa in the latter part of Atkinson's reign. He arrived with red Quaser boots for which he was paid £5,000, a deal which impressed us all greatly, and a reputation as the smoothest guy in town. He was another big character who could make me howl with laughter, especially on the pitch. As our goalkeeper got ready to punt upfield, Fash would be shouting, arms aloft, 'Oooh, baby, oooh, baby, just put it up there.' And as it went skywards, there would be more running commentary. 'That's Big Fash's ball. That's for Big Fash, baby. Come to Big Fash, baby.' It was hilarious – but it worked. Fash was an intimidating figure and his talking constantly unsettled opponents. When Villa played a UEFA Cup tie against Inter Milan at the San Siro in 1994, the Italians did not know what to make of this glistening giant, stripped down to his shorts and all oiled up, going through a kung fu martial arts-style routine in the communal warm-up area before the players' tunnel. The Inter guys just looked at Fash with 'What the hell is that?' all over their faces. But it worked for us.

Cyrille Regis was another key influence during the Atkinson years. As a footballer, he taught me the only important thing is what happens when you cross that white line. 'This is where you are judged,' he would say. 'You will make mistakes, don't take everything to heart. You will have down periods in your life and you will have to find the desire to come back.' He was a great mentor, a privilege to play alongside, if only for a brief spell.

By the time my twenty-first birthday party arrived, I was no longer the naive, wide-eyed newcomer from the Caribbean. I was much more settled into the ways of the world and had decided that I would not let this special night pass without arranging a suitable party – and breaking my booze embargo.

At the time, I was going out with Lisa but my social circle was now very active and I spent the weeks leading up to this bash at Villa Park inviting just about every single woman I bumped into. As a result, when the party came round, the place was wall-to-wall with extremely attractive young girls. I'm not sure some of the older lads in the party were so grateful to me. They had to explain to their wives that this array of female loveliness was nothing to do with them. But I was on a high that night and had the time of my life.

Having not touched alcohol beforehand, I had to find a drink to my taste and settled for Baileys, the closest I could find to what I recalled of the flavours of the Caribbean. I got merrily drunk although not drunk enough to follow the ways of one of my teammates. At one stage in the bash, one of them asked me to accompany him to his car because he 'needed to get something'. When I got there, he was smoking a spliff, an aroma I knew only too well from growing up in Tobago. He handed it to me and, I guess intimidated by his seniority and a little bit the worse for wear, I took it and had one drag. It was pointless. I couldn't tell what it was supposed to do for me and handed it back immediately. It remains to this day my only ever contact with drugs. I didn't do drugs. I didn't gamble or even bet on the horses. I didn't smoke. I had two great passions. Football – and spending time in the company of women. It didn't have to end up in bed for me to enjoy myself. But often it did.

I had bought my first house in Sutton Coldfield for £95,000 before my twentieth birthday and that naturally made entertaining a little easier. Sheila, particularly, was devastated when I left and it was daunting at first, realizing I would have to fend for myself, cook for myself, choose furniture and decorate. But the independence took the restrictions off my social life.

Now I don't want this to sound arrogant but I realize that is probably unavoidable. But by the time I was making a name for myself at Villa, I could have done with another two or three Dwight Yorkes to take care of the attention I was receiving. Trying to please everyone was taxing; there simply wasn't enough to go round. And, yes, I know how that sounds but I am only telling the truth. I don't feel I should have to apologize for this. I know that there is a certain resentment attached to the fact that a young man who engages in a lot of sexual activity enjoys a certain reputation while a woman who does the same is frowned upon. I can't do anything about that. But there were never any false promises in my adventures. Despite some of the claims that would later appear from women – some I had met, some I had not – in the tabloids, I never took any girl to bed under false pretences. She knew how things stood. I wasn't looking for marriage or even a steady girlfriend. But I was looking to live life to the full. And if you are a professional athlete, trained to the limit of his physical capabilities, and up for it, what else are you going to do?

There were some famous escapades, some of which made the headlines but many didn't. Like the time I ended up bedding four women in twenty-four hours. That may sound pretty far-fetched but, such was the life of freedom and excitement I was living at the time, to me it was perfectly natural. This particular episode began on a regular night out with my Villa drinking buddies, including Ugo and Smally, on a trip to Birmingham's party strip in Broad Street.

We would meet up to pass away a pleasant evening in our favourite haunts, not doing anything outlandish but, yes, looking to pull girls. On one such occasion, I recall leaving with a girl whose name – try as I may – I cannot remember but with whom I ended up enjoying a night at my house. No strings attached and, with her dashing out early the next morning to get to work, no awkward 'I'll call you' moment.

But the night had given me a taste for action and, with training finished by 1 p.m. the following day, my thoughts turned to a sequel. Time to call a girlfriend whose routine I knew well and who worked locally, Sue. I knew she would be finishing around 3 p.m. that day and she knew what was on my agenda when I called her that afternoon to 'catch up'. She would only be able to stop for a while but there was still time for round two before she had to hurry off to collect her daughter.

I was only just recovering from that escapade when my phone rang a little while later. This was another well-established date, a married woman whose identity I should therefore protect, although she was so unhappy in her relationship I would be surprised if she remained in that marriage. When she called, I knew what she wanted and I was more than happy to oblige. She would be able to get round for an hour or so, making her regular excuse about going to the gym, between 6 p.m. and 7 p.m. It was a workout I had not anticipated but despite the activity of the day I rose to the challenge.

Enough you might say and I was absolutely knackered by then. But these were days when my phone would be going constantly and it wasn't long before a girl I knew from Tamworth was calling me. Did I fancy dinner? Well I hadn't eaten so why not? A little wine, some conversation, some food and I could feel my energy levels returning. Lynne made it clear that she wanted to come and spend the night at my place and who was I to reject the offer? Or the invitation to bed later.

That was not something which happened every week but, at the same time, it was not something which I found particularly amazing. It was pretty much indicative of the life I had come to take as normal once I had left Sheila and Bryn's. I didn't behave any differently at Manchester United than I did at Aston Villa; it's all about perception. What surprises me is the scale of amazement whenever I tell that story.

And by this period in the mid-1990s, with my Villa career blossoming, chance dictated that I was joined in Birmingham by none other than my old pal who I had once caught out as wicketkeeper in that inter-island cricket match. Lara signed a contract to play cricket with Warwickshire and we could not believe our fortune.

Now he was 'The Man', probably the finest player in the world at that moment as his record-breaking innings throughout the mid-1990s would suggest. While we had never been out of touch, now we could team up all the time. We felt like kings of the hill. I would watch his back, he would watch mine. We shared accommodation, he would stop at my place and I at his apartment; we shared cars and maybe even a little rivalry to out-do each other in our chosen fields. Anybody who was around at that time knew where they could find us, at the Bel Air nightclub at the Belfry every Monday night. We would party hard but we played hard. We're still really tight, and I am godfather to his daughter Sydney.

It was a pivotal moment in my career when he came to Warwickshire. He was on fire at that point. He scored 501 runs in one match for the county club. And, I remember when he scored that record breaking 375 for the West Indies against England in 1994, Ron Atkinson took me into his office and popped open a bottle of champagne! Brian inspired me and spurred me on to greater success. He had become a major superstar and was breaking record after record. Although I was doing well at Villa, I hadn't yet reached the top of my career. He may not realize it but he helped to make me the success I became. Every time I heard about a hundred, I wanted to go out and score a hat-trick. I remember joking to him, 'How can I compete with you? I've got to go and win *all* the trophies!' And I did! But there were more years of hard work to get close to Lara's achievements, and it is somewhat down to him that I did.

The two of us were pretty much inseparable at that point and we had some great fun. I was back in Trinidad on a home visit at one point in 1995 when Brian was in Port of Spain for a one-day international match against Australia. We decided to hook up before the match. It was a Friday night, and Brian came out to meet me. He said, 'I'm just coming out quickly for a drink because you're here, but I've got cricket in the morning and so I can't stay long.' Well, those were famous last words. We were still out partying at about three in the morning. Brian didn't drink as much as I did, but we had a fine time.

I was due to go and watch him that next day, but the combination of alcohol and jet lag meant I overslept and woke up completely disorientated. 'Shit!' I thought, 'I'm supposed to be at the cricket!' I switched on the telly only to find that not only had I missed half the match, but there was Brian batting and already well past 100 runs thwacking balls all over the place. He had managed to not only get up and get to the ground on time, but he was putting in an amazing performance. I could only lie in bed and marvel at what a genius cricketer he was. That was just one example of the fun we had. It was the best time of our lives and, away from the media bubble that encircles sports stars in London and Manchester, we were able to enjoy ourselves relatively discreetly.

I dread to think what the headlines might have been if I had enjoyed such a fine time as a Manchester United player. I'm sure I would not have been able to keep it so quiet. In fact, I know I wouldn't. Witness one other memorable, crazy and funny night a little later on in my Villa days which would ultimately end up splashed all over the tabloids.

By now my crew had been joined by the Australian goalkeeper, Mark Bosnich, a character who shared our love for fun and adventures when the hard work had stopped. Bozzy, Smally and myself were, as usual, on our Thursday night patrol when we met up with a bunch of girls we knew and headed back to my house. Now a few weeks before this, a technician pal of mine I knew only as Keith had been round to fix me up with Sky on my bedroom TV that already had access to several porn channels. Anyway, he asked me if I was aware that I could get a camera link from downstairs up to my bedroom and I thought to myself, 'Yeah, why not?' I was a young man up for ever-more interesting experiences.

Anyway, I swear I thought nothing more of it and certainly had not taped anything before that night and the drinks and laughter started flowing. Suddenly, somebody pipes up about the camera and thinks it would be fun to tape the antics. It doesn't bother me or anyone else. So why not?

There were three girls with us and the idea to play a game popped into the conversation led I think by Bozzy who has – or had – a freak nature. He could be mad one day and then undergo a complete personality change, leaving you wondering if he was the same guy you were talking to twenty-four hours earlier. 'Let's cross dress,' he declares, 'the girls get our clothes on and we go for theirs.' Well, it sounded like harmless fun – and I'm sure it was as three hulking athletes tried to slip into three slinky dresses

– and the drinks were still flowing. I think one or two of us might have been hoping it would turn into an orgy. But that never happened. Bozzy got into some spanking and toe-sucking and what have you, which was all very freaky but typically Bozzy, before the night kind of fizzled out. That's my recollection anyway. As I recall, the only person who got lucky at the end of it all was Smally.

I never watched the tapes and later put them in with my football and porn tapes which a guy used to collect when bringing me new ones every so often. This guy took them by mistake and what happened after that I have no idea. My theory is the world would never have known about them had it not been for my move to United. But the moment that happened, somebody, somewhere realized they were sitting on some valuable private tapes and the next thing I knew, they were all over the papers. The newspaper tried to portray the night as some kind of sordid, seedy episode but it was nothing more than a bunch of young, like-minded folk having a great laugh at a time of their life when they could. But it all seemed so much worse in the cold light of newsprint and caused much embarrassment for all of us.

Don't ask me why, with all the lovely girls whose company I have been fortunate to enjoy, but I have never fallen in love so fully that I found myself thinking: 'This is the one.' I've been smitten more than once, seriously smitten. But never to the point of thinking I wanted to settle down with just one girl. I always felt during my Villa days that there was something more ahead of me, something that I had to achieve and moving in with a woman was only going to get in the way of that ambition.

There were other reasons for this feeling. Players are often under pressure, subtle pressure but pressure nonetheless, to get themselves sorted out with a wife and family. Managers clearly like the notion of their players, always the subject of the kind of attention that I enjoyed, being taken out of the firing line, so to speak. But do you know something? Pretty much all I have seen from this culture is misery. Painful, bitter divorces. Or players cheating on the side. People in and around the Villa team at that time were getting divorced and the only message I detected from the dressing room was: 'Don't get married – it only brings problems, pain and heartache.' Especially for a man so young and so focused on football. That was also strengthening my resistance to those who wanted me to change my ways. It didn't seem to have done so many of my teammates much good. I was a young single man having the time of his life and I was quite happy for it to stay that way.

We didn't even look at our payslips in those days. Well, I didn't. I must have scores of them unopened scattered in boxes somewhere. You may imagine that to be another display of arrogance but it wasn't meant to be.

There was never any trouble, never any fights and all the high jinks were harmless, consensual fun. It was just a subplot to my first passion, football. And the football made sense of everything. The team that Brian put together, with some terrific new players arriving to replace the Atkinson group, was exceptional. We could party all right but we could play, too, and we didn't get the two mixed up.

It's funny how over such a long career, you can recall

big, big moments which are down to instinct as much as anything else. But they are moments that shape your life. By the time we went to play an FA Cup fourth round tie at Sheffield United in January 1996, I was a very secure twenty-four-year-old feeling extremely settled in the Villa line-up. In the build-up to that game, I had been larking around taking penalties against Bozzy, who by then had already established himself as one of the League's brilliant young keepers. I gave him the double-bluff on one occasion, luring Bozzy to commit himself before gently chipping the ball down the centre while he lay sprawled on the goal line.

'And that's how I'm going to take my next penalty,' I declared to the sound of much ribbing from my teammates.

'Naah, you won't have the bottle, Yorkie!' they shouted. 'Doing it in training is one thing, but you'll never have the balls to do it in a match.'

But I did. And it was one that counted too, the only goal of the game in a really tight, tough match at Bramall Lane. Alan Kelly, the Blades keeper, took the bait as my gentle nine iron dropped into the net. And that was quite a moment for me, especially with the match being beamed on live TV around the country. Suddenly, the football world was very aware of this cheeky young buck now leading Villa's attack who had dared to execute such an outrageous spot kick. I definitely detected an increased interest in me after that match. I sometimes wonder what would have happened had Alan stayed still and just caught it.

A couple of years later, it was a penalty repeated successfully against David Seaman, the England goalkeeper, in scoring what would be my last goal for Villa, one which helped us qualify for European football. Seaman, to his credit, just laughed as it gently floated by him. But that type of goal was very much part of my nature; I was here to enjoy myself and hopefully entertain people and it was the confidence Brian displayed in me which really brought out this side of my game.

And I wanted the headlines, I can't deny that. My career had levelled out under Atkinson and I had watched Bozzy, just by way of an example, really propel himself to the forefront, removing a Villa legend in Nigel Spink from his path to become the number one keeper and probably one of the best in Europe. It is a natural part of a goalscorer's make-up to demand the same kind of status and I was no different. Sometimes, it is that basic. The goalscorer gets the headlines and you will rarely meet one who doesn't revel in that attention. I was no different. And I was determined to reap the rewards.

I love life. I love living. I come from a background which makes me treasure every single second granted on this earth. I feel so, so fortunate to have achieved what I have done so far, and I have enjoyed it all. And that smile on my face, which was the tag the media latched on to as my career blossomed, was not contrived. I was having the time of my life.

The finest moments came in that 1995–96 season, Brian Little's second year in charge. It culminated in another League Cup triumph at Wembley, the fifth in Aston Villa's history, and there was absolutely no doubt I would be in the team. Our semi-final conquest of Arsenal produced another one of those games when I got myself noticed by the top dogs in football. We were two goals down to the Gunners in the first leg of the semi-final at Highbury, with Dennis Bergkamp on fire for them, and pretty much everyone thought the tie was over and done with after barely half an hour. But that was to be some night and I'll never forget it. I think I played one of my best games for the team, scoring twice to draw the match. Thanks to the increased confidence I felt after the Hendry moment and the backing of my new manager, I went to Highbury no longer frightened by anything or anyone, even though the legendary Arsenal back four were notoriously intimidating – Adams, Bould, Winterburn and Dixon. But I was full of confidence by then. We remained goalless in an absolutely epic second leg at Villa Park, a game that proved football can still have drama and tension without anyone scoring.

And the final? We could not have asked for a better performance against a Leeds team we totally outplayed. Townsend, Mark Draper, McGrath, Ugo, Gareth Southgate, Gary Charles, Ian Wright, Bozzy, Alan Wright . . . these were all top players and we were supremely confident. Our 3–0 victory was as comprehensive as the scoreline suggests. And so it was, on the Monday morning of 25 March 1996, two years after that crushing disappointment on Villa's previous League Cup final trip, I woke up at our Wembley hotel after a night celebrating our victory with a beautiful blonde beside me wondering if it was possible life could ever be sweeter.

I had flown over my mentor, Bertille, to watch his protégé at Wembley. I knew back home the entire island would have been huddled around their TV sets to watch their boy in action. I rounded off the victory scoring our last goal and if you look very closely at the TV pictures of those moments you are not mistaken – there were tears in my eyes, so emotional was the experience. I think Bertille must have shed tears too. I had so wanted him there to see me finally step out on that turf on such a magnificent occasion; the little kid he had to slap down on the street to put him back on the straight and narrow and then bundle into his boot to give him a ride home from his simple coaching sessions. I had wanted my family to come too but they were unable to get time off from work. I knew at home the country had been on lockdown for that match. And the pride, the joy and happiness I suspected they all felt was written all over Bertille's face when I saw him after the game.

It was a momentous day that has been burned on my brain for ever. The sheer numbers of supporters, especially our own, was unbelievable. I can still hear them singing the 'New York, New York' anthem they had adapted just for me as we drove through the streets to the stadium. 'It's up to you, Dwight Yorke, Dwight Yorke.' Oh man, it was just incredible . . . the excitement of the build-up, the scale of that setting, the game itself . . . it was breathtaking. Two years earlier, I had been heartbroken when left out of the Villa team which beat Manchester United in the final but I had returned as the main man in the attack of a rebuilt team.

Yes, a fantastic day was followed by a night of wild celebration, a fact confirmed by the blonde sleeping on my shoulder the following morning. Her name was Nicki, a friend of Mark Bosnich's fiancée, Sarah. Nicki was stunning, a beautiful model with whom I had shared a few dates before the final. I was quite smitten with Nicki, I don't mind admitting. Not only was she dazzling but wonderful fun as well. She had the whole package, you might say, and at that moment in my life I could not have asked for more arresting company.

In the months that followed, I would see her less frequently before we drifted apart. I was far too focused on my football and a single man's lifestyle to consider anything more serious. But many's the day since then that I have thought of Nicki, that exhilarating night we spent together and wondered: 'I wonder what would have happened if . . .'

I had it all surely? I had remembered in my earlier days at the club marvelling at the stature and confidence of David Platt. He would stroll into the dressing room and start getting stripped for the game even before the team had been announced. Some might say that was arrogance but for me, waiting anxiously to see if I had made the bench or even got in the starting XI, it was a statement I longed to make. 'I am The Man.' And now I could make it. Now I could walk into Villa's dressing room and know that, providing I was fit, I would be playing. My football was where I wanted it to be. At last, I was The Man.

I never had any issues with my teammates throughout my Villa days save for one. Stan Collymore disappointed me, I'm afraid. He came to the club in the summer of 1997 as a big, big signing who, Brian hoped, would help move us from a top six team to one which could maybe challenge for the championship. Stan was one of the game's big personalities in the mid-1990s and a forward who had a strong pull towards Villa. As a local lad raised in nearby Cannock, he had watched the famous team of the early 1980s which had won the League Championship and European Cup. He made his name at Nottingham Forest and then transferred to Liverpool in a big money move, where he had mixed success. Nevertheless, Brian was trying to take us to the next level and clearly saw Stan as a man to help us do that. He certainly had talent, no one could deny that, but there were rumours he could be a bit moody.

Nevertheless, when Villa brought in Stan for a club record £7m fee, it was to the acclaim of Villa fans who were excited by his arrival. But I felt Stan's arrival brought an unsettling tension to the team. He had left Liverpool, undoubtedly a bigger club, and to me gave the impression that he could swan into Villa and just take over the place. As I had just finished the club's top scorer for the second year running, having scored 45 goals over the two seasons, and I had been named Villa's player of the year, I certainly felt insulted by this. I could not help wondering to myself who the hell he thought he was?

I am a great believer – as is obvious – that if you have warranted success and a high profile then you should be free to enjoy them. And I had worked very hard to get myself into a key position at Villa. I had earned it too. I wasn't the only one. Ugo, too, had gone through the same process. Bozzy as well. And yet here we saw someone who was basing his authority at the club and inside the dressing room on reputation alone. And that's how it stayed. We never saw Stan deliver anything on the pitch with any consistency that warranted his big attitude around the place. He talked a great game which he rarely, if ever, delivered and to me that simply wasn't acceptable. It has since come out that Stan was troubled at the time and had his own issues. And who knows if that contributed to what seemed to me like a bad attitude. But I found it hard to bear.

I had so much time for Brian but I felt he indulged Stan too much. He was allowed to miss training, for example, and that undermined the manager's authority. It sowed seeds of discontent in the dressing room and instead of providing the trigger point for an even stronger Villa challenge, it all went horribly wrong in the autumn of 1997. We made the worst start to a season in the club's history and, frankly, we never recovered. Brian, battered by the pressures and downturn in our fortunes, would ultimately walk out early in 1998. And while I wouldn't lay all the blame at Stan's door for that, I think he certainly played a key role in ending a management regime that I will always cherish.

7

OLD TRAFFORD CALLS

I don't read the papers now – for different reasons – but at this time they were essential reading. I was a headline junkie, wanting to get on the back pages, wanting to make a name for myself. If they were not talking about me, that translated as me not doing my job.

I don't remember precisely when I first saw my name and 'Manchester United' appear in the same story, but it must have been early in 1998 because I do recall this was the first time the idea registered with me. You don't really take too much notice because the stories are kind of two-a-penny and, to be honest, United are that little bit different to every other club and there is no point in denying it. I remember seeing it and thinking: 'Well, that's never going to happen.' At that stage, I could not see beyond Villa; this was the club where I had made it, where I had found my true self and proved myself as a footballer in England. I was happy and settled.

Brian was replaced by one of his former coaches, John Gregory, who had left to take up his first managerial appointment at Wycombe but now returned to Villa bringing a breath of fresh air and a release of pressure. We began a surging recovery in which I played well and had a really good goalscoring run. And then, suddenly, the talk about me and United was hotting up.

Throughout pretty much all of my Villa years, I had been guided by the Birmingham-based adviser – he hated to be called an agent – Tony Stephens, who had built up a formidable portfolio of football's blue-chip players. He had masterminded David Platt's career, which was how I was introduced to him, and from there he took on players including Alan Shearer and a promising young midfielder at Manchester United named David Beckham. Two years earlier, I had been in Tony's back garden while he thrashed out the details of Alan Shearer's move to Newcastle. So I knew the kind of financial territory these people were moving in.

United, Tony began to tell me, were not the only interested party. After playing against Atlético Madrid, who squeezed by us in the UEFA Cup quarter-finals, we met with their president Jesús Gil and a party of their representatives in London. The money being talked about now seemed incredible – I think that offer was £1.3 million a year. After tax. Far cry from the £200 a week I'd considered a fortune in 1989. We met them at the Conrad Hotel in Chelsea and left thinking that a deal was all but done.

But then talks began with Sir Alex Ferguson and the prospect of a transfer to United became a little more real. Not that I dared believe it would happen. I was still the kid from Tobago at heart who had already reached way beyond his wildest dreams. And no matter how things would later turn out, I also felt a strong sense of loyalty to Villa.

And it was wise not to get carried away. One of the big hitters on the European scene, the Dutch striker Patrick Kluivert, was also being linked equally heavily to a move to Old Trafford. Alongside him, I felt, my profile was dwarfed. But talking with Tony and then Platty, who had been propelled into an outstanding career in Italy, I began to get excited.

What surprised me was the response this generated from Villa. Tony met Doug Ellis, Villa's chairman, to discuss a new contract. He made it clear he was ready to offer a then staggering £27,000 a week. In terms of cold, basic pay, this was actually more than the Man United offer and it sent my head spinning.

'You don't want to leave here, Dwight,' Doug was saying to me. 'This is your home, you are part of the furniture now.'

I remember reading that another of my heroes John Barnes was going to be paid £10,000 a week by Liverpool. It had seemed a massive amount at the time and now I was going to nearly triple that. It seemed crazy, absolutely crazy.

Villa then offered to throw in a £1 million signing-on fee and the guarantee of a testimonial if I would sign there and then. I was in that meeting, listening to this offer and thinking: 'Can I really walk away from this?'

So why did I? Deep down, I was torn between dedicating the best years of my career to the club I owed so much and taking a chance of even greater things a hundred miles up the road. It was a little scary. I would be pushing out on my own again, just as I had done when I left Tobago nine years ago. But it was also incredibly exciting.

There was something about going to United that left me tingling inside. As Liverpool had dominated the 1980s when John Barnes was playing, so United were dominating the 1990s. They were the best club at that time. They had won the Premiership four times since it had been formed, taking the FA Cup in two of those seasons. They had amazing players. All I could see were the images of Roy Keane, Paul Scholes, Peter Schmeichel, Ryan Giggs and the rest of them holding trophies in the air. It was unreal to imagine I could be alongside them. But I could be. I could be.

We walked away from that Villa meeting pleading for more time and as the season then wound down, that cheeky penalty against Seaman helped us qualify again for the UEFA Cup. The team took on an end-of-season trip to Marbella, and when we ran into contact with Villa supporters they immediately struck up the now familiar song: 'It's up to you, Dwight Yorke, Dwight Yorke.' They were right. It was up to me. That was the problem. It was up to me and these guys were making me feel so special. I felt a real conflict of loyalties.

'You need to get away, somewhere where the media won't bother you,' Tony told me and, helped by Bozzy's Australian contacts, I headed for Sydney with 'the crew'. Bozzy, Ugo and I were a tight-knit little group and we had the time of our lives – although escaping the buzz about joining United was not quite so easy despite the holiday of a lifetime.

We really lived it up, so much so that we booked for two weeks and stayed for three. We threw a party on the roof of the Hyatt Hotel in Sydney and arrived to find 300 people there. Don't ask me how 300 people turned up but they did. We were living like rock stars, flush with money, dating beautiful girls, bumping into people and saying: 'Hey, we're having a party, you must come.' And never in any country have I seen so many outstanding women as in Australia.

Apart from the presence of some Aborigines, black folk in Sydney were still fairly scarce at that time, so I think Ugo and I were a bit of a novelty to the locals; we gate-crashed parties and even a wedding. But we were in such good spirits we never ran into opposition. We made a bond that trip – Bozzy, Ugo and myself – that no matter where our careers took us or what happened, we would reserve a week of our lives every year to go on holiday together. Like most promises, it was easier to make than keep. Especially with Bozzy. As the whole world would later discover, he would fall victim to a cocaine addiction which would cost him so dear and it may be easy to presume that this was the kind of setting in which that addiction started. If so I never saw it.

In fact, let me deal with something here. In all the partying I've enjoyed, never once did I take cocaine or any drugs for that matter. I've been labelled with it a few times; I have heard people whispering about 'Yorkie being into this or that' and it angers me. Yes, I saw Bozzy smoke some weed and on that trip I saw cocaine once when a local soap actor indulged.

Bozzy drifted into a spiral that brought him the wrong sort of headlines and a premature end to his career – he didn't play football for six years after his ban in 2002. But,

I will always be there for him if ever he needs me. Yes, he could be arrogant. He had that ruthless streak and could be nasty at times and there will be a good many people who only saw that side of him. But he could also be charming and great company. His descent into addiction saddened me greatly and I regret that our friendship has drifted from the halcyon days of Sydney 1998. And I will always defend him.

Despite the party time we were having, my phone on that trip was ringing constantly, the demand for updates impossible to resist. By the time I got back, the story was still running. 'Grego' had been first a great coach under Brian and in very little time as manager had made a big impact. He was again stressing how important I was to Villa and how desperate they were to keep me. But for all their best efforts, I wanted the move to United.

The transfer would drag on and on and I rolled with the speculation and Tony's advice to keep calm, stay focused on my football and let the rest take care of itself. I completed a good pre-season and settled down happily again with my Villa teammates. The fuss died down a little, I began to relax. But that was until the transfer deadline came.

It began with a phone call from my old gaffer Brian. 'How ya doin', son?' he asked.

'Fine, fine,' I said. I was always delighted to hear from Brian.

'This must be quite a moment for you, with all the rumours,' he went on. 'Well, I think I might have helped get you the move you're looking for.'

'What? What do you mean?'

'I've just come off the phone with Fergie and he has been asking all about you. What sort of lad you are, what kind of player etc. I've given you a good recommendation.'

That told me that United were interested for real. Despite all the Kluivert stories, despite the delays and Villa's staunch resistance, maybe I was the one they wanted.

Villa by now had changed their tack from fighting to keep me to fighting for every penny they could. Grego pointed out that I was as important to Villa as Shearer had been to Blackburn. And Blackburn had got £16 million for the mighty England centre forward. That's what Villa wanted. It was heating up now as the hours ticked away. I think Brian mentioned that United valued me at £10 million – not the £15 million to £16 million Villa were asking for.

There was time for me to play what would be my last match for Villa, the opening game of the new season at Everton – and I think that must have been my worst performance for the club since I arrived. It was not through any deliberate policy on my part; it never would be. I know Villa fans have always accused me of 'playing to get away' that day but there was so much going on by then, so many distractions, that it was hard to focus on the game – anyone who has been in that position will tell you the same.

But as the weekend rolled into Monday and then Tuesday, even Tony was beginning to have his doubts this deal could be pushed through. Villa were holding out for their valuation and United's third offer of £10 million had been rejected. There was talk of Andy Cole coming in the opposite direction but as we approached deadline day, and with my phone red hot from friends and family wanting to know what was happening, the transfer looked dead.

One morning of that week, I had awoken early at around 7 a.m. – and that is not like me at all! – having hardly been able to sleep for thinking about what was going to happen. I found myself knocking at the front door of the Villa chairman's house within half an hour.

He was surprised to see me, invited me in and we sat there and had a chat.

'I feel you've got to let me go,' I can hear myself telling Doug even now. 'I've come this far but it's time. You've got to let me go.'

'I can't,' he told me. 'You are too important to this club.'

I kept on pleading with him, to the point where there were tears in my eyes, but I was not sure I had convinced him. I left in a bit of a sulk thinking that there was no way he was going to let me go.

I awoke on transfer deadline day in August 1998 knowing the parties were still talking but resigned to the fact it was too late for a deal of this magnitude to be done. That was the last day a player could be registered to play in Europe that coming season, and United weren't going to pay top whack for me if I wasn't eligible for every match. Tony called to remind me to take a change of clothing, '. . . just in case . . .'

Normally, I'm a chirpy, smiley fella but as I arrived for training that day, I guess the misgivings about everything were obvious. Dressing rooms can be cruel at such times and the lads ripped into me mercilessly. 'You're going nowhere, son,' they taunted me.

Steve Harrison, the coach, came in and read an imaginary note on his clipboard: 'Now don't shoot the messenger, Yorkie, but I've got you down here for training – it looks like you're with us, son.' Very funny. And when he said it, I did think, 'Well, that's it.'

But then everything changed. Tony rang me on the communal phone outside the treatment room. I listened. Congratulations, Tony was saying. You're going to United . . .

Into the manager's office. Confirmation. 'I don't want you to go but they've accepted an offer now.' Villa had compromised at £12.6 million. Less than they valued me at, but they had still forced a record sum out of Man United. I was to be their record signing, which wasn't bad for a lad from Canaan!

And then a strange feeling. While I was waiting for it to happen, it was all excitement. Now suddenly it was happening and a moment of doubt ran through me.

Still the lads were taking the mickey. But there were a lot of warm handshakes from the coaches and teammates to the kit men and canteen girls.

But in my head there was sudden apprehension. This transfer that had been on my mind for months was now becoming a reality. This anchor in my life, Aston Villa, was being taken away and I was heading for new, uncharted waters. I was leaving everybody behind, so many great times and so many fun memories. They all flashed before me now – Sheila and Bryn, the games, the laughs, the goals, Paul McGrath, Ugo, Bozzy, Smally, the managers. I had not had this feeling since I left the Caribbean all those years ago and landed in the deep winter of a strange country wondering what on earth would happen to me. I thought I would be at Villa for ever. I was very emotional as I realized I was saying goodbye – again – to another family.

'Wait a moment, do I really want to do this?' I heard myself asking. 'Isn't this where I belong? Maybe I'd be better off staying?'

It wouldn't be too long before I had those questions answered.

8

IN THE BACK OF THE NET!

It was transfer deadline day, 20 August 1998. I needed to get to Old Trafford quickly to get a medical done in time. Tony zipped me up the motorway to Manchester. I changed out of my training gear into a suit in the back of the car. Tony advised me to ring my mum because what was about to happen would be global news.

As we neared Manchester I called. 'Mum, just wanted to let you know I'm joining Manchester United.'

'That's very nice, dear,' she replied as only mums can. 'Are you sure it's what you want?' She had no clue in those days about what was going on around her son in England.

But her understated response also reflected my own state of mind. Of course, I had been in England long enough to know United were one of the biggest clubs in the world. But that was from the outside. The truth is that unlike every football fan in the country, I was not so genned up on the story of Manchester United as you might imagine. This would prove to be invaluable to me in the first few weeks, which passed by in a blur. Back home, Manchester United was the club everyone supported. Growing up,

United were the team in England all my pals spoke about. But I wasn't as familiar with the legend of United – the Busby Babes, the Munich air tragedy, Best, Law and Charlton. I had no idea of the true scale of this institution I was about to join and in a strange way that would make settling in a lot easier than maybe other players who were brought up on United stories from the moment they kicked a football.

I was already aware that United's offer of £23,000 a week – mind boggling enough – was nonetheless significantly less than Villa. But as Tony was David Beckham's agent I knew that he would know the pay scale at Old Trafford and would be negotiating a contract on a par with the top earners. It was a five-year deal with endorsements and such like but, do you know, I didn't really take it all in. I was joining United and that was a big enough concept for me to deal with at that point.

After the medical, I recall there being one final haggle with Villa. They wanted me to waive the substantial signing-on fee I was due based on the enormous profit they were making on my sale. Villa would not release my registration until I had signed the waiver. Time was getting close; we were five minutes away from the deadline when Tony spelled it out to me in one of the offices at Old Trafford. 'You will more than make up for it with endorsements,' he said. 'But if you really want this transfer, you've got to let the money go I'm afraid.'

And I did because money wasn't my motivation at this point. I had spent the many weeks of the on–off saga daydreaming about the players and the team I could be joining.

I have huge respect for other players, always, but there are special ones you particularly admire. Paul Scholes was one. He was an incredible natural talent. He was a quiet lad who never gave interviews or put himself in the public eye off the pitch, but I would get on with him so well. Giggsy was another. Before I got to Old Trafford, I had met the United winger on a few social occasions and liked him. He had always shown me respect, which I really appreciated, and always gave me the time of day. As time went on, and I got to know Giggsy better, I realized my initial impressions were right. He is an exceptional guy. You look after him and he will look after you a thousand times over.

But the cast-list at United did not stop there. There was David Beckham and his passing range and crossing ability, Roy Keane the driving force, Peter Schmeichel, probably the best keeper in the world at that point, Gary Neville, Denis Irwin, the two fullbacks. You play against these guys and only then do you truly appreciate just how good they are. I had watched their big European games avidly on TV thinking: 'That's what it's all about.' Those were the images that were flooding through me that day, not the money I was saying goodbye to.

We signed the waiver with minutes to spare. And then for the first time – but by no means the last – I found out what it was to be a Manchester United player. 'Jeezzzuuussss,' I heard myself say as I walked into the huge media room to be confronted by more cameras than I could count and what seemed like more flashbulbs popping than for the Oscars.

I had never experienced anything like it in my life. I had

done interviews in my time with two or three TV crews in attendance; but not the fifty or more who were focused on me now. I had wondered what it was like to be a United player. I gulped now at the reality of the biggest press circus I had ever seen. Sitting next to the manager in front of all those cameras, as a record signing for United, was when it sank in.

I later learned that there had been some dispute between Fergie and his coach, Brian Kidd, over the signing. Kiddo felt the team needed a player with bigger physical presence and suggested John Hartson. Fergie's response, so legend has it, was: 'Do you really see Hartson as a Manchester United player?' But Fergie saw me as precisely that – a Manchester United player – and he had plans for me to be his number one striker.

He later told me something which shows this man's incredible knowledge of football. Nine years earlier, I had scored a hat-trick for the Trinidad and Tobago U19 team against United's, which, at that time, included his son, Darren. I think I had just joined Villa at that point but was far away from a first team profile. But what I never knew was that my performance had clearly got back to United's manager and he had watched my progress ever since then. I couldn't believe it!

I wasn't scared. I was excited. I had absolute and total faith in my ability and the raw excitement of the day and now this frantic media interest meant those earlier misgivings disappeared. Let's get this show on the road, I thought.

That first night at the Copthorne Hotel – the first of three hotels which would be my home for the next four months – was crazy with all the calls coming in. From Birmingham, from Tobago, from Australia, from everywhere. My name was all over the sports news and my brothers were even calling from the States telling me it was on the bulletins over there. Journalists and cameramen went out to Trinidad and Tobago wanting to interview my mum, my friends, the locals, anyone who knew me. Crazy, crazy, crazy. I had been thrown into superstardom.

That first morning I was driven to the training ground to be greeted by hundreds of supporters waiting outside. At Villa there would maybe be fifty or sixty. But this was on another level – fans screaming my name and security guards holding them back as we went through the gates. I signed a few books but I was keen to get into the dressing room and finally meet the players. I was full of nervous excitement. What on earth was I stepping into?

I remember it so clearly. United's much-loved kit manager, Albert Morgan, one of the club's stalwarts who would remain a great friend to me, was waiting to greet me. 'Hello, son . . . this is where you'll be . . . this will be your shirt number . . . if you need anything I'm happy to help.' The defender David 'Maysie' May and one or two early birds were already there and offered a nod of welcome before, one by one, the players arrived. Teddy Sheringham, Keane and Schmeichel, who was a huge presence in the dressing room. There's me sitting down like on my first day at school, waiting to be acknowledged I guess, not sure of how they were going to respond to me.

I wondered what they knew about the manager's plans for me. Fergie had told me that I was to be his number one striker, playing down the middle. But what would the other senior strikers, Teddy, Andy Cole and Ole Gunnar Solskjaer, think about that? Did they even know? The manager clearly had confidence in me and so did I. I didn't doubt my ability for a moment. What I wasn't sure of was how they would react to me.

And then the man himself, Fergie, came into the dressing room.

'OK, everyone, this is Yorkie,' he said, walking over towards me. 'Make sure you look after him, he's one of us now. Make sure you make him feel that way.' I needed that. He had his arm around me, and that was when I got my first taste of the legendary United dressing-room humour. After he'd gone the lads start teasing me. 'So are you Fergie's son?' Giggsy quips. 'Dwight Ferguson, is it?' The other lads joined in and I got my first breaking in. And with that I was part of the team.

And then I was out there training with them, doing what I had been brought in to do. And Keano is pinging a pass at me first time as if to say, 'Let's see how you cope with that then?' Smashed it at me he did. He caught me a little off guard because I never thought he would hit it so hard from such close distance. I didn't control it properly and he said: 'Welcome to United – Cantona used to kill them.' That was his little dig at me. He was saying, 'They've paid £12.6 million for you so you better be able to control them.' OK, I thought, I get it. And I caught on pretty quickly after that.

That first session, in fact United's training generally, was one big buzz – hugely enjoyable even though that first day rushed by. It was now Friday and the opening game of my career as a United player was a little more than twenty-four hours away at West Ham.

The main thing I remember about that match was the nightmare Becks was enduring on his return from the 1998 World Cup. It had finished infamously – for him and for England – with that red card against Argentina. It appeared to have turned half the country against him.

He was the focus of all the attention and I could sense this whole occasion amounted to a moment of genuine anxiety for him, which when you recall all that ridiculous effigy-burning rubbish that was going on was understandable. But that first match day gave me an immediate glimpse of one of United's strongest features: the camaraderie of the dressing room.

As the months and years rolled by, it was clear that some players didn't particularly like one another. I don't think Coley and Teddy ever got on, for example, and as for Keano . . . well, he didn't want to get on with any of us! As far as I could tell, he and Schmeichel absolutely hated each other, a clash perhaps of two giant characters who want the same thing and both believe they know the best way to get it.

But, whatever the internal dynamics of that United team, when a mate was in trouble, look out. The players put a ring of steel around Becks that day which made a big impression on me. Every one of them would have jumped on anyone trying anything. It would be the same out on the pitch whichever of us was the target. If anything kicks off then you would have ten mates fighting your corner. I really had joined something special.

The attention on Becks that day helped me get off lightly with what would be a pretty unremarkable debut in a pretty unremarkable game. This first weekend was more interesting for the way it laid bare the spirit of United. I felt like I was now part of an elite group. At 12.45 p.m. on match day, a team meeting was staged at which everyone attended in their club blazers and ties.

By now, Fergie's aura of authority and calmness was making a huge impression on me, as did his first team talk. After the tactical issues, he sent shivers down my spine with his words and the tone of his address. 'Don't let this crowd intimidate you. Just remember the shirt you're wearing and who you're representing,' was his message.

I sensed at that moment the aura of Manchester United, and in the years to come I would see it on the faces of other people, including players, when we walked by them in hotel lobbies or filed into the dressing room. It came from the manager and I felt it for the first time in that opening team talk.

At Villa, those moments had been far more informal. We would arrive and, especially with me being laid-back, it would be, 'Hey, howya doin'?' Not with United. The team coach pulls up, we all put our game face on, and follow the manager into the dressing room. It is sending a message that something different, something special has just arrived.

And my first home game against Charlton was certainly special. I had to wait two weeks while international matches were played and I was dying to get out there. I knew the importance of this game; I had barely been able to stop thinking about it. Tony had even let Becks know it would be much appreciated if he could just stick one of his trademark crosses on my head! No need for special favours. I felt confident.

Even now, after hundreds of games and so many incredible experiences, that first, magical night at Old Trafford comes back to me so easily. Close my eyes and I can replay it whenever I want to, one image after another. As required, I arrived three hours before kick-off, again club suit and tie. The fans were already there waiting for more autographs; I truly had never known anything like this before. I signed a few before a steward parked my car and with screaming fans on both sides of the barriers, I headed inside thinking: 'This is like being a movie star.' I met up with the boys and went into the pre-match players' room where the players, and only the players, are permitted to congregate. No wives or partners. All the food and refreshments you could want were laid out and we idled away the time chatting before heading to a second lounge, just off the dressing rooms, for another hour.

I noticed little groups developing as the dynamics of this team unfolded. Then suddenly it was nearly kick-off and we headed to the dressing room, which was the first time I had seen it in all its glory with its huge spa and jacuzzi. By then, I was dying to get going but first there was another team talk to confirm the line-up. I was playing, this time with Solskjaer, Becks on one side, and Scholes behind me. How could anyone fail with that support cast?

What happened after that was just a blur of colour and emotion. Emerging into a packed Old Trafford wearing a

United shirt for the first time was a massive attack on the senses, the scale of that roar, bigger than anything I had ever known before. And it felt great. Electrifying. I knew at that moment this was where I wanted to be. I wasn't scared or intimidated by the stage. I was relaxed.

I had to score and the quicker the better. Right at the end of the first half, Becks picked me out perfectly from a free kick, just as Tony had demanded, and I watched my header drop into the bottom corner of the left-hand side. I wanted to run and throw myself into the crowd but there is a ditch just at the back of the goal and there's no way I would have got back up from there. So it was time for a little restraint, back to my teammates and Becks first of all because he knew how important that was to me.

And that was it. Off and running. I got a second goal that night, just after we kicked off for the second half, and was enjoying myself so much I couldn't believe it when I got substituted. I think there was still another twenty minutes to go and I felt that the manager must have got that wrong. He couldn't take me off! I wanted a hat-trick! Still, I had a huge grin on my face as I left the pitch knowing I had made a near-perfect home debut. And what happened after that has passed into the folklore of the game; this dirt-poor skinny kid from Tobago found himself at the centre of English football's first Treble.

9

A GAME TO REMEMBER

My integration into the United camp was also helped by the fact that this winning team knew how to let its hair down. I saw this first on a trip to Chester races, something of an annual event for the United lads but a whole new experience for me. It was a great early-season bonding exercise. We had a great day in a VIP box during which it became clear the gaffer was crazy about racing, something which had never caught my imagination (and still doesn't).

If I was expecting that session to end after the last race I was happily mistaken. All the group headed back to Manchester and hit Barça, the bar run by Simply Red front man and United fan, Mick Hucknall. It was the hot place to be at that time. There the personalities within the group began to come out. I think everyone got smashed in their own way. I lapped it up. I never drank beer, always spirits, brandy and Coke being my tipple of the time. I was thinking: 'Is this how it is going to be? If so, bring it on!' For some of the foreign lads, this level of drinking was not something they were used to – Ole, for example, while

Keano, Giggsy and even the quiet-natured Scholesy were a little more resistant. Even so, everyone had a really good time enjoying a carefree evening.

I'll certainly never forget that night. I met a cool girl, a tiny thing with an amazing figure which caught my attention. I remember taking her out of the club and stumbling a bit worse for wear down some steps and then hearing water lapping against a shoreline. 'I must be back home,' I thought to myself as we got down to business. Never before can the Manchester canal have been mistaken for the Caribbean! I saw the same girl three years later when she reminded me of our 'beach-side' encounter. We both had a good laugh about it.

My new teammates knew how to party. That may not have been their public image but they knew when to work and when to let themselves go. The manager knew it too. I think Fergie considered it a vital part of team bonding, along with celebrating every goal with all your teammates. He always stressed to us the importance of everyone joining together to celebrate to display the unity of the team. It was the same with partying; it was the culture he had been brought up in, don't forget. And everyone was included. If something was happening everyone turned up – well, everyone apart, perhaps, from Keano, who really was a law unto himself.

But I always got on with our captain. Even though we had such different personalities, I felt we clicked. Don't be fooled by his gruff persona. At that time, even though he was a family man, he loved to go out and have a good time and unwind. Keano was old school and understood the culture of winning together and socializing together. Having a bevvy on a Saturday night. That was the norm.

Down at Highbury at the same time, Arsène Wenger was starting a crusade which would change this part of our game for good. But drinking only water wasn't for us. We were about to begin a three-year domination of English football in which the bond within the dressing room was cemented by some memorable nights out. And I think the manager trusted us to know when it was time to stop and get back to work.

The pressures of becoming a United player were difficult to adjust to. I spent the first months in a hotel and company was always precious. On one occasion, I arranged for a girlfriend to come over from Australia and, already aware that an awful lot of eyes seemed to be watching me, took great care to keep the visit secret. The flight was booked through my agency office and nobody would know who she was and who she had come to see. I was also seeing a girl in Birmingham at the time and . . . well, let's just say a little discretion was sensible. She came to Manchester, we went out for lunch just around the corner and stayed in my room all night, chilling out. The next morning the papers show pictures of the two of us chatting in the hotel lobby and leaving the restaurant. They had her name, origins, when she arrived, pretty much everything.

I was really shocked. Where were they getting this information? This was a new level of prying way beyond anything I had experienced before. To know everything about this girl, who had never been to England previously . . . how could they do this? Occurring in the first weeks of my time at United it took some getting used to, if, in fact, I ever did. At Villa, I could go out with whoever I liked, when I liked, where I liked, without it being splashed over the papers. Now all that had changed and it changed me as a result.

I began to exit by the back entrances of places to try to escape the endless cameramen. I became convinced my phone was bugged; how else did they always seem to know where I would be? I seemed to be changing my number every two weeks.

If the publicity that began to follow me concerned the manager, he did not show it at this time. In fact, my first home game had coincided with the lurid tabloid story about that tape featuring me, Bozzy and Smally. I knew it was innocuous, harmless fun, but it isn't the sort of attention you want to be associated with your debut. But if Fergie ever heard about that story he didn't let on. I think he was happy with my game.

The football was my release, my comfort zone by then. As the football and goals flowed, I relaxed and began to feel part of this special moment in football history. It was off the park that life was becoming a little uncomfortable. For three or four months, it felt like I was a regular target for the Sunday newspapers especially – at the front and back.

Of course people would sell their 'stories' to the press, which ratcheted up the whole feeding frenzy around football. These stories were often completely untrue but I suppose they helped sell newspapers. Yet it wasn't always the case. I remember having to go up to Scotland for a visit. I had been there many times and I thought I would contact a girlfriend who worked up there.

The night before I was due to return, I stayed the night with her but made sure I booked a taxi for 6.30 the following morning. Knowing I couldn't get back in time to catch the team bus, the cabby would have to take me back south if necessary. The most important thing was to be there for a 1 p.m. training session that day.

When the old black cab turned up, the driver agreed to the journey and at the last minute I said to my girlfriend, 'You fancy coming? You got anything else on this weekend?' To my surprise, she agreed to come with me and off we set on a long journey which, with the cab's top speed of about 70 mph, was going to take a few hours. A few boring hours. Now what could Alison and I do to pass the time? What else but make out in the back of the cab. There was no way the cabby didn't know what was going on. In fact most of the Glasgow commuter traffic that morning must have. There were legs and arms everywhere and I recall that more than once we got stuck in traffic jams, which, for anyone looking in at our cab, would have been a little more colourful than usual.

But it was great, great fun and what better way to pass the three hours it took us to get back. That journey cost me £300, which I handed to the cabby and he gave me a cheeky wink as he set off on the journey home.

Although there's an even more curious footnote to this particular story.

I braced myself for some unwelcome headlines over the next few days after that cab journey. Someone, especially the driver, is going to tip them off about that, surely? But nothing ever appeared. And three years later, I was back in Glasgow hailing a cab from outside my hotel. I saw the driver looking at me through his rear-view mirror. 'Is that you, Dwight?' he said.

'Yeah. Do I know you?'

'You don't remember me, do you? I'm the cabby who took you down to the training ground with that wee lass.'

I couldn't believe it. This was some coincidence.

'That was fantastic. The pair of you looked as if you were having a fine old time,' he went on.

We did, I assured him, before satisfying my curiosity. 'Tell me, man,' I said, 'how come you never went to the papers with that. You could have made a nice little packet with that story.'

'Not my style, Dwight,' he said. 'It was nobody's business but yours and the girl's. Two kids having fun as far as I could tell. And you weren't doing anyone any harm were you?'

Now that's my kind of cabby and for the second time in his life, he found himself getting a nice little tip from a grateful footballer.

I finally moved into a house, bought for £400,000 in the smart suburb of Bramhall, thinking that would give me more privacy but how naive was that? The paparazzi soon found out where I lived and I realized I had made the mistake of choosing a property which was far too open to prying lenses.

Of course, some of the lads who had dealt with this

intrusion for some time were more than happy to see me. Giggsy, the most obvious eligible bachelor at the time, particularly. Probably Becks to a degree as well. 'Thank God you've come, Yorkie,' they would say to me. 'It takes the pressure off us now.'

And thank God the football was at least one part of my life where I could relax. I knew the rules. I wasn't going to start shouting my mouth off or bragging about any exploits. I had to show this dressing room that I was worthy of their respect and a place in their team and that is what I set about doing.

Even so, the boys would recognize that small but cheeky grin on my face in training after a day off and the laughter would strike up: 'Come on, Yorkie, what have you been up to? Tell us all about it.'

'Well, fellas, you won't believe me if I tell you . . .' And so the laughter would begin.

I was a natural target for this type of attention as the only determinedly single guy in the group. And I was determinedly single. I was always straight with the girls I would date, and, I like to think, always kept in touch and remained friends as a result.

But life became a dream, the ultimate dream I guess. Playing great football with great players under a great manager at the greatest of clubs. And meeting and dating beautiful women. All of it accompanied by the increasing sense of what United could achieve that season. United's old training ground at The Cliff had been good enough but now we moved into a state-of-the-art complex at Carrington which symbolized the club's status. And the players' bar would be like a Who's Who of the high rollers. Actors, sports stars, TV faces. I would be chatting with Colin Montgomerie alongside the cast of *Coronation Street* while exchanging greetings with Scary, the Spice Girl I fancied most, whenever Becks's missus brought her gang with her.

And among all this came a great friendship, a friendship I truly appreciated, which helped me settle so easily and smoothly into life in and around Old Trafford.

My opening months at United had been spent with a variety of partners up front – Giggsy for one game, then maybe Ole for a couple and Teddy bought on as sub – which left Andy Cole not getting much of a look-in. I'd made my debut alongside him at West Ham, but after that he wasn't picked. He was still being linked to a possible move to my old club, Villa, and it looked as if the manager had put the other strikers ahead of Coley at that time. Despite all of this, despite having every reason to resent my arrival on the scene, Coley became a great friend, the man who showed me the ropes. He knew that while a single man's life could be exciting it could also be lonely, cut off as I was from my old Birmingham friends, stuck in a hotel to begin with and then on my own at my new home. He wasn't too worried as he knew I was getting out there, having fun. But maybe Coley felt he should keep a protective eye on me. He invited me to his home for dinner with his lovely wife, Shirley, and became the first man I turned to for advice, be it where to get a haircut or which was the best route to the training ground.

My arrival might have pushed him out the door, but if

he thought that, you would never have guessed it. That was the measure of this man and a side of him that not everyone knew or understood. Shirley was a huge help getting my furniture sorted out and involved herself in the move to my new house because I had no one to help me with some of those decisions.

We even went out and bought two convertible Mercedes together. Coley wanted to buy a new car, a convertible for the summer, and I offered to take him to a mate of my mine, Eugene, a Mercedes dealer I knew in Tamworth. When we got there I decided I would buy one too. Same purple colour, same model, separated only by one digit on the number plates. And £70,000 worth of business for which Eugene was very grateful.

Now I know what people will conclude as this friendship took root in my new life. This is where our partnership on the pitch came from. Right? Wrong. That just happened. Honestly. Did we talk about it? Plan things? Work things out? No. Not really. It just, well, happened. I wasn't even that aware of it. I was playing in such a good team. No matter what players the manager chose, it all balanced beautifully and everyone was contributing. But when Coley and I came together a little bit of magic happened, something born out of pure instinct. The supporters felt it because, wherever I go and whenever the subject of United comes into conversation, everyone talks about Yorke and Cole.

To this day, I have not sat down and watched any videos of our games together. This book is the first time I have had a chance for any kind of reflection. I can remember some of them but the night that first stood out was at the Champions League group phase match against Barcelona at Nou Camp in November 1998.

I know from how people talk to me about that night that it was 'that goal', United's second in a 3–3 draw, which made an indelible mark on the game all over Europe. But the whole night was an eye-opener for me. I mean, Old Trafford had been spectacular enough but Barcelona's stadium was like a huge football cathedral complete with that famous little chapel on one side of the dressing-room corridor.

What's it like playing there for the first time? Well the turf is to die for. It is a paradise pitch for footballers. I will never forget our training session on the eve of the game. I was like a little kid back home in Tobago again trying out all sorts of things, chips, flicks, scissor kicks, overhead volleys, everything and just from the sheer joy of feeling my feet and the ball on that magical pitch. I wasn't the only one. Becks, Scholesy, Giggsy, Coley, we were all the same. The ball just zipped across the grass and I knew, absolutely knew, that we would be playing in a spectacular game the following night. When the session finished, Fergie couldn't get us to stop. All of us were like children being called in for our tea. 'Come on, boss, just five more minutes, just five more minutes,' we kept imploring.

'Albert, get those balls in the bag,' Fergie boomed out to his faithful kit man. We had to be dragged out of the place in the end. Players who had, even by then, won championships and cups and played in huge international matches, just wanted to stay out there and practise,

practise, practise. The passion and joy those boys showed for their football in that training session was one of the many reasons why this United team was on its way to making history.

So I knew the game would be as special. And what a setting. When you walk out at Nou Camp the scale of the stadium blows the breath out of your body. I can't find the words to truly describe what went through me as we stepped out that night but even today it sends tingles down my spine. The game was amazing and that second goal – my stepover and exchange of passes with Coley before he scored – was the outstanding highlight for us. It was purely instinctive on our part but it sealed the Yorke–Cole partnership in the minds of the public and as we went on to share 53 goals between us in that first season together, the reputation which followed us home was probably deserved. I don't believe I've heard of another strike partnership achieving that. People are still talking about it. It's only now I'm coming to the end of my career that I can appreciate how huge that was, but back then I just thought: 'Ah, that's nothing!' But it was a bit special!

The only blip we had in our relationship was not of our making, but was unfortunately down to lies in the media. We had been on fire for a good six months, and our friendship was tight off the pitch. We were inseparable. And then a story broke in the press that Andy and I had been with a girl. We had just won a great victory over Internazionale in the quarter-finals of the Champions League, and we were on course for our showdown with Juventus in the semis. We were all in a buoyant mood, and then a fabricated story was splashed all over the tabloids. As the single guy, I was used to this sort of attention, but this had never happened to poor Andy before. It was a real blow for him and it was so upsetting for Shirley.

It was utter rubbish of course – he hadn't had anything to do with that girl (besides she wasn't even his type!) – but it brought unwanted attention for him. He's such a shy guy. We tried to stop the story, but the papers felt that the girl's word was enough evidence to go ahead and print. That was all they seemed to need in those days. I tried to give Shirley my assurance that it was all lies, but understandably, for a short while, my friendship with Andy was under a bit of strain. I took a step back so that he wasn't associated with my single life, until it all blew over. Thankfully, it didn't take long and we were soon firm friends again, which we remain to this day.

Everyone felt United and Barcelona were the two best footballing teams in that year's Champions League and probably represented the dream final Europe wanted to see. But that draw was not enough for Barça. They were knocked out. For our own prospects, I wasn't too upset to see such a fine team eliminated from the competition. 'Just as long as we don't have to play those bloody Germans in the final,' I remember thinking.

The standards the team set for itself were remarkable and woe betide anyone who slackened off. That wasn't likely. We were all gelling and the manager was happy. There was no sign of his infamous 'hairdryer' rollockings; in fact, it only kicked off once that season, at Sheffield Wednesday, where we were beaten 3–1. I remember playing a great one–two with Coley giving him a great ball to equalize. But by half-time we were down 2–1 and when we got back into the dressing room it all started. Keano began ranting and raving before we even had time to sit down. He was having a go at Peter for having given away a soft goal. Unusually for Schmeichel, he had made a mistake or two, but he wasn't the only one that Keano had a go at.

And then it was Fergie's time to talk. He always picks his moments. Everyone went silent (although Keano was still huffing and puffing to himself in the corner). The gaffer went through the team, picking out who wasn't pulling their weight. I'm listening, thinking we didn't need to panic yet as we were capable of getting the game back, and suddenly he was in my face and shouting at me, 'Get hold of the ball! You're not doing what you're supposed to be doing. You're giving soft balls away, allowing people to come through you.' That may not be the exact phrasing, but that was his message! I'm looking at him and thinking: 'What have I done?! Haven't I set up the goal?' I was too shocked to even defend myself. That was the first time I'd been on the end of the 'hairdryer' and it was the first time I saw it kick off in the dressing room. I was pretty shocked. This was mid-November and everything had been going wonderfully. Now, suddenly, one bad half at Hillsborough and my teammates were at each other's throats: 'If you don't pull your effing finger out . . .' and such. What happens with this lot if they lose two games in a row, I thought?

At full-time, the intensity of the underlying tension between Schmeichel and Keano meant they had to be separated before coming to blows in the dressing room. If the standards dip in this team, I realized, all hell breaks loose. Fergie was always trying to enforce the need for consistency, pointing out how crucial it was to maintaining our top spot. And that was probably why the reaction was so strong to the defeat at Wednesday. It might sound over the top, but it was this ferocious desire to be the very best and insistence on standards that carried us through to the Treble.

Thankfully, that game was one of the few wobbles of the season and the rest of the time we were playing with confidence. Two games that showed our total domination were our 6–2 victory over Leicester City in January 1999 and the 8–1 away win over Nottingham Forest the following month.

The first game saw us playing away to Martin O'Neill's Leicester, a game we knew would be tough. They had been playing well and we had struggled against them in previous matches. They were a gritty, tricky team and we had to start well, or we'd have been in for a hard game. But that day, I felt there were goals to get, despite the quality of their defence. My first goal came after ten minutes. Jesper Blomqvist reached the byline and laid the ball back to me. I took one touch, another touch – that's how much time I had and how confident I was – before I tucked away the chance. Leicester put up a good fight and it wasn't until the fiftieth minute that Andy added a second for us. And then the goals came. Andy got a second, followed swiftly by my second. Me and Coley were playing really well supported by Keano and Becks and Giggsy. We were in control even though they managed to get two past us that day.

So, two mates on two goals apiece were literally fighting for the ball to get a hat-trick. Coley brought the ball down on the left and hit a sweet strike, but it came off the crossbar and I was there to tap it in. That was such a special moment for me. I think it was my first hat-trick for United. The ball was signed by all the players and it's still in pride of place on my mantelpiece.

The other highlight of that game was the final goal in the dying minutes, which was Jaap Stam's first for the club. This big centre half came up and scored with a real quality side-footed volley that any striker would be proud of. Jaap went berserk! I think he was a little bit surprised. That was how much fun we were having that day. It was a very happy dressing room at the end of the match.

The second rout was against Forest, and my old gaffer, Big Ron, had just taken over. I think it was his first home game. Perhaps that was how he ended up in the wrong dugout! It was so funny. All the media were waiting for him in the Forest dugout but he strode into the Man United side completely oblivious. Suddenly he realized. 'Oops!' he says. He saw the cameras and said something like 'Oh Christ!' and hurried off. It was a classic Big Ron moment. He saw the funny side of it but I don't think he saw the funny side of the result that followed.

We'd gone to the City Ground aware that it wouldn't be an easy game. Forest had a reputation for playing good football and even though we were pretty fearless at the time, we still had a healthy respect for the opposition. But that season, if we were on song there was very little the opposition could do.

I kicked off the scoring after two minutes. Forest equalized soon after but one minute later Coley put us ahead again. I nearly scored with a volley after the break and Coley pounced on the spilled ball. I made it 4–1 with a tap in soon after.

We were in a commanding position constantly bombarding their goal, and I felt there was a third goal for me that game. In fact, me and Coley were wondering which of us it would be to go home with the football.

There were about fifteen minutes to go and I looked around and saw my name had come up and the manager was substituting me and Keano for John Curtis and Ole. I bet the Forest players must have been glad to see the back of me, but I was thinking: 'What are ya doing?!' The gaffer explained I needed 'rest' and should 'think of the other games coming up'. But instead all I could do was watch the Norwegian assassin come on and score four goals to make it 8–1! He completely demolished the defence. It was the biggest away win in league history at the time. And so Ole went home with the football that day. I was delighted for Ole, we all were. I had nothing but admiration for how he took them apart. But I don't mind admitting that I was cheesed off at the time as I had really wanted to repeat my hat-trick at Leicester. But who can argue with the manager when he makes a substitution like that?

Ole was a super player. I called him a goal-scoring machine. In my eyes, he deserved more credit for what he achieved. He was a true team player. He respected the manager and his decisions and understood when he was left out. He always trained well, was never late, and he was a clean-cut family man. Exactly like his squeaky clean image! People think he must have minded that he was always a sub, but he just loved the club and playing for United.

Around this time I scored one of my favourite goals of the season during our 4–1 victory over West Ham at Old Trafford. It wasn't so much the goal, which was our first of the match and came in the tenth minute, but the fact that I scored against my old mate from home, Shaka Hislop, who was in goal. It was also Shaka's first season for a new club, having left Newcastle for West Ham at the same time as I moved to United. We had been teasing each other before the match about who was going to get the better of the other, and we had made a bet. A goal for me would require him to buy my drinks for the night and vice-versa. Winning that bet made the goal even sweeter and Shaka kindly stumped up the drinks after the game.

In Europe we would have to get past two giants of Serie A, Inter Milan and then Juventus, to reach the final and we could not do that without touching the very peaks of our game. Peter, the subject of Keano's rage that afternoon, produced two monumental saves against Zamorano and Ventola in the home leg against Inter as we held on to a 2–0 lead. Up front, I was just breezing along without a care in the world and scored twice (both supplied by Becks's amazing deliveries), making like it was easy getting past Italy's finest in a Champions League quarter-final. It was all still the most magical time of my life.

We got through the return leg before, famously, finding ourselves staring into oblivion in the second, Turin leg of the semi-final against Juventus in April. Giggsy had scored a vital late goal to give us a 1–1 at Old Trafford but here were Juventus on their home pitch 2–0 ahead in ten minutes. We were in a state of shock; I looked around the pitch and didn't recognize the swaggering side I had played with up to that point. Uh-oh, I thought, this is going to be a very long night. That Juve team had Zidane and Davids ('The Rash' we called him because he was all over you) in midfield. They were at the height of their careers and were pulling us apart.

And that's when the team dug deep and remembered our standards. It was our captain who took hold of us that night and dragged the team up by its bootstraps. The run that he made to meet a great Becks corner was brilliant and his headed goal sent a surge of relief through the team. These were the standards Keano had fought hard to maintain. That was the pivotal moment in the entire campaign.

I scored an equalizer and I thought: 'Wow, 2–2; that's it, we're going through.' You could see the impact we had made on the Italians. Their reputation for great defending goes before them and at 2–0 they must have thought we had been tamed. Now there was doubt in their football and anxiety on their faces.

In the dressing room at half-time, Fergie gave a classic performance, perfect for that moment. He spelled out the challenge that lay before us. It was time, more than ever he said, to take responsibility; for every pass you make, every tackle, not to blame each other, not to leave it to a teammate, and to stick together like never before, no matter what comes at you. And most importantly 'have belief'. That was the phrase I took out with me on to the pitch, forty-five minutes away from the biggest game of our lives. 'Have belief.'

Coley and I looked each other in the eye before the second half started and knew, without speaking, what we felt. We had it within us to beat this team. We fancied it. As a group we were more buoyant and we sensed Juve's growing unease. We did, indeed, score the third goal that killed them when I got pulled down in the area for what I thought would be a stonewall penalty. It didn't matter because, as the ball spilled loose, there was my pal doing what all great strikers do and following up.

We knew at that moment we were through. Juve couldn't score twice now; they knew it too. And this is when it went crazy. All I remember is the fans going ballistic and jumping up and down, and I was screaming at the top of my voice when the game ended. Those moments last for ever and yet pass in an instant; it's just so unreal. The scenes in the dressing room were sheer madness. I was singing my head off, drinking champagne and pouring a glass for the gaffer. Just as he was about to drink it, I took it from him and said: 'It's OK, boss, I'll drink that for you.' He knew I was being cheeky but Fergie was in no mood to chastise anyone. Not that night.

I don't know when it was – maybe about eighteen or twenty games from the end of the season – but I started counting down the games we needed for the Treble. After each win, I would be standing on the benches shouting,

'Come on, boys, only fourteen games to go' or however many it was. And all the time, the boys would look up at me and raise their eyebrows as if to say, 'Oh come off it, Yorkie – like that's going to happen.'

But that night, having already secured the FA Cup final place and with the championship in range, there was real gusto in my voice when I heard myself shouting, 'Come on, boys, only eight games to go now. Eight games to the Treble. Oh yes, boys.' And for the first time I think we all started to believe it was possible.

10

SCHMEICHEL'S CIGAR

The most incredible achievement in the history of the club game happened over ten days in three momentous games. They were like the final chapters of three amazing stories woven in one book. You are desperate to find out how it is all going to finish, hoping for the happy ending. But at the same time you want them to go on forever.

Three games in ten days – the Premier League title, the FA Cup final, the Champions League. One by one they came at us and one by one we ticked them off. There will be some whose hatred of all things United is so irrational that they have erased the events of those days from their memory banks. I had been warned about the hatred United had to deal with but it had never bothered me too much. At Villa I didn't like them – but only because they were always so successful. I think United would take it as an insult if they were not hated so much because it would mean they were no longer as dominating.

But for any other football fans, and particularly for Manchester United's, I cannot believe they will ever forget the trail of drama which climaxed on that epic night at Nou

Camp. It will be with me for ever. I'm sure it will be the same for my teammates. Hopefully, we will all live to be old men and one day have the time to meet up, knock the top off a beer, and relive it all, step by step. Probably at some distant anniversary reunion dinner.

Being the top dog in England is something I had only dreamed about until the morning of 16 May 1999, a Sunday, broke fine and clear and I began to think about what was ahead. The title race had come down to the final round of fixtures and, at its most simple, if we beat Spurs at Old Trafford that afternoon we would be champions. Anything less and a victory for Arsenal over – wouldn't you just know it? – my old mates at Villa would open the door for our closest rivals to take it from us and regain their title.

Despite some of the embarrassing headlines that I could have done without, the season could not have gone any better for me. The FA Cup fourth-round match against Liverpool in January was one of my best games. We had been 1–0 down with two minutes left when I scored from Coley's knock down, a goal followed immediately by Ole striking a winner in stoppage time. I don't think I have ever been so emotional on a pitch as I was that day, especially in the seconds after I scored. Never felt like that before or since. Maybe it was the atmosphere, the special cocktail that comes from United–Liverpool games, as they are bitter rivals. But I found myself shouting into the cameras and reacting more wildly than ever before. That really wasn't my style but something got to me that day.

I played well, too, absolutely at my peak, and the team's ability to win it back at the last minute never ceased to

I was obsessed with playing football when I was growing up in Tobago.

Kicking back with some friends including my best friend at the time, Rama (front right).

Bertille Sinclair's coaching school, where it all began.

Representing Trinidad and Tobago.

Playing for my national side against the USA in the World Cup qualifier in 1989. I was heartbroken that we didn't make it to the finals, but it freed me up to join Aston Villa.

Playing for my first club in England, Aston Villa, where I had nine happy years.

I first met my great mate, Mark Bosnich, at Villa. We were later reunited at Manchester United after Peter Schmeichel retired.

Lining up for a photograph before the 1994 League Cup final against Manchester United. The manager, Ron Atkinson, is clowning around with me.

Celebrating winning the 1996 League Cup with my teammates Savo Milošević and Ian Taylor.

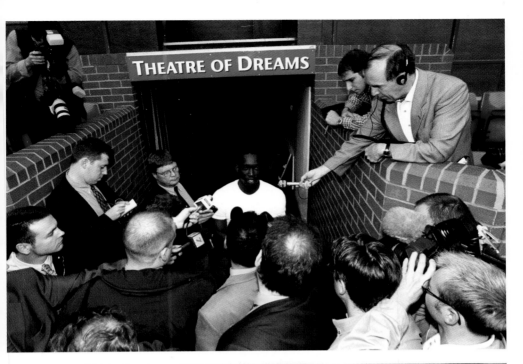

Arriving at Old Trafford, I had a little taste of the media attention that came with being a United player.

With the gaffer: Sir Alex Ferguson.

Lining up with some of the amazing players at United.

Reaching for an overhead strike.

Treble glory! Celebrating the 1999 Champions' League Cup with some of the other players including a jubilant Ole Gunnar Solskjaer in front and Teddy Sheringham to the left of the cup.

The crazy scenes that greeted our bus as we paraded the trophy.

With my strike partner and great friend, Andy Cole, celebrating winning the second trophy of the treble.

Above and left: Some of the awards I have received. Carling Player of the Month at Villa in 1996 (which I also received at United in 1999), and United's Player of the Year 1999, presented here by Alex Ferguson.

amaze me. Without that dramatic finale, the Treble would have gone there and then.

We came even closer to the precipice in that incredible semi-final against Arsenal, of course, the one won by Giggsy's legendary goal in the final minutes, the best I have ever seen on any pitch. He took the ball from behind the halfway line and ran with it to the six-yard box throwing off all the Arsenal defenders as he went before burying the ball in the top of the net with his left foot. I hated not playing in that game but what did that matter when someone you admire and respect as much as I do Giggsy does something like that. Special. Just like the man himself. And now everything had come down to these three final challenges. Spurs for the title. Newcastle for the FA Cup. Bayern Munich for the Champions League. In the space of ten days? Bang, bang, bang.

What do I remember? Calmness to begin with. The gaffer demands a quiet day before games and I would just chill out at home and try to stay calm and rest up. When I arrived at Old Trafford at about midday, the excitement was incredible. Supporters were clamouring for autographs when I drove in and all the players felt the anticipation. During our pre-match meal, we were having precisely the same sort of conversation that was going on in thousands of pubs and households at the same time. How would this day play out? How would we do? How would Arsenal do? But really we all knew that we just needed to take care of our game and the title would be in the bag.

Fergie gave a great team talk and went over our tactics. Until then, we did not know the team but we had all spent the week playing our own guessing games. But at that stage, I always felt confident that I would be in. I was to play with Teddy up front.

When Fergie started talking about Spurs, the mention of one name we had to watch brought a rueful smile to my lips. A few weeks earlier, David Ginola had been voted first the PFA's and then the Football Writers' Player of the Year. I was runner-up and frankly felt robbed. In fact, I was angry at what I thought was a decision heavily influenced by a media which favours London-based players when their careers are going well. I'm not knocking David's qualities as a player. He had helped Spurs win the League Cup and scored some memorable goals. But did that really compare to being top scorer with a team now within touching distance of the Treble? I know Fergie was furious, so much so that he pulled the plug on any of us attending the awards dinner, and I was devastated. I was doing everything right. I played the game in the right way and with the right spirit, always with a smile on my face. I felt I should have won those awards. I know there are some of the greatest names the game has ever produced on those trophies and I longed to see mine among them.

With Coley not starting the game, it left me clear to follow my one superstition. Like him I liked to run out last. Not that my superstitions seemed to do us any good. Ginola limped out of it quickly enough but our chances came and went and left me thinking: 'It's going to be one of those days.'

After twenty-five minutes, Ferdinand put Spurs ahead, which was a big blow. But there was no panic. I knew what the rest of the boys would be thinking – don't panic, keep playing.

Thankfully, Becks put us level before the break. At half-time, Fergie swapped Teddy for Coley – which gutted Teddy – but Andy came on and scored the winner. And with that we were champions!

And come the FA Cup final, against Newcastle six days later, it was my turn to be dropped. I had no idea of the surprise Fergie had in store for me that day until the morning of the game. I knew the whole of my homeland would come to a standstill for this match, one of the most prestigious fixtures on the football calendar anywhere in the world, fully expecting me to play. So did I.

Again, we all had our guesses about what team the gaffer would choose but I had no inkling of what to expect. What you dreaded most on the morning of a game was 'The Knock' on your hotel room door. That was the nickname for the gaffer's visit to you because it usually meant he wanted to explain why you would not be playing. The morning of that FA Cup final, Fergie came to see me to tell me I wasn't playing. I looked at him aghast.

'You must be joking, gaffer,' I said. 'This is why I'm here – to play in games like this. I want to play.'

But it was a waste of time. He explained that he didn't want me to get injured with the Champions League final to come four days later. It did nothing to ease my disappointment. But how could you argue with the man? All through that season he had been juggling his selections with such effect that here we were, the title in the bag and two games away from something that had never been achieved before.

At the team meeting, when he announced his line-up, my

heart sank a little deeper. But my job now was to back the boys who would take the battle to Newcastle. Whatever I felt, it could not have been worse than for our captain that day. Keano already knew he was suspended from the Champions League final but lasted less than ten minutes of this game before having to come off with an ankle injury. He sat next to me on the bench, his season over, poor guy. I really felt for him.

Teddy scored just after coming on and then my boy Scholesy produced another in the second half to make it a fairly comfortable win. I learned that it was the tenth time United had won the cup, and the fourth under Fergie. But it was the number three we now had our eyes on. Something bigger – the main event – was still to come. And this time I knew I would be playing.

There wasn't much time for celebrating the FA Cup final as we were soon on our way to Barcelona for the match just four days later. The trip was kicked off in style as we flew there by Concorde. The Hotel Arts, where we were staying, matched the plane for luxury and exclusivity and we were treated like VIPs. Everyone had their own room, the weather was beautiful and the food was exquisite. It was my first trip to Barcelona and I was impressed.

We trained on the Monday afternoon and the Tuesday, and then retired to the hotel to rest up for the match ahead. I tried to get to sleep that night but I just couldn't. Everybody was on the phone to me, all my mates and people from home calling me to wish me luck. I was talking to everybody from New York, to Mexico to the Caribbean. I dread to think what my phone bill was like! But there was one phone call I really wanted to make. I had to talk to Graham Taylor. On the night before possibly the biggest match of my life, I wanted to thank him for having given me my first break and the opportunity to come to England. He had made my dream come true and here I was at the pinnacle of my career. I had to talk to him and let him know how much I appreciated it. But when I rang, all I got was his answerphone. I left a garbled message for him trying to express all I had to say, but I felt like a bit of a geek speaking to a machine. I bet that message would be so embarrassing if I heard it back again now, and perhaps Graham still has it, more for its comedy value than for its meaning! But at least I told him.

On the day of the game we had an itinerary set out so we knew what time we had to meet, when we were due downstairs, what we had to wear, when we would head off. I was pretty relaxed as I knew I was playing. The manager had said, rest assured you're playing, so I was cool. The day slowly went by. We watched some TV, had lunch, I made some last-minute arrangements for the two friends from home who had come over for the match. None of my family came. I think it would have been a bit much for them! But they were watching it back home and ringing me to wish me luck. We then had our team meeting and Fergie analysed the opposition for us. And then we were off to Nou Camp for the evening match. This is when I started to think, this is where I want to be as a footballer; this is the stage I want to be playing on. There were 90,000 people watching at the ground, and millions would be tuning in around the world.

And so the biggest game of our lives kicked off. To be honest, we didn't have the best of games. It certainly wasn't a classic. Bayern were playing extremely well and they were a tough team to face. We had faced Bayern in the group stages and drawn each time. We knew what sort of game we faced. For my part, I wanted it so badly that perhaps in the end I tried too hard and didn't let my natural game come out. I had dreamed of scoring the winning goal and playing my best game ever. I had played it over and over in my mind, but in the end I didn't play as well as I wanted. In fact, I think we were all trying too hard, and that was why it wasn't flowing for us. Keano wasn't playing and Scholesy was suspended. The team's shape had had to change, and to my mind we were missing our two most influential players. We knew the Germans were resilient, and a hard team to break down. We knew how to do it but we ended up doing the exact opposite.

Bayern went ahead early on. We battled on for the rest of the match, and arguably Bayern deserved to win. But the way we had won the league by one point, and had scraped through some of our close matches meant we had a gritty determination to fight on and squeeze a win. It was our season. People don't talk about the performance when it's all over, they talk about the result.

It was right at the end of the game. I got a touch from a corner, and Teddy scored the equalizer and put us closer to extra time. And then the Norwegian Assassin scored the winning goal that has gone down in history.

All I can remember was screaming, unable to believe what we had just done. It was madness, absolute madness.

And all I could do was scream. We had done it. I wish I could tell you more but I never saw some of the scenes that capture that moment. I never saw the great Ghanaian Samuel Kuffour collapse to the floor distraught. Or the rest of the carnage we inflicted upon Bayern Munich. I just remember screaming. There was no champagne on the pitch but we were all drunk on the moment. I think we must have stayed out there celebrating and dancing in front of our fans for an hour; but it felt like five minutes.

God knows what happened in the dressing room when we finally got back in there. There was so much champagne in huge, huge bottles, swilling around and everyone was celebrating like crazy. The image I recall best was the look on the manager's face . . . well, it was like you could see the little kid in him again. He must have been scratching his head and wondering how that had just happened.

People might say it was a fluke but before you dismiss it likewise be aware of this. It is Fergie's creed, drummed into his teams from the outset, that you never, ever, give up. That you keep playing the way that you have been coached to play. No matter how long is left, no matter how you want to panic. You keep playing. And during that season there had been more than one occasion when we had pulled results out of the fire in the dying minutes and even seconds. I think I had done it myself with a goal against Charlton when I had scored in the final throes of the game.

Every manager or coach tells his team that of course. The trick is getting them to truly believe it. And that was what Fergie had pulled off with us. We believed even if my faith had waned in those dying seconds at Nou Camp. So yes, we got a break; but it was not as big a fluke as you might imagine. Fergie's United never stop. And that is still going on to this day and will do until the moment he retires.

Coming from the Caribbean, I didn't really get a big handle on the animosity between England and Germany in sporting combat until that night. But having been accustomed to the anti-Man U culture, I realized from the amount of texts and messages coming in from Liverpool and Manchester City supporters that the whole nation had been caught up by the drama and wanted us to win. I just sat there in the dressing room for half an hour, drinking it all in with the champagne and thinking: 'Boy, am I going to get pissed tonight!' But first we had a gala dinner booked for our hotel with our families and close friends. Wives and girlfriends were all booked in; straight up to the room, dump your kit bag, on with the club suit and downstairs for dinner. But I was by myself.

It was in the reception that Big Peter, who had just played his last game for the club having announced his retirement, handed me a big cigar. Now, as I have said, I don't smoke and not even winning the Champions League was going to change that; but I stuck it in my mouth and pretended to. It would be my companion for the amazing thirty-six hours that were to follow. I didn't go anywhere without that cigar.

I don't think I ate. I was too excited to eat. I just drank, danced on the tables, danced with the chairman, Martin Edwards, danced with everyone, kissed all my teammates, thanked them for a wonderful, wonderful time. The party didn't start until 1 a.m. but by 4 a.m. the couples are all heading for bed. Not this guy. I was ready to party but with who?

Stroke of luck. Jordi Cruyff, a United player on loan to Celta Vigo, was one of the few single guys like me as his girlfriend was not about; as someone who had grown up in the city he was a good guy to hook up with, I figured. It was by then 4.30 a.m. and I heard myself saying, 'Come on Jordi – this is Barcelona, we're Manchester United and we're the European champions. You must know where to go.'

So off we ventured to one or two more bars, where we were treated like royalty and continued the party mood until – somewhere around 5.40 a.m. or 6 a.m. – we stumbled across another bar which turned out to be a gentlemen's club, no less. I didn't really notice what it was until I walked in and suddenly found myself staring at the most unbelievable collection of attractive women walking around in knickers and not much else. We sat down and were soon surrounded with Jordi speaking in fluent Spanish to them. I was surrounded by four or five beautiful, half-naked girls and I've just won the Champions League with Manchester United. You've got to be kidding me.

'Come on, Jordi, organize the man,' I pleaded, knowing I would need his Spanish to get past the language barrier. He knew full well how I wanted to end this incredible night. 'One of them has got to come back.'

One girl was outrageously stunning. 'Come on, Jordi, you can do it, man.'

My teammate did not let me down. Having explained what was on my mind, this girl agreed to come back with me to the hotel. Trouble was, time was now pressing. United had a private charter plane booked which required us to be on the coach outside the hotel by 9 a.m.; I looked at my watch and it was already 7.30 to 7.45 a.m.

The taxi driver hurried us back to the hotel where the staff were probably a little surprised to see Dwight Yorke of Manchester United sprinting through reception tugging at the hand of a beautiful if somewhat bewildered local girl. There again, maybe they were not surprised at all.

I swear to you, not a sentence passed between us. To this day, I know nothing about her, not even her name. But when we got to my room I all but ripped off her dress, ripping off my suit at the same time; I just couldn't wait to get hold of her. I fell off the bed three or four times because I was so drunk and impatient but, laughing like loons, we managed to make love three times with me looking at my watch thinking, 'Hell, I've got to be downstairs for 9 a.m.'

I ended up leaping from the bed, throwing on the same suit, saying 'muchas gracias' and stupid made-up words like 'fantastico' to this bemused girl, kissing her feet, trying to explain that she was absolutely the most beautiful creature in the world but there was a plane I just had to catch. And when I rushed out of the room, I still had Schmeichel's cigar in my mouth.

I remember walking on the bus and singing as I walked down the central aisle. But there was not a lot of action by then. Everyone was quiet, exhausted by the events of the last twenty-four hours, and not in the mood for further celebration. I tried to get a power sleep but it wasn't going to work. I was still wired. We got the VIP treatment straight on to the plane and it was only on the flight, when I ran out of people to talk to because everyone was so tired, that I managed to get some shut-eye for a while.

Did I know what we would be stepping into back in Manchester? Not really. We got a sense of it at the airport, which was already flooded with fans. Even on the tarmac, the baggage handlers and airport workers were all waiting excitedly for us. It was an amazing feeling. But nothing like what awaited us in the city itself as we boarded the open-top bus for a drive to the M.E.N. Arena, where a salute to our incredible year was planned.

I think the entire party was drained on leaving the air-port, emotionally wrung dry but we were all recharged by the sight of Manchester's streets heaving with people. I later read that a million people were estimated to have gathered in and around the city that day but it reaches a point where the numbers are just meaningless. All I can tell you is the wonder I felt looking down at the happy faces from the top deck of the bus.

The scale of the celebration was just impossible to take in. I had never seen anything like it and never will again. Folk were hanging out of windows, leaning over balconies, screaming for our attention. I saw one woman whip her top off and swing her bra around her head . . . the crazi-ness just went on. And every time I looked ahead of me it seemed as if the throng was getting thicker and thicker, so much so that the bus could barely move.

For me – I'm sure for everyone – the attack on our senses was just overwhelming. 'What am I doing here?' I kept thinking. 'How on earth did this happen?'

As for sleep, what was that? I had not slept well the night before the game and had barely slept since. But still I was wired. In the Arena itself, another 17,000 fans were gathered waiting to acclaim the manager and the team as he walked in and the place went absolutely berserk. By now, I could see that fatigue was returning on the face of some of my teammates; but they were running on empty. They wanted quiet time; to go home with their wives and families and probably soak up what had just happened. I could feel they were impatient to leave. But not me. I was thinking: 'When is this going to happen again? Never.' I was far from finished celebrating.

Manchester was a mess with roads blocked off and litter and rubbish everywhere. But the most important thing I had established was that Bernard, my 'man' at the Reform Club where we had spent so much of our downtime, was open for business.

'Yorkie, you can't be serious – you're not going out for more?' the lads were saying to me. But I had no one to go home to, no wife or girlfriend. A big empty house was all that awaited me and that was no way to finish a day such as this. So I hooked up with my old mate Kona Hislop and headed for the Reform Club where everybody was still going crazy. All I can remember is staggering out of there at 2 a.m. in the morning thinking: 'How on earth am I going to get home?' The taxis could not get through, people were just roaming the streets in a state of delirium, Manchester was on a lockdown.

When I stepped outside, still dressed in my club suit, I saw one of those riot vans and through the haze heard a police officer saying to me, 'Yorkie, what are you doing? Where are you going?'

'I've got to get home,' I mumbled. Which is how the last member of Manchester United's 1999 Champions League winning team to be standing that day ended up in the back of a riot van being driven home. And still with Schmeichel's unlit cigar in his mouth.

I hit every corner of the walls when I staggered through my door but even after a shower and sleep, I awoke to find that I had not yet come down from the high of the week's events. Still I needed more. I was conscious of the fact that I was flying to New York to see family on the Monday, which only gave me the weekend to milk the moment.

The mood everywhere was still ecstatic. I could not cross the road without people tooting their horn and Friday was a beautiful sunny day spent just chilling out with friends before heading to The Rectory in Wilmslow at about 7 p.m. to find the place rammed with hundreds of partygoers still celebrating our feats. Once again, the drink started to flow and I recall climbing up on a table and dancing, feeling like a rock star, taking my top off and waving it around my head, with three fingers in the air to symbolize the Treble. I shouted to the barman to make me fifty B52s – coffee liqueur, Baileys Irish Cream and Grand Marnier – and he did, lining them all up for me to hand out. Naturally to the women first. It just got crazier and crazier; the most fantastic night. And this went on for another two days, inevitably finishing each night at my house with girls and pals and just the best of times. I may have ended up with someone but I honestly can't remember.

I did not want it to end. It had to in the end because there was a plane to catch on Monday. But what a party, what a three-day party. That was what life was all about. Great achievement bringing great joy.

And somewhere at home I've still got my constant companion through it all. That Schmeichel cigar, still unlit, locked away and preserved in a glass case. I'll always be able to look at it and remember some of the happiest and most satisfying days of my life.

11

A PLEASURE MACHINE

That incredible summer of 1999 I found myself struggling to comprehend the world into which I had now been catapulted a year after leaving Birmingham. I seemed to be flying from one part of the globe to another, jumping from New York to Dublin to Ascot to Australia . . . it flashed by at a bewildering pace. And everywhere I went – everywhere – I no longer had any anonymity. No, I was Dwight Yorke, Manchester United Treble winner, and it seemed to create hysteria in people. It was lovely but also claustrophobic even for someone who by now was wising up to the constant flash of cameras. I couldn't even escape them in New York, where I visited family and friends. You don't imagine the Americans have any notion of our football but they knew about Manchester United, the Treble and me all right. I can vouch for that.

And when I went to New York, it had to be by Concorde. I built up a picture in my head of what this flight would be like – packed with sexy, available women or maybe exotic heiresses. I climbed aboard to discover that it was, in fact, packed with old business-type folk; I think was the only guy under thirty on the flight. But it was still incredible. Three and a half hours to get to New York and as we begin our descent the old Manchester United magic works again.

'The captain would like to know if you would like to join him in the cockpit to watch us land, Mr Yorke,' said a stewardess. Did I ever. I wish I had taken photographs because that was just another incredible experience to add to all the others. But, of course, you think it will happen again, so not to worry. It never did.

Yeah, that summer found me in some strange places I would never have imagined. I think there are some pictures of me looking extremely ridiculous in full . . . well, what is it you call them, morning suits? Whatever it is the English wear for Ascot. Complete with top hat. Ascot? I mean, what was I doing at Ascot? And yet I found myself mixing and schmoozing with high society after Lara had secured a VIP box.

I also had a box at Old Trafford cricket ground when I went to watch the West Indies against Australia in the World Cup. I was with some friends, including Bozzy, and Lara was playing. It was only a few days after the final at Nou Camp and I was still in full party mode. I was sponsored by Pepsi at this time, and along with the sponsors, we thought it would be fun to surprise my countrymen with some drinks at a break in play. They organized me to drive a little golf cart-like wagon with refreshments on to the pitch when the Windies were fielding. The look on their faces as I came motoring towards them was a picture! They were pretty surprised. They had a bad result that day, so

I hope I livened up a disappointing match for them. I ended up in the commentary box talking about the match, which rounded off a really cool day, only dampened by the West Indies losing.

I was having so much fun at that time that even sponsorship obligations could feel like play. One time I was doing a shoot, again for Pepsi, when the cameraman took on a wager he thought he couldn't lose. But he obviously didn't know about the time I won my first pair of boots to an outrageous bet! If he did, he might not have challenged me, especially as it turned out he was a Liverpool fan. 'I bet you can't hit the crossbar from the halfway line with one shot,' he said to me. I shrugged and said, 'I'll give it a go', quietly confident that I could do anything at that point. And so I spied my target and nonchalantly struck the ball from the centre circle and watched it float all the way to the crossbar, which it struck with a sweet *boing*. The rest of the production team fell about laughing as the cameraman's face fell. He took it well, given that it must have choked him to be outdone by someone from Manchester United. I think I probably enjoyed that shoot more than he did!

The thrills just kept coming. I had to get back to Dublin for the 'wedding of the century' as it was being labelled but, having been introduced to the city by Paul McGrath and enjoyed many subsequent trips there with my Villa teammates, I promised to get there a few days in advance to hook up with a network of friends. I had not even looked at the invite to the Posh and Becks bash that I had brought with me. It was only in conversation with Giggsy the day before the wedding that I realized we were all expected to wear a certain style and colour of suit. Apparently, the dress code was black and white. I had everyone scouring Dublin for someone who could get me this outfit; again, a task made a lot easier when money is no object.

I didn't go to the church ceremony; unlike my mum, I'm not one for churches. I was, however, looking forward to the celebrations afterwards. Having got to know Becks in the last year, I knew they were not going to be anything too ordinary. It was as outrageous and spectacular as it must have doubtless been described to everyone in the days and weeks that followed. Although, once again, I felt a little bit out on a limb as the devout bachelor in our party. All the lads were there with their wives and girlfriends. Well, that's not strictly true – Keano wasn't there but that's just Keano. I don't think we really expected him to show.

The bride and groom did the whole routine, changing outfits and returning to their guests, and Becks was clearly in love. But again, there was nothing I saw or felt that day which filled me with a desire for marriage. I just couldn't see any reason to change anything in my life and why should I? I had no reason to suppose my life would be different the next year. It was a fantastic event unlike anything I've ever seen in my life. But it was very much an affair for couples.

By 2 a.m., I knew there were other parties happening in the city and I wanted to be part of them. The marriage of Becks and Posh may have been the most talked-about, most lavish and most publicized wedding of the century. But this particular guest headed back to Dublin to finish the night dancing on the tables in a bar yet again surrounded by ecstatic, celebrating United fans.

And incredible as it may seem, all of that was about to be topped. The club had arranged that summer to undertake a pre-season tour to the Far East and Australia, taking in Hong Kong and Shanghai and finishing in Melbourne and Sydney. I can safely say it remains one of the greatest trips I've ever undertaken, made extra special for me by my meeting with the most extraordinarily beautiful girl it has ever been my pleasure to know.

The possibilities for a slightly more relaxed excursion than normal were raised by the fact that the manager and Keano would not be there while the absence of a recently married and therefore otherwise-engaged Becks lessened some of the hysteria which might have engulfed us. Fergie stayed behind to collect his thoroughly deserved knighthood while the captain was absent because of injury. With the gaffer's iron fist missing, the lads felt that they had a bit of leeway. Or at least I did.

They all missed an amazing trip from the word go. We flew in a private Boeing 747, chartered by the Australian promoter Rene Rivkin, which is simply one of the most luxurious planes. It had everything – leather seats, wonderful spacious beds, everything you could wish for at your disposal. This really was the high life.

We would play two games in Australia, the first in Melbourne and then on to my old party ground in Sydney. The locals were even more excited because one of their countrymen, Mark Bosnich, was on board. Bozzy had taken on the hardest job in football – following Peter Schmeichel as

United's new goalkeeper. (Pete had stuck to his word and left English football with the Treble as his farewell prize. It was a hell of an act to follow but I know Bozzy was a goalkeeper of the highest quality. He was a big character and was up for the challenge. He'd been at United before with the juniors, and he felt he could come in and achieve.) It was great to have my old Villa teammate in the team. At each game, the place went absolutely crazy for us while we went absolutely crazy trying to find ways round the intense security in place at each of our hotels. No one was more determined than me. There cannot be anywhere on the planet with so many beautiful women as Australia. Everywhere I looked there were stunning girls to entice any young man and I wasn't the only one who was eager to be enticed.

Naturally, Fergie's assistant, Steve McClaren, wanted to make sure the trip went as if the gaffer were there; naturally we didn't. At the Melbourne hotel, we were under a strict lockdown and curfew with no visitors allowed and security guards stationed in the lifts just to make sure.

On my first morning there, I received what had become a regular morning call from Albert the kit man, who would knock on the door, check I was up and about and more often than not come in for a cup of tea and a chat. He did so that morning, casting his eye around the room for any signs of revelry. There were none. Or so he thought.

Albert and I chatted for a short while before he finally left my room, reminding me that we were due down for breakfast in ten minutes. What he never knew was that all that time there was a girl hiding motionless under the crumpled sheets of the bedding – lovely Vanessa, a girlfriend from my previous adventures in Oz. The night before, I had beaten security through the oldest trick in the book – bribery – to sneak her into my apartment and as Albert left and she emerged from under the sheets, we burst out laughing. I've since confessed to Albert who was able to share the joke. 'I thought you were up to something,' he said.

I guess that trip was the one time I didn't give my all to training. I was having too much fun. One night, I went out with the lads, and there were Teddy and Giggsy with me. Giggsy headed off back to the hotel early, leaving me and Teddy to continue our party. Steve had imposed a curfew but we ended up getting carried away and broke it.

It was nearly morning when I sneaked into the hotel, but I still made it to training. Steve had us running, which would normally be fine for me, but we seemed to be running round and round in circles. I'm lucky that I don't get hangovers, but after twenty minutes my head was starting to spin and I started to wonder what he was playing at. I might have been OK if we were doing criss-cross, or relays, or even changing direction and going round the other way! Now I think about it, perhaps he knew all about our late night and was getting his own back, but I'll never know! So when I finally got to stand still, my head was still spinning. I was so relieved that we started to do some stretches and I thought to myself I'll just take the opportunity to lie down for a minute and do some gentle quad and hamstring stretches. Big mistake! Within two seconds I was fast asleep. The next thing I know I was being drenched with water and I woke up with a start to find the lads killing themselves!

They'd heard me snoring and thought they'd have some fun waking me up. They had a great laugh. I guess Steve McClaren got his own back!

We played our game in Sydney and I scored in the 1–1 draw but the real highlight was to come at a nightclub we were invited to that evening. I think every member of the party could have fallen in love on that trip so beautiful were the women.

But I was on the look out for one in particular who I had been told would be there; one of the hottest babes in Australia. Gabby Richens was also known as 'The Pleasure Machine', a nickname she apparently got from an advertising campaign in which she had steamed up the screens with a striptease on behalf of Virgin Atlantic Airlines. I've never seen it but was intrigued by her. And when I saw her, I was transfixed. She was breathtaking and there was no time like that moment to approach her.

We were introduced.

'Everyone tells me you are the one to meet,' I said. She certainly was. Gabby had beautiful brown eyes and mesmerizing curves. We hit it off straight away and had a pretty good night getting to know each other. We exchanged numbers and kept in touch with a good vibe coming through in text exchanges.

Finally, we arranged to hook up one night for a date and I broke the curfew and sneaked out of the back door of the hotel. I would have broken down the door itself to meet her! Gabby picked me up at the back entrance and we set off to enjoy Sydney.

We parked up at a spot which gave us a panoramic view

of the city. We kissed. Beautiful. I seized the moment. 'Do you want to come back?'

I was expecting a rejection but was pleasantly surprised when she said 'Yes'. Actually, that's an understatement. Pleasantly surprised? I was doing cartwheels without moving. We parked outside my hotel where I knew I was in for a problem with security.

'Listen, wait here for five minutes and then slip in through that door there and catch the lift to my floor,' I said. 'I will be waiting for you.'

'Are you sure?'

'Yes, it will be fine.'

I flew upstairs, hardly daring to hope that she would go through such a tortuous subterfuge just to come to my room. I had to strike before she changed her mind, I told myself. That meant I had to get to the guard who would be covering the lift from which one of Australia's most photographed, famous and beautiful women would soon emerge.

'Listen, mate, I've got Gabby coming up.'

'Oh yeah?' he said. 'Gabby who?'

'You know. The Pleasure Machine.'

His eyes nearly popped out of his head as the name registered. She was big, big news Down Under. I think he was possibly more excited than me on hearing that. I gave him a hundred US dollars but I would have parted with a year's win bonuses if necessary. And I think he felt rewarded enough just to see Gabby arriving a few moments later to slip silently into my room. He was still staring in disbelief when I closed the door gently.

Which is as much as I am going to tell you other than to say we had a spectacular night until Gabby left at about 6 a.m. We stayed in touch for a time after that and she came to England for a while but I have since lost contact with her. But she was one more extraordinary adventure at the end of an extraordinary twelve months.

The summer of 1999? Unforgettable. Simply unforgettable.

12

JAILHOUSE ROCK

'Yorkie, it's me. Bozzy.'

'What time is it, man?' A look at the clock by my bed-side told me 5.30 a.m. 'What the hell's going on? Where are you?'

I was having to talk quietly because I had a girl sleeping next to me. She had ended a fantastic evening arranged to celebrate Bozzy's last night of freedom. Now we were in the early hours of his wedding day and he was calling me . . . from where?

'I'm in the police cell. I've been arrested.'

I cannot tell you how quickly my heart sank to what felt like somewhere below my knees when I heard those words. This was a Friday, 4 June, and just when I thought the golden summer of 1999 could not get any crazier . . . well, that phone call meant it could.

I was Bozzy's best man, a role I was more than happy to take on, and now the last words his bride-to-be Sarah had said as we made our plans for his stag night came thundering back as Bozzy told me where he was: 'Dwight, whatever you do, look after him. Don't let him get into any trouble.'

Oh my God, I thought, she is going to kill me.

Not only that, but Bozzy had just joined United and the publicity – for it would be all over the papers the next day – would have alarm bells ringing up at Old Trafford and the manager wondering just what he had done.

The night before, Bozzy, myself, Ugo, Lara, Smally – the old Villa crew – had reunited in Birmingham for the stag night and I felt it was a very calm, restrained evening. Conscious of the fact that the wedding was the very next day, and that meant anything too excessive had to be ruled out, we spent a very relaxing evening touring our old haunts, hooking up with old girlfriends and generally enjoying a good time. No one went over the top and no one got drunk. By the time the clock was turning 2 a.m., it was time to turn in – especially as by now the girl whose company I had enjoyed during the evening was clearly in the mood to return to my hotel.

Bozzy was perfectly sober as we left the last club but then suddenly declared that he wanted to finish the night at a casino. We tried to dissuade him but there was no changing his mind. He wasn't ready to go home. He seemed fine and so I could not see the harm in it; neither could the rest of the guys. And that was the last I heard of him until the phone woke me with a start.

It emerged that Bozzy had got himself involved in a row with some photographers outside the Legs Eleven lap-dancing nightclub, one of whom had reported him to the police. His release was eventually secured before we all hurried round to his house first thing in the morning to find out what the hell had happened. When Sarah confronted me about it, she was as angry as I had feared – although not half as angry as she was with her husband-to-be.

She felt humiliated by the whole episode and for a while it felt like it was touch and go as to whether the wedding would go ahead. But everyone calmed down and we all made it to the wedding venue, a beautiful old abbey on the outskirts of Coventry, on time.

The brigade of photographers and media gathered outside as everyone arrived was a further sign of what had gone on just hours before and the ceremony itself, in a tiny little chapel next to the main hall, was loaded with tension. And I mean that. You could feel the atmosphere. And when the priest asked that question about anyone knowing a reason why the couple should not be joined in matrimony, you could have heard a pin drop. I had played in some of the biggest and most intimidating stadia in the world the previous season but at no time did I feel as nervous as I did at that point. Marriage? Not for me, I thought, definitely not for me.

Thankfully, the ceremony was completed without any more hitches and with a sigh of relief we started to relax and enjoy ourselves and, in my case, the company. Particularly one of the female guests who I had already met on a number of occasions and with who I had always got on; she was beautiful, lively, great company and with a real sense of fun. We hit it off that day and I began to hope that after all the tension and trouble of the previous twenty-four hours, the night was going to end in a much more enjoyable fashion.

Just one problem. She wanted to be discreet in front of

her parents. As a result, we danced and partied the night away and waited and waited until everyone else had gone to bed before secretly sneaking up to her room.

We were trying to be as quiet as possible but that was difficult on two counts – we were both quite merrily drunk and her evening dress was one of those fitted affairs which she had to be helped into – and out of. I had no idea how to get her out of it and the pair of us collapsed in hysterics more than once as we tried and failed. In the end it was ripped away impatiently. The next morning our sleep was abruptly interrupted by the sound of knocking on the door.

'Are you in there?' enquired a woman's voice.

'Oh God, it's Mum,' she said in a panicky whisper. 'Won't be a moment, Mum!'

'Why's your door locked, darling?' asked her inquisitive mum.

'Just give me a moment.'

Oh God. What to do? There was nothing for it but to scramble together my discarded clothes and dive under the bed while my friend played for time in answering the door. This was no ordinary bed. It was an antique four-poster under which there was barely enough space to fit a child never mind a fully grown athlete.

I squeezed in, held my breath and then cursed silently as her mum came in, sat on the bed and settled down for a cozy chat about the day before, oblivious to the unwelcome guest jammed beneath her. It was like a scene from a *Carry On* movie: me not daring to breathe, the daughter trying to hurry the conversation along and usher her mum away – but her mum particularly keen to know how on earth she had got out of her dress. 'Oh look, darling, it's all ripped . . .'

After what seemed like an age, her mum did leave and I crowbarred myself out from underneath the bed, gasping for air – before we both broke down in laughter at the absurdity of it all. In the end, I managed to slip back to my room unnoticed, change and then re-emerge for breakfast, passing my accomplice and her parents along the way. Hopefully, when we exchanged morning greetings, they didn't detect the secret smile between their daughter and me.

During that first, unforgettable year at United, someone had coined the nickname 'The Smiling Assassin' to describe my football and I guess that was true. I loved scoring goals and smiling was second nature to me. At this stage of my life, my smile was particularly wide.

When I came to England never did I imagine the fortune that I would end up earning. In less than ten years, I reached a seven-figure salary and what else is any young man going to do but spend it. As soon as the big money came in, I would send home around £1,000 a month for my mum so she could live the way I wanted her to and not have to worry. You could get about twelve T&T dollars to the pound sterling back then so it was a really handsome sum. I made sure the house was refurbished and extended as well. It was not long before my sisters, brothers, nephews and nieces and everyone else besides were looking for their little brother or uncle to bail them out. I wouldn't change anything; in the end I got myself into a position which was financially beneficial to my family and I would like to think that had my fate befallen any of them, I would have received the same.

But I was in an unreal world, a universe no generation of footballers had ever occupied before. You do lose touch with the realities most people have to deal with because money is simply no object. I would go shopping for shopping's sake and began spending, on average, maybe £100,000 a year on clothes. Instead of buying one Prada T-shirt, why not buy four or five? Once they have lost that brilliant white, they don't look so good. I would find shoes I liked but then buy two or three pairs for the same reason. In my wardrobe, there must have been thousands of pounds worth of gear that I never actually got around to wearing; over the years, I lost track of the family and friends who would be visiting and see something they liked.

'Hey, do you want this? You've never worn it,' they would shout over to me. And I would say, 'Fine, take it.' Sometimes, without even looking at what it was they had selected.

Cars? What boy isn't going to buy fast cars if he can afford to? I know it sounds silly now but I wanted one for each day of the week. I got close. I think at its peak I stockpiled six, which I know included a Ferrari Maranello, two Mercedes, a Porsche and a Range Rover. I can't think for the life of me what model the sixth was. But of course, after a while you can't get one out of your driveway without moving another and another and it became stupid.

But all the players went down that road. It became a matter of pride to drive the latest model. Becks, Giggsy and

Coley were the three other car fiends in the team; when Becks bought his Maranello, within three weeks to a month all three of us had one too. And they were costing £180,000 a time. Someone was doing a lot of good business somewhere.

Was I a fool to satisfy this material craving? No, I wouldn't say that. I have absolutely no regrets. I had years of my contract to run so money was not an issue. I was twenty-seven with the world at my feet and loving every minute of it. Eventually, as you get older, the novelty wears off. Believe you me, I speak as a man who has been there and done it. There has been much criticism of our excesses and I can understand it to a certain extent. The money in the game couldn't have been imagined a decade before and we were earning incredible sums. I suppose to the average person, we were spoilt, but let me tell you I earned every penny through hard work and dedication. It had taken ten years to get to that position.

If there's one thing guaranteed to get me angry these days it is seeing young players being rewarded with contracts way, way before they have earned them and shouting their mouths off about their big cars or fancy homes or luxury holidays. Yes, we were at the forefront of the most extravagantly paid footballers in the history of the game – but we were at the top of our profession. Some players today get the cars, the home, the holidays, the luxury lifestyle without being fit to clean the boots of that United team.

I spent that first year at United walking on cloud nine and with a growing sense of feeling ... well, of feeling invincible. On the pitch that was certainly the case and off it I seemed to be in the thick of an incredible round of parties and beautiful women.

It was glamorous and exciting and I drank it all in eagerly. In the spring of that year, for example, I had met and dated the *Coronation Street* actress Tracy Shaw. We got on like a house on fire from the outset and enjoyed a wonderful fling together without it ever becoming anything too serious. By then, the biggest challenge I faced was trying to avoid paparazzi who continued to track my every move and I can vividly recall having to escape out the back of Tracy's pad and make my way home skipping over garden fences, unsure who was lurking around the other side of the house. You couldn't blame me. Tracy and I both knew where we stood. But you get pictured together and it's 'Dwight can't take his eyes off her' or 'Will they end up hitched?' That was rubbish. We were never boyfriend and girlfriend really. We had our fun and moved on and, anyway, Tracy became serious about the man she would marry and I wasn't going to get mixed up in anything like that.

And I must tell you about my first Christmas party at United. Now that was the stuff of legend. Christmas 1998 at our favourite, the Reform Club, was just immense and set the standard for years to come. I don't know how I got involved in helping to run it because it was generally led by Giggsy, who was the man with all the best connections and the guy all the pretty girls chased. But I got in on the act and suddenly found myself holding for distribution 200 of the 250 tickets printed. How was I going to find 200 people to invite? There was only one thing for it – I went on the prowl around Manchester, firstly to clubs and then even into the Trafford Centre, to invite the girls. Any girl who made me go 'wow' I would stop, introduce myself and simply hand them a ticket for the Manchester United Christmas Party.

By the time the night arrived, I had no idea who was going to show. We had security arranged, searching the bags for cameras or recorders, while the players' pool had plenty of money set aside to meet the bill. Come 8 p.m., perhaps 8.30 p.m., and we were all sat down with just maybe one or two girls there. Nothing outrageous. I hoped it wasn't going to be a flop. I began chatting to friends and the next thing I remember is looking up at a clock showing 10.30 p.m. and the place had just exploded – 250 people were there and it was clear my female targeting had worked a treat. There must have been a 3–1 ratio of girls to boys and that's just how I wanted it!

The night was outstanding, absolutely outstanding. There were plenty of United players who if they did drink only did so in small quantities. But that night something came over them and I don't think any could have gone home sober. The bar bill was £35,000. I would help organize two more Christmas parties after that when we probably spent even more but I cannot tell you how any of them ended up for me. I'm sure there was a girl or two involved but it's like that thing they say about the Sixties – if you can remember them, you weren't there.

It was all part of the unique camaraderie of those players and of that time. I was the happiest man in the world surrounded by the most closely bonded teammates I ever worked with and in a team which was just purring on the pitch. We were all different. Some only got on when they crossed the white line. But we were all strong. Gary Neville for example. You could not imagine anyone more different from me. 'Yorkie, you will never meet a girl in one of these nightclubs,' he told me, meaning of course, a girl to settle down with. Well, putting aside the fact that Gary met his future wife in a club, who wants to settle down? But as a teammate, I couldn't choose a better man.

Giggsy I've told you about before. He is a top, top bloke.

And Becks was by then in a world of his own in terms of profile, having famously paired up with Posh Spice and become one of the glamour boys of the age. But he was always just one of the lads in the dressing room or at the Christmas party. We were soon next-door neighbours and became good friends and have remained so over the years. I last spent some serious time with him when I played in a testimonial match during his Real Madrid spell and he treated me royally.

But still there was something bigger than all of us and that was Manchester United FC. And it was something that I was going to learn the hard way.

13

'IT SEEMED LIKE A GOOD IDEA AT THE TIME'

In all my time at United, Sir Alex Ferguson's word was law. Indeed, I only ever saw one player take him on and it will surprise no one that it was Keano.

We were on a training trip in Portugal when one session became extremely tense for reasons I could not understand. The players were flying into each other, trying to take pot-shots with the ball; it was unbelievably charged. In the middle of it was our coach Steve McClaren, trying to referee a short-sided game but not to the liking of Keano, who was tearing around the pitch unleashing some ferocious tackles and challenges that were a danger to his teammates. He had one on him that day all right.

Every call Steve made was wrong in Keano's eyes and you could see the steam coming out of his ears as he continued cursing back at McClaren for each decision. Watching it all from the sidelines was Fergie who must have shared our alarm when Keano exploded after one decision too many was called against him. He swore viciously at McClaren, a half-a-minute rant of 'effing this' and 'effing that' which eventually forced Fergie to step in from the touchline.

'Come on now, calm down, Keano,' he said.

'Fuck off,' was the reply.

Now nobody, but nobody, had ever taken those kind of liberties with the gaffer before. You could have heard a pin drop. And this, as I recall, was a training session for the Treble winners. Unbelievable. Fergie called it off there and then and how he dealt with Keano's rant in private I never found out.

The captain lived to tell the tale but you never, never challenged Fergie's authority. And yet, with the defence of the Treble only just underway, I found myself taking chances, like in the first weeks of the following season. We had a match at Coventry which was to be followed by a flight to Monaco to play Lazio in the UEFA Super Cup final. A footballer's life is packed with glamour but it can also be tedious. Club to hotel, hotel to game, back to hotel and on to the next port of call. That Friday night in August brought us to the Forest of Arden hotel between Birmingham and Coventry on the eve of an early game in the defence of our title.

I was lonely. And within just a few miles were any number of friends from my days in the Second City who I could trust to pass the night away discreetly. I called up one such girlfriend, Zoe, and asked if she wanted to come and stay over. This was, of course, strictly against protocol. I would be for it if the manager found out. But I was aware of his habits by now and figured it was a chance worth taking. Fergie would either take his staff out for a meal somewhere or entertain them at the hotel. I knew, or thought I knew, that from around 10 p.m. he would be occupied and this would be a good time for Zoe to make her way to the hotel.

As we spoke on the phone, we began to cook up a plan to smuggle her into my room. I gave her precise instructions. 'Go into the lobby, keep your phone to your ear, in fact call me, and I will guide you in. Take the first stairs to your left, come up to the second floor and my room is . . .' Well, I can't remember what it was but you get my drift.

Zoe agreed to the plan – and then promptly ignored everything we had mapped out when she arrived. Possibly nervous at the consequences of this secret meeting, she walked into the lobby and headed straight for the lift. Which would have been fine had, as the elevator doors were closing, another hand not forced them open again. It was the manager's. Into the lift stepped Fergie.

Fair play to Zoe for keeping her cool at this stage but I have since imagined exactly what went through the great man's mind. A beautiful girl had just got into the elevator of an otherwise quiet, golfing hotel full of middle-aged businessmen and dinner-dance couples. What's more she was heading for the same floor where his multi-million-pound collection of footballers were bedding down for the night. And it was a stone's throw from Birmingham. I think he worked out a prime suspect. Me.

I was upstairs oblivious to this, still waiting for Zoe to call me on arrival but with my camouflage well set. I had left the room on the latch so it could be opened soundlessly. I had the TV on quietly and I lay under the duvet, feigning sleep.

Back in the lift, and without exchanging a word, Zoe got out at the second floor only to be immediately conscious of Fergie following her. Not a word was spoken. As she passed my room, she glanced quickly at the half-open door but then carried on walking. The next thing I heard was that familiar, gruff Scottish accent barking out of the darkness from the doorway.

'Who's that in there? Whose room is this?' said a clearly suspicious manager.

It was time for some acting. 'What?! Eh?! Who's that? Oh it's you, gaffer. What are you doing here? I must have nodded off watching the TV,' I said.

'Your door was open, Yorkie.'

'I must have just nodded off like I say,' I explained. 'What's up? You could have given me a heart attack.'

'Well, just be more careful in the future.' And with that, he headed away, not hearing my sigh of immense relief.

I was congratulating myself on my deception but suddenly realized I didn't know where the hell Zoe was. Ten minutes later, my mobile rang. 'It's me,' she said.

'Where the hell are you?'

'I'm hiding behind the plants by the exit door at the bottom of the corridor. Your bloody manager was following me! Is it safe?'

It was and Zoe eventually made it safely to my room. And all's well that ends well. I scored against Coventry as we beat them 2–1 the day after as well.

But it was never wise to take chances with this manager. To me, that was no more than a bit of harmless fun. Throughout my career, I have never been one to place much store by this 'no sex before games' nonsense. If there was a night game especially. What better way to kill an otherwise long day waiting?

I still didn't have the settled, family life of my teammates and was enjoying my freedom. I was the guy out there indulging in the life now commonly associated with today's super-rich footballers. And when you're a super-successful United player, the invites just keep flooding through the letterbox and it is difficult to say no. I certainly wasn't going to pass up the invitation to fly to Dublin in the November of my second season, for example, to attend the European Music Awards.

In the VIP area that night, I mingled with some serious A-listers. Puff Daddy, Whitney Houston and Bobby Brown were there, the Irish boy band Boyzone, Denise Richards and, most amazing of all, Carmen Electra. Wow! Now there was a beautiful, stunning woman. And yet people were just as interested in screaming for my autograph as all these showbiz stars. It was a real eye-opener for me.

There was a little intrigue among these US-based celebs as to who exactly this guy was they didn't recognize and I found myself in Carmen's company, introducing myself and just generally chatting as the music started banging out. What else do you do when the beat is thumping and one of the most coveted women in the world is talking to you? You dance of course. And we did. I even began to think I might have a chance with her. I could have sworn she gave my arm a little squeeze as we talked. But then a fight broke out – to this day I don't know why or how – and before I could imagine anything else, a team of burly security guys had whisked her away. One moment she was there, the next gone.

But while that was the sort of red carpet treatment which was now on offer to me, I didn't think I took too many liberties. I wasn't jumping on planes to fly here, there and everywhere. I wasn't, at that time, dating famous girlfriends or behaving any differently to before. I've always been a man who, in terms of organizing his life, lives on the edge. I would zoom in for training at the last minute. But always in time. That was my style. I knew the other lads would look at me and be thinking: 'What's he been up to now?' And no wonder. I had a grin on my face from ear to ear because I was just ecstatic about life.

We were the new rock and roll stars and I felt I had earned my place at the top table. I had top scored in the Treble year and then again in my second season – I had been a success playing for the top club in Europe, arguably the world – and that's why I could choose between a Ferrari or a Porsche to drive to training. I was proud of my achievements and my hard work and I didn't mind people knowing it. But, listen – and I want to stress this – I never abused my fitness. People behind the scenes knew I was still working hard to stay on top of my football. I may have been the last in but I was also the last out, always in the gym, sticking to the disciplines that had carried me this far in the first place.

But the headlines on the front pages did get worse as that second season wore on. I'm not saying I was a saint but not everything that was written was true. I think I was a very easy target. The sheer volume of it is too hard to keep up with so in the end you just accept it as part of being a Manchester United player. Unfortunately, other people were not able to dismiss it so lightly.

Becks was in a similar situation. He was getting increasingly hassled about his lifestyle. But both of us would smash the 'beep test', the high-intensity running test which measures your fitness. Not many players can do that.

I looked after myself and always have done. I would go and have a great night out and end up with a woman who would then be left amazed by my getting out of bed after sex to do a hundred sit-ups or press-ups. 'This guy is crazy,' would be written all over her face as she turned over to sleep.

I was full of energy and life. Making love and scoring a couple of goals? Is there a better way to spend your time on this planet? Not when you're twenty-eight and playing for the best team in Europe. I don't know if envy or jealousy is involved. But you suddenly sense a shift in how people are looking at you. I was not doing anything differently in the third year to how I had lived at Villa and in my first two seasons at United. I am adamant about that. I took my job seriously and I took my fun accordingly. But suddenly, it felt to me, people were looking at me differently.

Again, I think Becks went through the same thing on probably a bigger scale. When we were in the dressing room he used to give me the heads up on what was going to come out in the press. He really looked after me. I'd get notice occasionally from my management team, but somehow Becks knew what stories were going to break. It was helpful to know when to keep my head down! I guess that made us tighter. People love to bring you down from the top of the mountain. You're young, you're good-looking, invited to all the top places but the moment you have a poor game . . . well, look out. Here comes the backlash. I hate that culture in this country but I'm not the first and won't be the last to suffer it. This is life. It is supposed to be fun. Enjoy it. Make people happy. Celebrate your great fortune. That was my philosophy and had been for as long as I could remember. Unfortunately, I suddenly realized not everyone agreed with me.

So yes, I had again scored a bagful of goals in that second season as we won the title by an incredible 18 points from our greatest rivals of that time, Arsenal, a record points gap between first and second. The football had again been electrifying, especially over the second half of the season when we scored buckets of goals – 124 goals in all competitions, 97 in the league alone – and nearly 1.5 million paying customers had poured into Old Trafford to watch it all. I had at least matched my previous season's goal ratio with 24 from 41 appearances.

My partnership with Andy was still thriving with Teddy and Ole complementing the attacking end of the team perfectly. Off the pitch, I was learning too. I had to. I had taken steps within my own life to try to control the madness that had come with being a Manchester United Treble winner; no one could have prepared me for the frenzy that now surrounded us and my first home. As soon as I could, I moved to a six-bedroomed house in the 'footballers' suburb' of Alderley Edge where there was much more seclusion from prying eyes. We enjoyed a memorable house-warming party in which one of our younger players, Quinton Fortune, became so spooked by the tricks of a magician I hired he had to leave.

Celebrity now brought all sorts of strange goings-on into my life. I had total strangers turning up on my doorstep claiming to be long-lost family, people who were chasing favours, girls I had never met claiming that I was the father of their children . . . madness, all madness.

My new home, protected by electronic gates, gave me a natural barrier from such invasions while I could keep close to my friends and teammates. Becks was effectively my next-door neighbour and, with his profile, there was still no shortage of paparazzi in the village's leafy lanes. You can imagine how lively that street was when a story broke about both of us. It was chaos down there! But behind the walls there was at least a measure of peace and quiet.

And there was an aura of invincibility about the team which seemed to intimidate our opponents before they had left their dressing room. I carried with me a supreme confidence and I got off to another flyer, scoring in each of our first three games. Everything I touched, it seemed to me at the time, was turning to gold.

My respect for Fergie remains, to this day, enormous. For all the rows, for all the full-throttle old-fashioned bollockings that came my way in our four years together, he remains the greatest in my eyes. He was no coach and would not claim to be. In all the time I worked under him at Manchester United, I can barely recall him taking more than a couple of sessions with the players, both of which were as uncomfortable for him as they were for us. But his genius – and I believe it is a genius – in the art of managing one of the biggest football clubs on the planet shines through in other areas and especially in an uncanny ability to read the hearts and minds of his players, probably better than they can themselves.

I would be no exception. Only at United could you follow up the amazing triumph of the Treble by winning the Premier League championship again, this time by a record distance, and still have Sir Alex chill you to the bone with his damning verdict as that second season closed: 'Yorkie – you're failing.'

I can still hear him saying that to me now. 'You're failing.' And it was difficult for me to imagine how he could reach that conclusion.

That third campaign would be a difficult one for me for a number of reasons I can now recognize. Unfortunately, spotting the problems and doing something about them is not so easy when you are caught up in the whirl of the events that were engulfing me throughout this period. I can remember wondering what on earth my targets should be. What else could I hope to achieve after such a momentous first year? I recall saying to the manager as we gathered for pre-season training after the Treble, 'I think I need a year off just to get over this.' Fergie dismissed it as a joke; I can look back now and think that many a true word is said in jest.

And it was not as if it was possible to match the previous season because we were deprived of the opportunity of defending our FA Cup when the club decided not to compete in order to play in the World Club Championship in Brazil. It was a decision that outraged the rest of the football world and one which devastated the players. We were proud of our team, proud of what we were achieving, our dressing-room bond and belief were phenomenal and we would have backed ourselves to do in the Cup what we did in the League. The conversations within the dressing room were all the same – we wanted to defend 'our' Cup. If we couldn't repeat the Treble then we were pretty sure of our chances for a double. But the players were never consulted on a decision that brought an awful lot of criticism down on the club and fed the view that Manchester United were playing fast and loose with the great traditions of English football. That was never how we saw it in the dressing room.

Yes, there would be a blot in the Champions League when our campaign was ended at the quarter-final stage by Real Madrid, the one team we always felt would be the most difficult adversary. But that disappointment had long been put to bed as we won the title again so convincingly. No, the season had hardly been a shambles.

But Fergie is not such a great manager for nothing. There is only ever one game you can bring to the table and it is game A. Nothing else will do. And clearly he felt I was, along with one or two others, slacking somehow.

'You're failing.' To this day, I am not wholly sure what he meant. Was it my goals? Was it my play? Was it something else he had detected which I could not see? It wasn't long, however, before the tensions were beginning to show in my relationship with the manager and, as a result perhaps, my influence within the team.

Another person who was having a difficult time was my mate Bozzy. It had been hard for him to blend in straight away coming in after Peter. He had his own style and that didn't go down too well with some of the players. They were used to Peter and also Raimond van der Gouw. Bozzy took the pace down a little bit and I think some of the players got a little agitated. He was one of the best goalkeepers I've ever played with but, frankly, it would have been impossible for him to better Schmeichel at the end of a treble season. Bozzy was brilliant at shot stopping, arguably the best I've ever seen, but he was not as confident when kicking the ball. As the back pass rule was in force, goalkeepers needed to kick many more balls, and sometimes Bozzy wasn't consistent enough. He worked so hard at getting better but arguably the back pass did for him. He helped us regain our Premiership title in that second season, but he lost his number one slot when Fabien Barthez was bought to United in the summer of 2000. I felt for my mate. He left United for Chelsea at the beginning of 2001. I would soon know what it felt like to drop down the ranks.

It has always been difficult to balance the demands of a top-level club career in the most intense league in world football with committing wholly to the Trinidad and Tobago national team. There is a huge enthusiasm in my homeland for the national team and I am fiercely proud of my country. With me, Russell Latapy and Shaka Hislop playing for our country the anticipation of success was like never before.

I tried as best I could to accommodate both of my teams.

I had the choice sometimes to miss one or two less significant internationals in return for investing fully in the more important qualifying matches. By the time I reached United the pressure for Trinidad and Tobago's star export to play for his country intensified.

Back in Tobago, a new stadium was being constructed in Bacolet for the 2001 FIFA Under 17 World Championships and it was to be named in my honour. That was not something I took lightly and it added to the conflict I felt at that time. I wanted to focus on the demands of playing for United while helping my homeland continue its quest for the holy grail – a place at the World Cup finals. But it had not been easy. Back home, people saw pictures of me scoring goals for United and expected me to bring all the magic of that team with me and sprinkle it over the national side. I was the big star and they wanted the flying headers and spectacular shots they were seeing on TV. But it's not that simple.

Equally, things hadn't always run smoothly when I was out for six months at Villa under Big Ron. That was 1992 and the knee injury happened while I was playing for my country. I felt my home FA abandoned me to a lonely recovery – because, I reasoned, I was of no more use to them while I was injured. This left me angry and disappointed. A phone call or two – 'Hi, how are you doin'?', 'How's it going?' – was all that was needed. Instead I heard nothing. It was to be a major dawning for me. They had been all over me and now I couldn't play they didn't want to know. I realized I had to look after myself and started to put my club career first.

I started receiving some critical letters from Jack Warner, questioning my commitment, plainly accusing me of not putting in the same effort for my country as I did for United. I'm not proud to admit this, but I have to acknowledge there were times when I did not give my all for my country. I didn't want it to be that way and I understand why they would have then got upset with me.

But when I found out about the new stadium I knew I had to go back and take part in the new World Cup qualifying campaign even though – I rightly suspected – it would cause problems with Manchester United. Fergie was growing increasingly concerned about what he considered distractions from the business of Manchester United. I understood, but he did not have to deal with the wild excitement of having a Manchester United player for the World Cup qualifying campaign. And then I made a big error of judgement. I took another chance. And this time I wasn't so lucky.

In September of 2000, I played a vital World Cup tie in Port of Spain against Canada, who we beat 4–0. This victory secured our place in the final round of the qualifiers. And the islands went crazy. To accommodate the UK-based players, travel arrangements had been carefully put into place to ensure myself, Russell and company would get the first available flight back to resume our club duties. A helicopter was booked to take us to the main airport pretty much straight after the final whistle; we even had a police escort arranged to make sure we got to the chopper as quickly as possible.

Had we lost and seen our path to the World Cup finals

cut, things may have been different. But we didn't. We trashed the Canadians and the carnival atmosphere which had accompanied the match build-up gave way to absolute mayhem when the victory was secure. We duly stepped into the helicopter, glancing over our shoulders at the frenzy behind. We did our best to fight the temptation to stay. But we were missing out on something special, something that would pass into the folklore of our islands. This regret grew stronger as the chopper rose over the stadium and flew over homes on the way to the airport. Thousands of folk were out on the streets celebrating the result. I looked around at the guys who, I am sure, were thinking the same things: 'What are we doing? What are we leaving for?'

I must admit, my decision-making was affected by the fact that I had just picked up an injury, which I was fairly certain would leave me unable to play for United at the weekend. 'What is the point of rushing back for treatment and missing out on all this?' said the mischievous voice at the back of my mind.

The flight from Trinidad was waiting for us by the time we landed. And something just came over me. I turned to Russell, who I knew had been similarly affected by the sights and sounds that had greeted our victory, and said, 'Do we really want to miss out on all this?'

I also knew that, as I was the most senior player and the highest-earner, the other lads would be looking at me to lead the decision – and probably to pay any fine for wasting a helicopter and holding up a scheduled airline flight, which was now waiting on the tarmac with hundreds of passengers already depressed about flying back home from holiday!

It was no good; I caved. We had barely got out of the helicopter before we apologized for the trouble we were about to cause and requested the pilot take us straight back to where we had come. It seemed like a good idea at the time. For a start, we could blame our late return to the UK on a missed flight, an excuse that seemed good enough as we began an absolutely wild, wild night of dancing and laughing.

After catching a flight the following day, I braced myself for the consequences still hopeful that the delayed flight excuse would hold up in the cold light of day. And we might have got away with it were it not for the fact that one of the Canadian players made it back on time to play for his Scottish club. Fergie's intelligence network soon picked up the story from north of the border and it led to a direct challenge from the manager about my focus at United.

He lost his cool with me for the first time in the confrontation that followed. Did I really want to jeopardize everything I could do at Manchester United? This World Cup dream was all very well – but it could cost me everything I had at Old Trafford. He was angry and frustrated, I imagine.

I was still quite confident about my football but I was no longer the number one striker. What had been the Andy and Dwight show in the Treble season and beyond had begun to be replaced by a brilliant partnership between Teddy and Ole. I was still working hard and playing well but Teddy and Ole had hit a purple patch. Being away didn't help my position; Fergie's words of warning echoed around my head: if you are not 100 per cent committed here, you will suffer the consequences.

I certainly had no complaint with Teddy, who would go on to be named the PFA's Player of the Year that season. He is a good friend and a great teammate and he was playing some of the most outstanding football of his career at this point. The boot was now on the other foot. Where my form and success had forced Teddy to accept a support role in my first two years at the club, suddenly I was the one on the outside looking in. Flying off to answer my country's call was not the best way to persuade the manager otherwise.

I was in Fergie's bad books again later that same September when we prepared for a live TV home match with Chelsea. There is a routine about the team announcement at United. All the squad gather for the pre-match meal after which those who aren't playing get the call they dread – a summons to the manager's office to be told why they have not been selected.

I expected to be on the bench that day so it was a shock when I found myself in Fergie's office being told I had not made the sixteen. He gave me his reasons, suggesting Ole would be more flexible for the demands of that game but I didn't like it. I felt at that point that there was nothing I could do to please him. And I made a fateful decision. Instead of hanging around all glum-faced I left the stadium before kick-off, my departure observed by Sky TV technicians which, I knew meant it would find its way back into the manager's office. But I did not believe I was doing anything wrong; I felt my presence would only bring everyone down and I headed home to watch the match and brood over what was happening to me.

The next day in training, I got the call again. 'What have I done now?' I thought as I headed for Fergie's office, where I was reintroduced to the famed 'hairdryer'.

'What the hell were you playing at?' he was raging at me. 'You stay and support your teammates at all times. Do you think you are bigger than the team?' He was right of course – I know that now. But I had never been in this position before and I was struggling to know how to handle it. I think an awful lot of what subsequently happened to me at United stemmed from that weekend.

Before this period, everything had been so natural, so easy. I didn't have to think about my game. I had been calm and free in my football. Now I was starting to show anxiety in my play, snatching at opportunities, conscious that I was being judged in everything I did. I wasn't going out and expressing myself as fluently as in the past. I was becoming erratic.

One of the things I loved about United was the strength of the dressing room and never was that more valuable than when a player was going through a difficult time – as I was now. Take Keano, for example, a great player and a great leader. His care and concern for the players around him should not be underestimated; it was part of his captaincy which is less well-known. I'll always remember coming out of one difficult spell that season with a goal against PSV Eindhoven in a midweek Champions League fixture about a month after the 'Trinidad incident'. I'm sure he played me in and I ran on to score. Keano knew I was having a tough time and he was first up to me screaming, 'You're back, you're back' in encouragement. He was simply thrilled. That's what true top players are like. It was a brilliant show of togetherness, something so valuable to me at that time. But, unfortunately, my life was about to get even more turbulent, and it was not the football which would prove to be significant.

14

HEADLINING

In the build-up to Christmas 2000, we found ourselves with the chance to take some downtime in London after a 3–3 draw at Charlton. It was almost as if I knew something was going to happen because I recall vividly the build-up. We had been given a rare Sunday off the following day and this was an ideal opportunity to enjoy a night out in the capital. A lot of the guys were staying down, even Becks and Giggsy and Coley, and I recall us all discussing our plans for the evening as we showered after the game.

'Tonight, boys, I need to meet someone,' I said half joking, half thinking that something would happen. 'This is the night when I finally get it on with Natalie Imbruglia.' She was my dream date of that moment – sadly in my dreams is where she stayed – and there was much chuckling and banter about my prospects (or lack of them) of meeting up with her. It was all good fun and set the tone for the night. We were staying at the Sanderson Hotel, right in the heart of Soho and *the* best place to stay for reliable and discreet security and a suitably trendy setting. It was always a good starting point and I was relaxed and excited about the night ahead. I was meeting up with my old pal Kona and a more recent acquaintance Ade, the actor who had recently scored such a big hit in Guy Ritchie's *Snatch*.

When it was time to move on to a club there was only one choice at that time – Attica, just a short distance away and the place to see and be seen.

So I'm walking into the club and I'm in my own zone, scanning around when I suddenly feel a nudge in my back from Kona as he alerts me: 'Look, right in front of you – it's that Jordan.'

Jordan? Just a few yards away was a small but strikingly attractive woman I instantly recognized as the model who had been making a name for herself in the tabloids. She was twenty-two and originally from Brighton but all I knew about her that night was that she had become famous for what was staring back at me now. She was quite a picture with that famous, surgically enhanced figure squeezed inside what I recall was a sort of police uniform outfit revealing plenty of cleavage. This was the party season and I presumed she was on a girls' night out. It was difficult not to look at her.

As she walked by me I grabbed her hand and said the first thing that came to mind: 'How ya doin'?' Not the best opening line but it would have to do.

Her reply was equally tacky: 'Hiyaaaa.'

Could I get her a drink? I asked. Sure she replied before heading for the ladies.

We soon hooked up and stayed in each other's company all night. Our respective friends got on well too and as we settled in for drinks in one of the Attica booths, the night passed easily and effortlessly. If I'm honest, I was looking and hoping for a little action and she was perfect for that moment.

Come time to go, in the early hours of the morning, I had high hopes of locating a late restaurant for a bite to eat. Jordan, whose real name I discovered was Katie Price, had other ideas. 'I wanna McDonald's,' she announced to us all as we left the club and nothing would persuade her otherwise. That's interesting, I thought, but if there is a chance of spending the night with this girl, I'll eat some junk food if necessary. When we stepped outside, we were immediately greeted by the flashing lights of the paparazzi. They hardly had to snatch the pictures, though, as there was a McDonald's just a few hundred metres up the road and we walked there as a group.

A few moments later, and I was heading back to my hotel in a cab. Alone. We exchanged numbers and talked about getting together again soon. But my hopes for a more entertaining end to the evening were quickly dashed. Jordan made it clear that nothing like that was on the agenda – she even paid for her own McDonald's. And all I got that night was a bag of chicken nuggets and the definite sense of anticlimax. We'll see, I thought, we'll see . . .

The next morning I was on the phone straight away, relieved that she answered. Maybe I felt I had some unfinished business; I'm not sure. I was sufficiently interested to want to get to know her more. It had been a great night, I said. Did she want to catch up again? Sure, was the response but that would prove difficult with our different commitments. Our departure from Attica had hardly been secret either so there was the added inconvenience in the weeks ahead of trying to get to know someone while the gossip pages were stalking our every move.

We agreed to meet up when I had to return to London for a promotion with sponsors Nike and Pepsi. Katie and I were able to meet up briefly a couple of times in London before I invited her up to Manchester.

Back in the United dressing room, I was getting a fore-taste of what was to come. At training the next day, I knew the banter would be flying. So I might as well start it, I thought. 'Lads, you are not going to believe who I met on Saturday . . .' To roars of laughter and good humour, all they wanted to know, as young men would, is whether or not we had slept together. Naturally, they got no details.

Which brings me back to Fergie. I was still fighting for my place that season. But there would be one final, daz-zling hour in the sun for me thanks to Fergie's unique radar and his amazing instinct. What he couldn't pick up from observing a training session isn't worth knowing.

Arsenal were due to visit Old Trafford for a televised lunchtime game in late February. We were working towards our third consecutive Premiership title and this game effec-tively represented the Gunners' last chance to get back into the championship race. I had been a bystander for so much of the campaign I could not have expected to play.

Coley was suspended and the team had been short of goals in the previous games. But it was still a big surprise when the gaffer told me I would start while Teddy was dropped to the bench. I always like to think that Fergie knew I had a good record against Arsenal; but maybe he just saw something in training that week that told him to give me a go. I was certainly up for it, eager to prove myself. Why did he pick me that day? I imagine everybody was thinking the same thing when the teams were announced as it was only my second start in nine games. As if the occasion wasn't enough, it just so happened I had arranged for Katie to come to the game, take in a night out in Manchester and stay over. Everything was set. She was accompanied by a friend, Michelle, who was a big fan of Giggsy and hoped to get the chance to meet him.

To this day I still can't believe what happened next. I was beginning to think that after all the triumphs on the pitch and excitement off it, there was nothing that could make me feel like that again; I thought, if I am honest, that after two fantastic seasons there was no way back to the top of the mountain. I was wrong.

Once again the manager's incredible instincts had played their part. It was as if he knew something special was going to happen. In my mind, I knew this was a chance for me to show the world Dwight Yorke was not finished – and I'm never more likely to be inspired to do that than when I have got a woman to show off to!

Fergie's other great gift is his inspirational delivery of the team talk and before we left the dressing room that day, he had lit the touchpaper to a special performance as only he could. Take care of this game today, he told us, and the title is ours. That was the theme; the genius was in the delivery, which I can never hope to reproduce. This day was no exception.

In simple terms, I scored a hat-trick inside twenty-five

minutes in a scarcely believable 6–1 victory. We swept away what remained of Arsenal's challenge, leaving us 16 points ahead of them and needing only 15 more from ten games. For Manchester United, certainly for this Manchester United team, that was a stroll in the park.

That's it in simple terms but it does not begin to describe the intensity of what I felt at the centre of this amazing game. I scored after 2, 17 and 22 minutes. The first I played a one–two with Gary and shot from the six-yard box. Thierry Henry equalized before Keano picked me out, shooting over the Gunners defence. I got a right-footed strike on target. The last goal I scored, Becks sent over a killer pass and I held off the defence to fire past David Seaman. I even set up our fourth, returning the favour to Keano, crossing to him and watching him finish the job. Ole and Teddy completed the six. What an amazing, amazing match.

I can still feel the tingle of that day. There I was, out on the pitch, stepping into glorious winter sunshine to score a hat-trick against our greatest rivals and watching from the stands was one of the most famous and coveted women of the moment. It's not as if I planned it to turn out that way but that weekend our relationship really took off. I'm not even sure Katie knew exactly what she was stepping into. She certainly knew precious little about football. The cameras picked her up immediately – which I'm sure Katie wasn't going to complain about – and people just went crazy. Here's this fella, scoring a hat-trick and look at the bird he's got with him!!? That old Caribbean thing kicked in big time; that need to be the top man with the top girl. Are you watching this, Rhonda?

I'm always one of the last to leave after a match and before I had got out of the dressing room that day, there were already pictures of Katie being shown on TV, cut into highlights of my hat-trick. By the time I reached the players' lounge, further held up by interviews and the man-of-the-match presentations, a lot of the lads had gone. But Katie was waiting for me. I was not sure whether to kiss her on the lips or, more gentlemanly, on the cheek. I opted for the gentle approach. When we left we saw the scale of interest this new relationship was provoking. At United, there's an area reserved for signing autograph books of the fans and there was obviously a big demand on me that day. But I noticed that there was a significant increase in the percentage of men who were watching Katie and I exit the ground. Hundreds and hundreds of fans were out there waiting for us, no doubt interested in this girl I was about to drive back to my house.

It was a journey which passed quickly and was full of jokes and laughter. We both loved the attention we had been given and the excitement we seemed to have aroused in the public and the media. Who wouldn't? For my part, I was hoping that my goals would bring me out of my most troubling spell since my early days at Villa. What a script. The perfect match, the perfect result. Now for the perfect night?

By the time we got home, five or six cameramen were outside my house but I was far too elated to worry about them. It occurred to me as I showed Katie and Michelle my house that we had spent very little time together. We were treating each other gingerly still, apart from a few giggles and the look she gave me when I told her to take her pick from one of the guestrooms. As I watched her and Michelle bring in enough travel bags and cases for a month. I wondered for a moment if she was moving in!

My mate Lara was already on the phone, talking about the game. The phones began to melt with family and friends calling for congratulations and an update.

Later we went out to celebrate, and at last Katie and I got to relax a little more in each other's company. Again I detected the incredible effect she seemed to have on men wherever we went. I could see them staring at her with a mixture of lust and wonder. That's not to say the girls were not fascinated too, mainly by the 'Jordan Look', which I suddenly realized they all seemed to be copying.

The whole city was throbbing that night, especially after the events at Old Trafford, and I was buzzing. As the night wore on we grew a little more intimate; a lot more flirty, holding hands. The wine helped us to relax even more and there was a very strong chemistry developing. And what healthy young male isn't going to get excited about that?

We partied and we danced until 2.30 a.m., maybe three in the morning, by which time Katie had persuaded me to break the habit of a lifetime and kiss in public. I'm not one for that, I even find it difficult to hold hands; but she was very insistent and in fact seemed to enjoy it. So what else could I do but respond?

We spent the journey home canoodling in the back of the car and listening to the music. But as we arrived back in the dead of night, I was still unsure about what was going to happen. For once I was a little uncertain about what was expected of me. After all, this is a woman who has made a name for herself as something of a sex goddess wanted by men all over the country. What should I do next?

She disappeared for an age to chat with Michelle while I, a little the worse for wear, made my way to my bedroom and got into bed. It had been a long, long day, full of adrenalin and incredible emotions. I was now finding myself fighting off fatigue as I waited to see if Katie would come to my room. I was damned if after all this I was going to fall asleep!

Thankfully, after about half an hour, she came through my bedroom door and, as she did so, let a little light into the room. I'm not sure whether she saw it but I know I was sporting the cheekiest of grins at that moment. It was misplaced.

Back she went into the bathroom – what do girls find to do for so long? – for another fifteen or twenty minutes before the mystery of that question was put aside for another time. She emerged in tight-fitting shorts and a vest top, and as she climbed into bed only one thought was on my mind. At last, I thought, the perfect end to the most perfect day.

We chatted for a few minutes before I leaned over to kiss her. Katie responded. And then broke it off to say, 'You're not getting any nooky, you know.'

'Whhaaattt?! What do you mean?'

'Not on the first night.'

'You must be joking me,' I stuttered.

'No. No nooky.'

We kissed a couple more times, enjoyed a nice cuddle and in my head I was thinking: 'It's just a matter of time, she'll come round.' But she was true to her word. No nooky for me. I just wished she had told me earlier because I could have gone to sleep.

After another rebuffed attempt in the morning, there was time for a look at the newspapers to assess the interest our very public Old Trafford 'date' had aroused before Katie headed back down to Brighton. It was now established in my mind that we were seeing each other and that we were going to be an item. Everyone around us especially seemed very excited about the prospect.

I got plenty of interest in the dressing room on Monday morning. David May, who had a particularly wicked sense of humour and who often got a laugh out of my antics off the pitch, always led the chorus of questions after my supposed exploits were reported in the tabloids. 'Great read, yesterday, Yorkie,' he would laugh. Or it would be: 'Come on, Yorkie – what have you got for us this week?' That morning there was extra special interest because of Jordan's profile and the language of the locker room was particularly blunt.

'Come on, Yorkie – we know you. Come on, talk us through it. Are those tits really as big . . .?'

I just smiled. I didn't want to say too much. I left it open-ended. I guess they may have been a little surprised I was not signalling any extracurricular activity. Anyone who had seen us out that night would have reached the same conclusion as the lads in the dressing room. Just shows you how wrong people can be.

If Katie's behaviour had surprised me – only because it was so at odds with her image and what that had led me to expect – it was nothing compared to the shock of the next few months.

I had already made adjustments as my fame increased. I had handled the shift up that came with moving from Villa to United and then winning the Treble and being the top goalscorer. There was nowhere I could go, nothing I could do and no one I could meet, no matter how innocent, without it appearing in papers. But a celebrity girlfriend brought a dramatic change. I knew the manager was concerned for me; I was concerned myself if I think back now. It was just that I didn't know what to do about it. The pressure on me now was a whole new experience.

Katie and I were trying to conduct a relationship over a long distance and with limited time to spend together. A picture of me talking to any other female, be it an old friend or just a fan who stopped to say hello, could be misinterpreted by mischief-makers and earn money for the photographer. It could also cast doubts in Katie's mind. I was forever being set up with these predators and it was an unnerving experience.

I tried to escape. Dublin had always been a trusted, favourite place to kickback for me since my early visits with Paul McGrath and I returned now in search of refuge. But it was the same story there, too. United have a big following in Ireland and I was an easy target. Incredibly, even more girls were interested in me because they knew they would be able to sell a story about sleeping with Jordan's boyfriend.

United's goalkeeper at this time, Fabien Barthez, became a good friend who took me to Paris on a couple of occasions, which provided some respite. Fabien was a legend in his native country because of the 1998 World Cup win but even so football does not have the huge profile it enjoys in England; I was able to relax there during our brief excursions.

But things were getting beyond my control. After one of my trips to Dublin I had a confrontation with the manager that shook me to my core.

I was due to catch a Monday morning 6.45 a.m. flight back to Manchester, which normally got me back in plenty of time to freshen up and head for training. Except on this occasion, I heard the words that sent my stomach churning. Flight delayed. And we sat on that plane with the sick feeling inside me growing. I had to be in for 10 a.m. I heard the captain assuring us over the intercom that everything was fine and they would be underway just as soon as possible. But all I was thinking was: 'Just shut up and get this plane off the ground.'

Eventually it did but it would be 8.45 a.m. before we left the runway. I thought: 'It's a forty-minute flight. I'm really pushing my luck.' I had Kona with me and when the plane touched down I left everything with him while I rushed through customs and straight to a waiting cabby.

'You get me there for ten, mate,' I said telling him to head for United's training ground, 'and it will be double pay.'

I phoned the ever-reliable Albert on his mobile. 'Albert? It's Yorkie. Is the gaffer there?'

'Been in since half seven, mate. Why?'

'I'm coming in. But I might be a little late. Just get my gear ready. And I'll come in round the front.' Usually, the first-team players arrive around the rear of the complex where they also exit for training. Maybe I could sneak in the front and escape the gaffer's glare. And if he was just a few minutes late going out for training himself, I might just get away with it.

I was five minutes or so late but the first part of the plan worked fine. I sneaked in the front and completed the quickest change into kit possible. I had hoped to make for the cover of some trees as I emerged from the building before sneaking into the opening running session I could see the lads now undertaking. Then, when they passed by those trees, the plan was to slip into the group unnoticed.

No chance.

'Yorkie, come here!' screamed that voice. And in front of the entire squad I was then subjected to a tirade that left me shaking.

'Until you show more commitment to this club, then this club doesn't want you here!' he screamed at me. 'And the rate that you're going, you won't be here much longer anyway. Now go in. We don't want you out here.'

It was crushing and humiliating.

By now we knew we had the third consecutive title in the bag and my lapse was no more than an irritation – but this was Sir Alex Ferguson and there was no way he would allow anyone to use that as an opportunity to take their foot off the pedal.

Effectively, I was now the fourth-choice striker and I was

beginning to lose hope of climbing back up the strikers' pecking order and finding favour with him again. The Arsenal game had felt like a revival but the following match at Leeds found me returned to the substitutes' bench to make way for Teddy. That killed me inside, hitting my confidence hard. Had he made up his mind? Used me one last time but given up on me for the long term? The doubts were there. I may not have realized it then, but perhaps it was affecting me.

Despite the Premiership contest being so obviously in our favour, West Ham had knocked us out of the FA Cup and Bayern Munich stopped us in the Champions League, again at the quarter-final stage. This was a manager who would not accept another league title as adequate compensation. The tension between myself and Fergie had been growing, fuelled by my widely publicized relationship, and his full-scale blast at me that morning was perhaps the culmination of the frustrations of seeing another player knocked off track by the celebrity culture.

There would be one more conflict with Fergie before the season's end. The title had been clinched by the middle of April with a 4–2 win over Coventry – always 'good' opponents for me – in which I scored two goals. Before the penultimate game at Southampton, we were given two or three days off. I was looking forward to escaping to Edinburgh and spending some time with Russell, who was enjoying a good spell with Hibernian. It was a trip that would end with some more disastrous headlines.

Russell and I whiled away a relaxed, late afternoon and early-evening session in a bistro just five minutes from his apartment, during which we were counting our lucky fortunes and reflecting on our achievements. It was a lovely May day and our spirits were good as we discussed the future and the unhappy decision we both knew was looming – retiring from our international duties in order to focus on our club careers.

'My season hasn't been good, Russell,' I was telling him. 'Something's got to give. And I'm afraid it's got to be the national side.'

I was presuming that we would be left in relative peace but quite the opposite – the appearance of a Manchester United player with a local favourite seemed to cause an amazing amount of excitement. I couldn't believe the reaction we provoked in the bar, yet another reminder of the breadth of celebrity United players at this time had to expect. Add to the mix my relationship with Katie and yet again here were fascinated men and hungry women chasing the scalp of the model's boyfriend. We got held up longer than we wanted but stuck to our pledge to leave by 10 p.m. I had to get back for training the next day and that meant an early flight. I did not want any more rows with the gaffer.

Unfortunately, Russell had had a couple of drinks and we were stopped by police on the short drive to his home; he failed the breath test. My heart sank as I knew the next morning's headlines would make grisly reading in my manager's office.

I wasn't wrong. Even though my role was innocent, I had been caught out breaking his rule of no drinking forty-eight hours before a game. I got another rollicking to ensure the season ended on a sour, sour note.

Of course, I can look back now and see things clearly. I had fucked up off the pitch and had been caught out too many times that season. I can see that now. I was skidding down a slippery slope. I possibly knew it then but tried to kid myself otherwise. In my mind I was only behaving as I always had. My life had been so natural, so instinctive, so perfectly uncomplicated but the wheels were coming off.

15

'YOU GOT TO BE CRAZY . . .'

Over the course of the next few months I would discover the two very different people inside this girl for whom, I don't mind admitting, I found myself developing strong feelings. Katie Price I liked very much. She could be warm and tender and very cuddly. The alter ego she would unleash on the world, Jordan, I was less thrilled about.

It was difficult to conduct a normal romance for all sorts of reasons. We lived at opposite ends of the country and both had demanding schedules. She would occasionally fly up to Manchester in the weeks that followed but that only brought with it attention.

My timing, I knew, was lousy. Having finished the season knowing my career was at a crossroads, I knew I needed to draw less attention to myself, to get away from the front-page headlines which I reasoned were making Fergie wince. So not the best time to fall for a girl who was probably one of the most photographed models in Europe and whose professional life was driven by a publicity team which relied upon steamy media coverage.

Whenever we stepped outside my house, it seemed the

paparazzi knew precisely where we were going. It was madness. Even when I changed a choice of restaurant or bar at the last minute, we would still arrive to be picked off by a battery of cameras. I always thought she may have been inadvertently tipping off the press through her people or that she needed to keep the press onside so much that this was just part of the game. But maybe it was a newspaper tapping my phone.

And there were also early signs of something we could never reconcile. We were two very strong-willed people who had become used to getting things our own way. Other girlfriends would ring me up because, as I maintain, I never fell out with any of them. They clearly knew I was with Katie by then and had no ulterior motive in contacting me other than to say 'Hi'. But naturally, my new girlfriend was unhappy about that.

Equally I didn't want to shut out my core of close friends who had come to rely upon me as the man to get a party started. 'Come on, Dwight, we need you down here, man, it's not the same without you,' was the message.

Katie bridled at these rival attentions. This is what I do, I told her. My life had a pattern and, yes, it was a pretty selfish and indulgent one at that time. If I wanted to go anywhere in the world, I could ring up my management office and have flights and hotels booked by the end of the day. It was a fantasy world in which money meant nothing. 'Just put it on the card,' was the answer to everything. I would never even ask the price.

As Jordan, she too was used to controlling everything around her and that was always going to lead us into conflict. But that was ahead. And I'm not going to say that there wasn't a time when I was crazy about the girl. It was probably about three weeks after her visit to the Arsenal game that we made love for the first time – she probably wanted to make sure this was not going to be a one-night stand – and it was everything I hoped it would be. Making love to Katie, however, could be an entirely different experience to making out with Jordan.

Katie was much more tender, much more loving, much softer. She would love to cuddle up after our lovemaking and who wouldn't want or to be snuggled up to her? When we went out for dinner or to the movies, I would introduce her as Katie, my girlfriend. She was very accommodating, very warm to be around. We would snuggle up in bed watching those horrible, vampire horror movies she loved so much but could hardly bear to watch. I'm not much better myself, much preferring action movies, but she used to cling to me when the scary bits came along and bury her eyes in my shoulder or chest. She could relax as Katie, give the make-up a miss, put some casual clothes on. Sadly, such is the ill-feeling that has developed between us, I had largely erased all these images from my memory banks. But thinking of them again now, they are clearly my favourite memories of her.

That was Katie, the girl I wanted to be with. But the girl the public wanted and her career demanded was Jordan. And as Jordan a very different person accompanied me; there were expectations and she changed herself, inside and outside, to meet them. Katie became this sex symbol she thought Jordan had to be, vamping it up with outrageous skimpy dresses which left little to the imagination. Even the way she carried herself would change. Suddenly there would be a strut in her walk which wasn't there before. She would put on a show for the cameras and the public all right.

And, of course, it was Jordan who was constantly questioning her appearance, wondering if she should have a bit more surgery here or a bit more there. I kept telling her to leave herself alone and that she looked lovely as she was. But she would not listen. And as for making love to Jordan, that too was a completely different experience; the fireworks could be spectacular. For Jordan the wilder the sex, the more she seemed to like it. She was uninhibited and fiery.

Never at any stage did I see her as a marriage prospect, not so much because of any reservations I held about her or our relationship but because, as much as I was enjoying spending what time we could get together, I realized I needed to re-focus on my football. I knew something had to change if I was to stand any chance of retrieving my United career and I began making plans to do just that. But as I say my timing was lousy.

When you are trying to tone down your public profile it is probably not a good idea to fly off to perhaps the most affluent corner of Europe and rub shoulders with the high and mighty at one of the glitziest events on the calendar. But again I am being wise long after the event. In mid-May 2001 I took Katie to Monaco as I had been nominated for, and invited to attend, the Laureus World Sports Awards. It was an unforgettable all-expenses-paid trip during which we were treated like royalty. And it would be riotous.

It was my first visit to this money-drenched dot on the Med and even though by then I had lived it up in some of the most glamorous locations around the globe, nothing quite prepared me for what I found. We were given the five-star treatment all the way. First class from Heathrow to Monaco and then a private helicopter to a stunning hotel. When the awards were over, we would then be taken to a second hotel closer to the harbour for that weekend's Monaco Grand Prix. It was just madness. I have never seen so much money, so much wealth and so much glamour.

On my first day there, I got to play a round of golf – which at that time I was becoming increasingly passionate about – but not just any round of golf. This was a round of golf with Seve Ballesteros, one of the ambassadors for the sponsors. I was shaking like a leaf such was the presence of this man standing by me on the first tee. After three or four holes I began to relax as Seve took sympathy on me and began offering tips and guidance. What a wonderful guy and what an unforgettable experience. A round of golf with Seve Ballesteros remains right up there with everything I have done in sport. And I am still blown away by the fact that Seve actually knew who I was.

For Katie and me, this was equally exciting. Monaco was buzzing, filled with people gathered for the awards and the Grand Prix that weekend. There were hordes of media everywhere and we found ourselves treated like movie stars, with red-carpet entrances and photographers howling for our picture; the place was dripping in money and we wanted for nothing. It was exciting, sexy, glamorous, the ultimate millionaires' playground. But along with the excitement came another clash of wills between us.

With so much media in attendance, it was a heaven-sent opportunity for Katie to adopt her Jordan profile. As we prepared to go out for dinner on our first night, out came the provocative outfits and sex-siren behaviour.

'Why do you have to dress like that?' I asked her, imploring her to choose a less-revealing outfit. 'Do you have to show so much cleavage? Does the dress have to be that short?'

To my way of thinking, she was my girl now and didn't need to put on such a show for all the men who were lusting after her. I was deeply uncomfortable with that. You ask any guy – what they enjoy looking at in other women is not how they want their partners to appear. But it was a waste of time arguing with her. She had to be Jordan – and this was how Jordan faced the world.

It wasn't long before the boot was then on the other foot. On our first night out we stepped from the car outside a restaurant to be greeted by eighty or ninety cheerleaders from an American football team who just happened to be passing by, all dressed in those skimpy little numbers they wear. I was desperately trying not to look but it was tough. These women, every one of them, were stunning.

'I bet you wish you hadn't come with me now,' said Katie. 'I bet you wish you were with your friends.'

'No,' I told her, 'don't be silly. I want to be here with you.' And I gave her a hug of reassurance. I suppose it was a little sign of her insecurity or doubts about me. But I genuinely felt good to be with her even if it was a relief when the cheer-leaders moved on to eat at a different restaurant.

But we lived it up. Boy, did we live it up. Everywhere we went we were recognized – again I had no idea United's profile reached this far – and treated famously. But, once again, the night would end up splashed across the papers back home.

The second hotel to which we were transferred for the Grand Prix was even more glitzy and by then Monaco included some familiar faces. Both Giggsy and another United teammate, Nicky Butt, had come out for the race and plans were made for some hard partying at Monaco's landmark nightclub, Jimmy'z. Eddie Jordan, who was then running his own Grand Prix team, was there as well as Rod Stewart's ex-wife Rachel Hunter and we all ended up having the time of our lives.

Rachel is a stunning-looking woman and it wasn't exactly difficult to spend a good part of the evening dancing with her and generally enjoying her company. Katie, who was dancing with Eddie Jordan, felt I was giving her far too much attention – flirting a little too strongly for her liking – and a strained atmosphere developed between us as the night went on and more and more drinks were consumed.

Well, maybe she had a point. Rachel was intoxicating and I might have gone a little bit too far. But the truth is that while I was revelling in the company of such a beautiful and striking woman, I had absolutely no designs on her whatso-ever. To be honest, I don't think I was ever in with a chance anyway; she was way out of my league. I was, however, making a move on her on behalf of someone else.

I should explain. Many's the time down the years I have been pictured with various girls, each photograph accompanied by one or two sentences which hint at something more serious than it ever was. The truth is that on many occasions I was the fall guy for the planned indiscretions of married teammates who could not be seen and certainly not photographed chatting up beautiful women.

Seriously, you would not believe the amount of times I found myself saying to girls, 'Listen, my pal over there is crazy about you but he's married or he's with someone and can't come over. Are you interested?' As always the single guy in the group, I was a fail-safe matchmaker. I would continue the task of trying to charm them while my married colleague waited for his moment. True. I promise.

I knew what was going on that night and it had nothing to do with my wanting to get into bed with Rachel Hunter, as delicious as she undoubtedly was. Because there was also in attendance at Jimmy'z a very famous, married footballer (not a team-mate) who was absolutely besotted with her. 'Yorkie, I need your help,' he said and I guessed what was coming up. I spent a good deal of the time chatting to her on his behalf to see if she would be interested in getting together with him away from the prying eyes of the other guests and the inevitable paparazzi outside.

Watching this, however, Katie became convinced I was up to no good and a row was inevitable, reaching crunch point in the early hours of the morning when it became clear that this party of high rollers had been invited to see in the dawn on a yacht moored in the bay. I heard something about a Saudi Arabian prince being the owner but, to this day, I have no idea whose yacht it was. But I was having a great time and didn't want to stop partying now.

Katie, upset by my behaviour with Rachel, wanted out. She went back to the hotel and I know I should have gone with her. But I just didn't want the party to stop. We were two stubborn characters who each wanted their own way and it was only ever going to end in tears.

So I joined the group heading over to what was laughingly described as a yacht. It was more like a small city! The rooms, the lavish decor . . . this was a whole new level of wealth even I could not imagine. The food and drink made available to the partygoers just left me looking at it in wonder. But the upset with Katie unsettled me and after a couple of drinks and with the sun coming up, I knew I had to get back.

When I returned to our hotel room, I found Jordan had long since gone to be replaced by the alter ego I so much preferred, Katie – a little vulnerable, clearly angry and upset, tears having been shed. I felt terrible at my indulgence. She was angry I left her and angry at the way I had danced with Rachel. And she presumed that I had been with another woman. I hadn't. Happily, we reconciled in the best possible way but I guess I knew then that this was an argument that would repeat itself in whatever lay ahead for us.

Pictures of this eventful night, and various accounts which appeared, were soon splashed all over the British media driving home the growing image of me as a heartless playboy. Me dancing with, and trying to bed, Rachel Hunter while a furious Jordan looked on; that was how it was portrayed. I had long since vowed to pay no attention to what was appearing in the press about me because it was mostly so much rubbish and so inaccurate that it would drive you insane if you allowed it into your life. And many of the reports of that night were no exception.

And the footballer? Well, he remains married and for the sake of his peace shall remain anonymous. But if he eventually landed his prize he would have had much to thank me for.

Katie and I flew home together happy enough after a brief visit to Cannes but it was not long before our very different agendas became all too clear. I wanted to get my focus back on football and stay off the front pages. It soon became obvious to me that Katie was loving the attention.

I was seriously thinking about my football now and the last thing I wanted was more front-page publicity. Those pictures can be very misleading. I never willingly took liberties with United's schedule. But you get snapped in a bar or a club on a day off only for it to be used later in the week when the game is coming up and it is presumed you have been out drinking close to the game day. So I resolved to calm everything down, keep a low profile and make my plans for the new season, my fourth at United, against the threatening backdrop of an even greater competition for places at the club. It was an open secret that the Dutch striker Ruud van Nistelrooy was joining United but then Fergie added another fantastic talent in Juan Sebastián Verón in the same month.

After three successive championships, the manager was

clearly anxious to add new dimensions to his squad. The Treble-winning team was changing shape. Teddy had gone back to Spurs by now and that left me, Coley and Ole to make up the quartet of strikers with Ruud. But clearly Verón would have to be accommodated and there was no way Fergie wanted to omit Scholesy. How would he find room for us all?

The word was out that I was a prime candidate to be eased out of the club, the manager having finally grown weary of my 'playboy lifestyle'. But it did not intimidate me; it inspired me. I felt I knew Ruud's game and thought that I could be the perfect foil for him. I wanted to get myself in the best ever shape for a pre-season programme I knew was vital to me and hired a personal trainer, Andy Clark, to devise a fitness schedule that would enable me to hit the ground running when we reported back and supplement my United routine.

At the same time, another clash of wills with my girlfriend brought fresh tensions between us. We were approached by *OK!* magazine to do a home photo shoot which Katie and her team of advisers thought would be brilliant publicity. The money was also handy, about £150,000 between us as I recall; they could not see a downside to it. And neither could Katie. I could. I knew how that would be interpreted in the manager's office; he hated his players appearing in that magazine. Yet another symbol of Dwight the playboy, Dwight the celebrity footballer, Dwight the party animal. Those were not the signals I wanted to send to Fergie.

It caused a lot of trouble between Katie and me; she was

With my good friend and countryman Brian Lara.

Surprising Brian and the West Indies team with refreshments at Old Trafford cricket ground in May 1999.

Golf is my other passion. Here I am getting my first lesson from one of the best – Seve Ballesteros. I now have a handicap of three.

After leaving Manchester United in 2002, I was reunited with Coley at Blackburn Rovers for two years before joining Birmingham for one season.

Scoring for Blackburn against the West Ham and England goal keeper, David James. I was the top scorer in my first season.

Playing for Sydney
FC. We won the
A League in 2006.

I was invited by my old United team mate,
Roy Keane, to join Sunderland in 2006.
Here I am playing against one of the next
generation of United players, Anderson.

The two captains. I faced my old neighbour and friend at the beginning of the England v Trinidad and Tobago match at the 2006 World Cup Finals in Germany.

Above: Reaching the World Cup Finals was a dream not only for the national squad but for the whole nation.

Below: In action during an incredibly close match. Here I am holding off Joe Cole.

My son, Harvey, came to watch me play football at Ewood Park.
Below: With Harvey on holiday in Barbados.

Above: Harvey's first birthday.

Below: My second son, Orlando, was born in 2007.

Me, 2009.

annoyed at my refusal to go ahead. It would have been a major publicity coup for her but it was the last thing I wanted. I put my foot down and said, 'No.'

I made other changes. After the excesses of that Monaco trip, I gave up alcohol for the rest of the summer. And how I wish that I had known the importance of water intake to anybody but especially athletes. If I didn't drink alcohol I would drink fruit juices but three or four litres of water a day for a professional athlete is far more beneficial. Having indulged greatly over that summer, however, it was time to cut it out altogether. I would meet up with Andy for afternoon sessions at a rugby club, trying to get even fitter. I felt it was working, I felt the old sharpness coming back.

And as much as we didn't want to and knew it would hurt our homeland, Russell and I went ahead with our retirement from the Trinidad and Tobago team. It had to be sacrificed if I was going to focus fully on this last chance at United. Again I hoped the message would be received in Fergie's office. Just in case, I drove home my point when I had the opportunity.

'I mean business this season,' I told him. 'Just you see.'

He looked at me and acknowledged my determination. 'Just be careful – don't overwork,' he responded. Maybe he had already decided he had only limited use for me, what with these new players coming in at vast amounts of money. (Ruud had joined from PSV Eindhoven for around £19 million and Verón, meanwhile, had broken the transfer record coming from Lazio for £28 million.) If so, I would change his mind.

And it began well. That summer we ventured to the Far East again for a pre-season friendly against a Malaysian team and then Thailand, winning both games, 8–1 and then 2–1. It was my best ever pre-season with United and, I felt, went some way to establish my claims to be the player who was most suited to complementing Van Nistelrooy. Even Fergie was moved to comment in the press about my renewed appetite, which I took to be an encouraging sign.

I came on as a substitute in the Charity Shield match against Liverpool in early August and I thought this was a step in the right direction. If I wasn't in his plans to start I was the next in line. That would do for starters. I was pumping and I don't think it wrong to say that the feeling in the dressing room was that I was the most obvious player to link up with Ruud. Unfortunately, persuading the manager was an altogether different matter.

This fresh enthusiasm for my football was clashing with my girlfriend's designs for us. I tried to tell her I was fighting for my career but she detected – and it was probably true – that my interest was tailing off. That heady summer had passed and now football was my passion again. Katie felt neglected and the rows about when we would see each other started to become more and more frequent.

Ultimately, my renewed hope for prolonging my career at United came to nothing. In fact the very opposite happened; it fizzled out in the most depressing circumstances. The player who had worked himself super fit and been so determined to show that there was fresh life in his game would finish the 2001–2002 season broken and dispirited, winding down redundant weekends with a group of pals in a bar to drown his troubles. And by then, there were plenty. The carnival was over.

After the first dozen games of the season proper, it was clear that the plans for the team did not include me. I started only one of them. Fergie was obviously under pressure to make the new line-up work but it was clear by the end of the autumn that it was not flowing as it had done in the past. He was trying to convince Scholesy to play in that support role alongside Ruud but it wasn't working.

Scholesy didn't want to play there. It was not a role he favoured. 'I know you don't like playing there but trust me, it can work,' I recall the manager saying at one team meeting. I honestly felt I could be the solution but Fergie was ignoring the evidence of his own eyes. He is, unquestionably, one of the greatest managers in the game if not the greatest, a man to whom I owe so much. But I think he got that wrong; it is the only truly disappointing move I have known him make.

There was only one thing I could cling to as my enthusiasm began to waver. This was the season Fergie had announced would be his last. He would retire at the end of the campaign. Would there be a chance with another manager using a fresh pair of eyes? I spoke to the people close by at that time. Platty, and Tony Stephens particularly. Their advice was to stick with it. 'You never know. Keep your head down and get on with it.'

And why would I want to leave this club? I wasn't being judged on my football but on my lifestyle. Yes, they were right. He's going to quit so why not wait and see?

But everything was about to get increasingly difficult. My romance with Katie was now about as happy as my football outlook. So much so that, to all intents and purposes, I did not see us being together any longer. We still had occasional contact but it was clear to me that we had run our course by then. Our little fairy tale was over. If I am honest, and there's no point in doing this book if I'm not, I had been unfaithful to her, which I took as another clear sign that anything special I may have felt earlier had long since disappeared. Our schedules made it difficult for us to see each other, especially as I was so determined at that point to concentrate on trying to save my career at Old Trafford.

The approach of my thirtieth birthday party in November found us at our worst moment to date. I was planning a big bash, something to take my mind off the cul-de-sac my career was now in, at Tiger Tiger club in Manchester. All the football community would be there and it was something I wanted to enjoy. Katie wanted to be there. I said, 'No.' I wasn't happy about how things stood between us and I did not want her to arrive in full Jordan-mode and make a scene.

'Bollocks,' she snapped in our final telephone conversation about the event. 'I'm coming anyway.' I was equally determined she wasn't. I even went as far as to tell the security staff that under no circumstances whatsoever were they to allow her into the club. Thankfully, she never followed through with her threat and the night passed without any incident. But if I thought that that was the end of it, and that Katie too would see the futility of our relationship and move on, I was in for a very rude awakening.

It wasn't long after that birthday bash that I took another call from Katie. This time the subject was even more serious. She told me she was pregnant and that I was the father.

My reaction was immediate. There was no way we could have this baby, I told her. 'Our relationship is too unstable,' I said. 'I don't think it's right. What's the point of bringing this baby into the world when we are not going to be together?'

The conversation continued along those lines and ended with her agreeing. It was the only right thing to do and she accepted it. Or she seemed to. I knew this was not something to be talked about lightly; I also recalled Katie telling me she had had a termination before, after becoming pregnant with a guy she thought she was madly in love with only to discover otherwise. And I understood the gravity of the decision I thought we had made at that moment. I looked forward to fatherhood; it was something I definitely wanted for the future. But it is not something that can be entered into lightly. It is a huge responsibility. I knew that. For Katie and me, it was just wrong.

But a couple of days later, she was back on the phone. And this time with a very different message. She told me she was having this baby whether I liked it or not. Of course, she had the right to change her mind and it was her decision to make, but still the words hit home like a sledgehammer. Right there, at that moment, I felt my whole world change.

'You got to be crazy,' I said. 'We're not together any more.' On more than one occasion, she had even told me how much she hated me. And now we were having a baby? 'Why are you doing this?' I pleaded with her.

But that was it. As much as I tried to talk her out of it, there was no dissuading her from her course of action. I don't know what changed her mind; I don't know what happened to bring about this turn of events. But I felt I was being pushed into something in which I no longer had any say and I was totally dumbstruck. We agreed, I kept telling myself; we agreed there could be no baby. It was impossible in our situation. The questions kept spinning around in my head.

I had always got on well with Katie's mum, Amy, who I knew harboured hopes that her daughter and I could work things out. I had met Katie's family towards the end of our relationship. With my commitments to United days off were rare and so I didn't get to go down south often. But when I did meet Amy and Katie's stepdad, Paul, we got on very well. They were good company, and Paul was a sports nut who enjoyed talking about all the things which naturally interested me. When I spoke to Amy, she was as bewildered as the rest of us. But Katie nonetheless told the press that she was pregnant, that I was the father and that she was having our baby.

All hell broke loose. The press besieged my house. I had never seen them in such numbers before. There must have been twenty or thirty of them outside my gates, imprisoning me in my own home. I certainly wasn't going to speak to them. I had to call a pal to get some provisions for me and bring them round. That day passed by in a sort of blur. I don't believe I was thinking straight. All I could hear myself saying was that 'I thought we had agreed not to have the baby.'

Our relationship has never been the same since that day. Never before have I felt so powerless; never. I didn't want to speak to her for a long, long time. Clearly I had to and when we did resume communication, it was by telephone and very, very difficult. I just found myself coming back to the same questions each time. Why are you doing this? You don't love me. You say you hate me. Why do you want to have a baby with me?

I don't think I ever got an answer.

I've got to say that despite our cool professional relationship at this time, Fergie was absolutely brilliant to me at this point. I went to see him, desperate for a father figure who could maybe guide me through the madness that had enveloped me, and he did not let me down. It had been difficult for me to go to see him with all my troubles because, well, we were a bit frosty with each other by then. But I am glad I did. Fergie sat me down and offered sound advice and a sympathetic ear. I had seen his infamous hairdryer rages by then but this was a side of the gaffer that few get to see. He recognized how upset I was and knew I was looking for someone to turn to. But, he told me, there was no escaping the fact, whatever the reasoning, I now had to offer as much support as I could to Katie. That was going to be difficult. Our relationship remained at telephone distance and was constantly spiked with bickering and arguments. Amy, Paul and Katie's brother, Daniel, were great to me throughout all of this as well. We all got on. What you see is what you get with me. I am not a complicated man and they liked what they saw. They know that I did not mean to harm Katie, or disrespect her. They offered me plenty of sympathy and counselling too. But as time wore on, I realized I had been presented with a fait accompli and I had to come to terms with it.

16

HARVEY

It felt like my life was falling apart, brick by brick. Nou Camp, the Treble, Schmeichel's cigar were just distant memories. Normally, I could find an escape from whatever was on my mind on the football pitch but even that had deserted me now. By the time January came round, I was hanging on to the fringes of the first team but one incident at Middlesbrough told me my career at United was irretrievable without Fergie retiring.

Steve McClaren, our former coach, was now in charge at Middlesbrough and they wanted to buy me. The deal on the table was staggering – a £55,000 a week contract, which was way more than I was getting at United. And it was not without plenty of temptations. A cluster of old Villa pals were now at the Riverside including my big mate Ugo as well as Gareth Southgate and the coach Steve Harrison. Even though the clubs were haggling over the fee, the deal was close.

As fate would have it, United then drew Middlesbrough in an FA Cup fourth-round tie on 26 January for which I was named one of the substitutes. It would be a game we would lose 2–0 but it is what happened before that which perhaps hurt me even more.

The dressing-room doors are on opposite sides of the corridor at the Riverside and you walk past Middlesbrough's on the way to that of the visitors. As we trooped down the corridor, the Boro door was open and there was Steve Harrison, who had coached at Villa under John Gregory, standing at the doorway. Walking beside me was Fergie. 'All right Yorkie,' said Steve as we filed by. Fergie reacted by pushing me towards the home dressing-room door. I knew what he was saying. So did everyone who saw it. 'Here, you can have him, I've no further use for him.'

It hurt. It hurt my pride. We all tried to laugh it off as a bit of fun but inside it hurt.

There were other clubs interested. I got angry when I heard that Gérard Houllier was interested in taking me to Liverpool only to be put off by Phil Thompson's damning verdict of the baggage of my lifestyle. But the big hope for me at the time was a dream return to my first home, Villa. Graham Taylor had gone back there as a director of football and, as we had always remained in touch, it was easy to find out if there would be a chance of going back. Graham indicated that it was a possibility and my spirits were raised. I knew there would be opposition from some sections of the Villa public because I had turned my back on them to sign for United. But I was confident that it was nothing a couple of goals would not sort out. And I had always been happy there. With what was going on in my life, Villa would be like finding a sanctuary.

And so with Villa a prospect, and Fergie potentially retiring, I deferred on Middlesbrough. It was a fantastic offer but it was also a long, long way from home. And there was not exactly a great scene going on up there, as Ugo frequently reminded me.

But one morning the following month, a typically blunt greeting from Keano told me my options had just been further narrowed. 'Yorkie – you're fucked, mate,' he said as I arrived for training. He was right. Fergie had announced that he had postponed all notion of retirement. I smiled at Keano's brutal assessment of where I now stood at Old Trafford but again it cut deep.

The news was crushing. Those were the lowest days of my career and now the most determined bachelor at Old Trafford was paying for his single life. There was no one around to find comfort with. Just a big empty house, packed with possessions and material wealth – but still just big and empty.

I started to drink again. I wasn't an alcoholic, not even falling-down drunk. But it helped to ease the loneliness. I was like a zombie. I would call my mates and go out in an effort to try to forget what was happening but it could not fill the emptiness inside me. No matter how I tried, I couldn't get Fergie to change his mind about me, even though I felt he was ignoring the obvious. But that only added to the frustration. Instead of showing him what I could do, I found myself on odd days training with the reserves. In my first year at United I had scored 29 goals in 48 games. My second, 24 in 41. Even in my third I was still on that goal-every-other-game ratio of 13 from 25, despite starting fewer games. Regardless of the mistakes of judgement off it, I did not feel I had ever let United down out on the pitch. And now I was training with the reserves.

There was no point in hanging on any longer. I knew I had to leave. As my career fizzled out at United I became a Sunday afternoon fixture at Brasingamens, a well-known bar in Alderley Edge. For the last two or three months of my Old Trafford career, I would sit there with Kona, my faithful old pal, and two of his work colleagues Joanne and Alex, watching the live game on Sky TV and slowly get hammered. It got so that the bar owners even reserved the table for us. It became a fixture in my life. But a depressing one. I had no appetite to go anywhere else. Just this bar. I still had a smile on my face, trying to disguise the hurt I was feeling but inside I was in despair with my football and with Katie.

Even my hopes of a move back to Villa crashed and burned, the only time in my life I have been angry with Graham. I had placed great store in that and was under the strong impression that he could make it happen. John Gregory had left by now and Graham was back in charge of the team. I was close to the manager and the chairman, the two most powerful men at the club. Surely this transfer was in the bag? But Graham bought Peter Crouch instead and my heart sank. Again, I sensed the same judgement that had come back from Anfield about my highly publicized lifestyle.

I was searching around for positives and my old mate Coley at least gave me a straw or two to clutch. He had by then already joined Blackburn Rovers in December 2001 and was sending me some positive vibes about reuniting our old partnership at Ewood Park. When you leave Manchester United, it can never be for a better option. But Blackburn were an established Premier League team who were enjoying a successful spell at the time under Graeme Souness. They had just had a successful season winning the League Cup against Spurs at the Millennium Stadium in Cardiff. That meant a place in the UEFA Cup for the coming season. Coley had scored the winning goal in that game.

Souness was a man with a big reputation in the game. As a youngster, my favourite English team had been Spurs but I liked Liverpool too and Souness had been a fearsome midfield player in one of their greatest ever eras. As a manager he had launched his career at Rangers, then overseen a four-year period at Liverpool before coaching abroad in Turkey, Italy and Portugal. He returned to the English scene for the new millennium. He was a figure who, it seemed to me, never walked too far from controversy but there was no denying his will to succeed.

And he could see the appeal in reuniting me with Coley. Could we do it again? Yeah, why not? Wherever I went, no matter what corner of the planet, it was still the opening line in any conversation. Me and Coley. I recall sitting in The Living Room bar in Manchester one night where four handsome dudes were across the way just chilling but causing an almighty stir among every female who clocked them. I did not recognize them at all but I could see the effect they were having on everyone.

Eventually, one of the guys got up and came over to shake my hand. 'I got to say Dwight, you and Coley were something else together,' he said. And it was always like that. No matter what part of the world I was in.

The guy I didn't recognize? Simon Le Bon with the rest of Duran Duran – they were gigging in Manchester that night – who could clearly still flip the hearts of all the girls.

So, yeah, why not? Maybe Coley and I could relight the old magic. And I certainly hadn't lost any of my fitness or my desire to compete. It was around this time that I was involved with the first Sport Relief charity event. I had been invited to compete in a rerun of the classic 1970s television sports competition *Superstars*, which was one of the highlights of the televised event. I remember it was the day after Becks's legendary World Cup party, which he hosted in aid of Children in Need. It was a white tie and tiara big bash, outrageously flash, with Japanese geisha girls in the garden, in a nod to the location of that year's World Cup. It was an extraordinary night and they raised so much money for charity.

The next day it was my turn to contribute to charity. The original programme pitted individuals from different sports against each other to see who came out on top. The other sports stars who gave their time included Martin Offiah, John Regis, Chris Boardman and Steve Redgrave. The event took place at a sports facility in Bath and was hosted by Graham Norton, who was absolutely hilarious. We competed in various events including swimming, canoeing, sprinting, a run and the infamous gym test.

At about the halfway mark, I was sitting fourth out of ten. Next up was the running event. Everyone thought I would only be good at the sprinting as a footballer but quietly I had this longer distance down as a banker! I went off last, but still managed to win, taking me from fourth to first. I could still compete with the best and was full of energy, despite my late night. So much so that, after that race, I spotted a cricket game going on in the next field, bounded over the fence and asked the players if I could go out and bat for one of the teams. I was in my *Superstars* competition strip and I think the lads were wondering where Dwight Yorke had suddenly appeared from! But they let me play, and I was having a great time, smashing the ball all over the place. I knocked about 40 runs from 20 odd balls! All the other *Superstars* contestants were stood watching and cheering me on! It was such fun. There was definitely life in the old Dwight yet, and I felt that I was ready for a new challenge. Joining Coley at Blackburn seemed like a great idea.

Souness came round to my house for a face-to-face meeting. He wanted to look into my eyes and see if he could see the appetite was still there. After such a long, slow and depressing exit from United, I sure wanted to get playing again. And I liked him; we got on fine. United was over and there was no point moaning about it any longer. It would be Blackburn for me.

In the office of my management company, my PA Marie Priest – who has been holding my hand and provided a constant source of support from the moment I set foot in the country – has doggedly kept a file of newspaper cuttings which provide a fairly colourful account of my life.

I wasn't aware of its existence until this project began and I was less aware of some of the content having decided long, long ago to simply stop reading newspapers. Some of the stories I have since scanned are works of harmless or absolute fiction, the kind of tittle-tattle Maysie used to rib me about in the dressing room. Some are funny. One or two take me back to my halcyon days at United, others to my troubles. But it is the lies about aspects of my life deeply personal to me which really hurt.

It is an unreal world. Laughable in its fantasy at times, filled with hangers-on and desperate folk who just want a piece of the celebrity pie. You must not take it seriously. There was a huge, double-page spread in one Sunday news-paper in which one such character, an Alicia Douvall, had claimed to have shared a threesome with myself and Katie. It is hard enough trying to conduct a relationship with someone without those kinds of headlines.

And this never happened. Never. Pure invention. It was printed in all its lurid detail. But it never happened. I had slept with her once, long before I had met Katie. And that was it. The sum total of our relationship was that we met at a club, went home, had sex, fell asleep and woke up. People can't sell boring stuff though, can they?

As much as you try to ignore the press, it is inevitable you pick up what's being said. My housekeeper at the time, Norma, was avidly following the whole sorry episode with Katie and her pregnancy being played out in the newspa-pers and on TV and keeping me in constant touch with the media hype surrounding the birth of our child.

I found the stories disturbing. Deeply disturbing. Katie

and I were barely in contact with each other, which is not surprising because I could hardly bring myself to speak to her. But there were reports of her partying wildly and dating new boyfriends, which only made me more angry. I know that you can't trust what you read in the tabloids and Katie has said since that she only had one glass of white wine when she went out – which wasn't even that often. But, at the time, the press reports got to me. She had been so determined to have our baby that I could not make any sense of what I was hearing.

And the tales were inevitably finding their way back to Tobago, where I knew my mother was becoming increasingly distressed at what her boy had got himself into and what she was hearing. She is a religious woman and cheap, nasty stories that the baby might not be mine or other stories of Katie going out on the town made her very upset. For all the sensational headlines my life provoked in the tabloids, I never thought I would ever embarrass or upset my mum. But with all this ugly publicity topped off by the insane notion, prompted by the woman herself, that she would give birth live on the Internet, clearly this had crossed that line and I hated that.

Very occasionally, I would call Katie, probably out of sheer frustration. 'Are you serious, woman?' was my tone. 'You are still going ahead with this? Why're you behaving this way?' They were not great conversations. She seemed very unstable, very out of control. Around me, my friends were telling me to let it ride, that today's papers are old news tomorrow; they urged me not to make things worse by responding.

So by the time I was getting my head around changing clubs in this final, miserable season at United, I wanted to get as far away as I could from what was happening to me. That meant Australia, Sydney in fact, and the chance to take stock of what was happening as May brought that miserable season to a close. I knew Katie was due to give birth later that month and I wanted to be there despite all the difficulties and nastiness. But my life had become an open book and I could not go on living like this. It was just a circus and I appeared to have absolutely no control over it.

I felt as if I was being painted as a cold, black-hearted lover who had turned his back on his girlfriend and the baby we were expecting. Unfortunately, it was an impression that was not helped by pictures of me innocently strolling on a beach in Australia with an old friend of mine, the Australian actress and TV presenter Tania Zaetta, which apparently made Katie furious.

That played out in the press back in the UK as yet another example of the heartless playboy lover ignoring his expectant ex-girlfriend back home. At the same time, there were those continuing rumours that had filled the gossip pages of the last few months, rumours that the baby might not be mine and of other boyfriends now in tow. It was deeply upsetting.

It was decided that we should recruit a PR specialist, Michelle Kelso, to try to steer me through the minefield I was approaching as I prepared to head back to England for the birth. I wanted to be there, of course I did; for everything that had gone on, this was still the birth of my firstborn. And Michelle was eager to make sure I could be.

When I reached the hospital and went to Katie's room, it was the first time we had seen each other for quite a while, the first time we had spoken since our last telephone calls. The atmosphere was strange but she was fine. In fact her eyes lit up when she saw me, probably grateful at a worrying time for any new mum to have a familiar face there. I gave her a cheeky smile and said, 'How ya doin'? How you feelin'?' We had barely been able to speak to each other but that was forgotten now.

Katie was under some stress in what was, I think, a ten-hour labour. At one stage I was holding her hand and doing my best to comfort her as she lay in the bath enduring the contractions. I should point out that I am not the bravest in these matters and had already declared that I could not go into the delivery room. But I wanted to do whatever else I could. I left the room when the baby was close to coming.

And then suddenly Harvey was with us. 27 May 2002. I was a dad. It is overwhelming, an amazing feeling. I went a little weak at the knees, I must admit. The nurses got him all cleaned up and I held him for the first time and took him for a little walk around the hospital looking into his eyes. 'Welcome to the world, little man,' I whispered to him. 'You're in for quite a ride.' Despite everything, all the hate and bitterness, all the resentment I felt about how this had all come about, that moment was great.

Michelle took one look at Harvey and, addressing what everyone was probably thinking but no one wanted to speak out loud, said to me, 'There's no doubt that baby is yours.' I never felt otherwise.

Unfortunately, if Harvey's birth had brought a truce between his mother and me, it was only temporary. When it came to registering his name, we were again at each other's throats. I asked Katie if she had thought about what she was going to christen him. She told me Harvey Daniel Price. Harvey was her grandad's name, Daniel her brother's.

'Well do I get a say in this?' I asked her, more than a little upset.

My middle name is Eversley, from my family line, and I wanted Harvey to have that too. We had a furious row about it in which I demanded she change the name and she was equally determined not to budge. She got her own way. It was as if she wanted to put up the barriers between me and my son and then hammer me for not climbing over them.

There was then a lot of unpleasant publicity about Harvey being 'too white to be Dwight's'. My advisers were telling me I had to be sure; that I did not want to go through my life supporting Harvey if I was not the father. And there was a simple, easy way to check it with a DNA test. Plans were put in place for the test to be carried out but I never went through with it. I had no doubt, absolutely no doubt, that Harvey was – is – my son. I would have been devastated to find out anything different. I wanted an end to any more unpleasantness around the wonder of a new baby.

There was one other matter to attend to before I left Katie's side following his birth. I didn't know where we were going to go from this point. We had no formal arrangement about paying the bills that any new baby brings to a household. So I wrote out a cheque there and then for

£10,000 and told Katie that it was for anything he may need, a contribution to any costs that might soon follow.

Clearly we were going to have to do some serious talking in the future but for now I felt that was a reasonable gesture. And Harvey was worth it. It was amazing how something so beautiful could come from such an ugly episode in my life.

17

THE RING

I was no sooner a father of one than a father of three. Or so it was claimed for Harvey's arrival triggered more hysterical nonsense. A woman from Trinidad, whom I could vaguely remember meeting only once, announced to the world, via any newspaper that would print her story, that I was the father of her young son too. I wasn't. Not a chance. And that was followed by my doorbell ringing one day while I was at home.

A girl's voice spoke through the intercom, claiming to have left her jumper at my house. I was fairly cagey about such intrusions by then so I went out to the gates that protected my driveway and saw a woman I did recognize. I could not remember her name though. Behind her was her car and inside that a little toddler in a child's car seat.

'I've got your baby,' she said pointing to the little one. It was ridiculous. She obviously wanted money; I wanted nothing to do with it. This was getting crazier by the day, I thought. I later discovered that she had been put up to this amateurish scam by the real father of her child who had threatened her when he discovered that she and I had

216

once dated. I sent her packing and never heard from her again.

But those incidents were typical of an unpleasant world from which I could not escape. Harvey's birth coincided with my transfer to Blackburn and it was far from easy to marry the two together. Katie was still living in Brighton and I was at the other end of the country. Our lawyers had thrashed out visitation rights, which gave me access on Wednesdays, providing I could get the day off from my duties at Blackburn.

Katie has constantly criticized me for not making enough effort to see Harvey. In fact there was nothing more I wanted to do than spend time with my son but what Katie has never understood is that I had duties as a professional footballer. You exist at the mercy of your team's season, your manager's whims. He can change his mind in an instant and completely rearrange schedules, not to mention games that were rescheduled at the last minute for television. If I could not make it to see Harvey, that was the reason, but Katie presumed I was up to no good or that I could not be bothered.

Our agreement states that if she went out of the country with Harvey, I was to be notified. The only time I was notified was when I read about it in the press. And the difficulties of eventually squeezing out time to travel down to see him were nothing compared to what confronted me whenever I got there.

I set to working out the logistics of somehow seeing Harvey while earning my living in a trade which demanded nearly every day of your life for eight or nine months a year. I had not wanted Katie and me to have a child together, that I know. But Harvey was here now and I had not forgotten our little walk around the hospital together in the first hours of his life. I wanted to see him and make as much of a contribution to his life as I could. Anybody who thinks I felt differently does not know me at all.

It was possible for me to get down to see Harvey if I could dash from Blackburn's training camp to Manchester airport, catch a 2 p.m. flight to Gatwick, jump in a cab and make the thirty-odd-mile trip to Katie's house. There I could at least spend a couple of hours with my son before dashing back to Gatwick to catch an 8 p.m. flight home for training the next day. It was a tight schedule which would take its toll on me but, it soon became clear, one Katie never gave me any credit for taking on. In fact, quite the opposite. If I thought our relationship would get easier now we had a child together, I was to be gravely disappointed.

As the weeks rolled into months, then it began – the drip, drip, drip of stories in the newspapers savaging me as a heartless, uncaring father, questioning my son's parentage, accusing me of giving no financial or emotional input into Harvey's upbringing. When some of the things she began to say about me in the media reached my ears I was furious. As the parents of a newborn child, I did not think it right for us to be warring in public. But I was so angry I wanted to lash out in the same way.

I spoke to the people around me at the time. I was still under the guidance of one of the game's most respected agents in Tony Stephens, who had a mountain of experience in dealing with the press and how stories would play out in the media. His advice was very simple – to let it wash over me and not be provoked into a response. The expression I have heard over here is 'Least said, soonest mended', isn't it?

Strangely, and purely by a coincidence of timing, I am reliving these events while watching TV reports of the England midfielder Frank Lampard choosing an entirely different course of action. Incensed by some of the things being said about him, he has reacted by ringing a radio station to take issue with the criticism. I hope that works for him. I hope he has not made it any worse for himself.

But Tony's advice had never let me down before and I was confident he was right this time too. 'It's tomorrow's fish and chip paper, Dwight, let it go,' Tony told me. 'You only make it worse and feed the monster by responding to it. Save it for the day when you can have your say.'

That day has come. How much did I care? Well, I'm not going to stand here and claim to be the greatest father in the world. I will openly admit that I have made mistakes, that I didn't react well on occasions and that I sometimes made the wrong decisions. I am not perfect, and I guess I had initially found the whole situation overwhelming. I had freaked out, and I hadn't known what to do for the best. I had conflicting advice from various corners, and perhaps my confusion came across as indifference before the birth. But it wasn't the case. From the moment I set eyes on the little fella, I have loved my son like I could never ever have imagined possible. I am not going to hear any more that I did not care for Harvey, or have any understanding of his needs or that I was not interested in his welfare. Katie has said that I did not pay any maintenance for Harvey for three and a half years, and that she has no idea why it took so long. This makes me look tight-fisted and like I did not care about my son, which is totally unfair. Only Katie and I know the truth about what really happened. Strictly speaking, I did not pay maintenance for that time (although I did contribute financially in other ways), but Katie knows that during this period our respective lawyers were negotiating the financial and parental consensual agreement for Harvey. She also knows this did not stop me putting my hand in my pocket to help with Harvey. £10,000 on his birth, £5000 for his first birthday party, as well as special sensory equipment for his bedroom for starters.

Don't forget, all this was happening before Katie was the hugely wealthy woman she is today. I knew that she needed financial help with Harvey and of course I was willing to give it. Once things were formalised, I paid £1,300 per month amounting to £15,600 per annum to Katie for Harvey's benefit; I was more than happy to provide a salary when her mum, Amy, took on the role of principally caring for Harvey, which amounted to £90,000 over a period of time; I paid over £14,000 in school fees for Harvey's special requirements. Then there were payments outside of or agreement: down the years nearly £22,000 went on presents for Harvey, a specially adapted tricycle and a special computer for the school Harvey attended for his and other pupils' use.

But that's money. I was a wealthy young footballer. So what? What really matters, I know, is just being there. Clearly, that was going to be difficult because Katie and I could barely be in the same room together but I began making those hectic, whirlwind visits to Brighton whenever I could to try to fulfil my parental duties.

I hated those trips – not for anything to do with Harvey but for what I discovered when I arrived at Katie's house. Motherhood did not seem to have calmed her. She was dating or partying with what seemed like a string of young dudes throughout the first year or so of Harvey's life; one guy, whom the newspapers told me was a nineteen-year-old tanning shop attendant named Matt Peacock, was forever hanging around. I felt like a prisoner whenever I got to her house. I would arrive and be marched into a room where I would find Harvey, and the door would be slammed shut behind me but not firm enough to shut out the presence of this kid next door. It was horrible. An unpleasant, extremely strained atmosphere to walk into when I had hurtled down from Lancashire.

Katie is not exactly domesticated and the house, I found, was invariably a tip which, with a newborn baby around, was another subject of concern. Neither was there any sign of her party lifestyle changing to take in the responsibilities of motherhood. I remember staying down one night and Katie's crowd were heading off to a big party in London. They all came back steaming drunk and making a terrible noise in the early hours of the morning, oblivious to the fact that little Harvey was asleep upstairs. I challenged her about this lifestyle. She had desperately wanted our baby, I thought, but was this her idea of motherhood? This had become the most distressing thing I had ever had to deal with.

She was undoubtedly still bitter towards me. She would never entertain the idea of bringing Harvey up to Manchester in order for me to spend more, less aggravated, time with him; I felt as if she wanted to make things as awkward as possible for me. And she succeeded. No matter which way I turned, I was trapped. She would not make any effort to bring Harvey to Manchester while down at her house the constant boyfriends in attendance and the atmosphere that generated made it a dreadful experience just being there.

I had no transport; in order for Harvey and me to have any time together away from that horrible place we had to be driven to a park where I could at least take him for a walk. You would not believe the number of strange parks I found myself wandering around in the Brighton area in those days.

As time wore on, I still think Harvey and I bonded. I think he knew I was his father and that he would connect with me by touching my baseball cap. As anyone who knows me will tell you, that cap is a constant companion and Harvey would often reach out for it when he felt my presence or maybe heard my voice. That connection became ever more important, of course, because on one visit I found myself with Katie in the car at a fast-food restaurant's drive-through lane when she told me she thought that Harvey had a problem with his sight.

I never felt included in any of the key decisions in which any father would like to have a say and I couldn't help but feel that, yet again, I was about to be told something everybody else already knew.

Harvey was barely more than three months old and seemed normal enough to me but Katie told me she was going to check it out. It would eventually emerge that Harvey suffered from septo-optic dysplasia, a rare condition which causes blindness and growth hormone deficiency. This was just another level of upset and trauma for everyone to deal with. He would need constant monitoring and medication. For me, marooned hundreds of miles away and trying at this stage to revive my career at a new club, it drove home my sense of isolation from Harvey. Still she would not consider bringing him up to stay with me, no matter how much I pleaded. And yet she must have known how difficult it was for me to get down to Brighton.

I managed to persuade her to come up one time with the whole family. It was near Christmas, and my mum was over visiting me. I really wanted her to be able to get to know her grandson and so I had planned to bring Katie's family up from Brighton, take them to the game and then bring them to my house so that my mum could spend time with Harvey. Thankfully, Katie agreed. I flew the whole family up and put them in a box at Ewood Park and laid on hospitality. But after the game when we finally got to my house, they literally only spent a few minutes there before Katie wanted to go back down south. I'll never forget it. I was so disappointed for my mum.

I had a room specially decorated for Harvey in my house. I had professional artists come in to decorate the room with little details, and the words 'Harvey' and 'Daddy loves you'. It cost me eight grand but it is still there unused. Harvey has never slept in it.

After a while, I could not cope with going to Katie's house at all. Fortunately, there was an alternative. Her mum and I had still continued to get along and I even wondered if Amy hoped that one day Katie and I might get back together. Despite all the tension between Katie and myself, Amy and I were able to communicate easily. And we chatted about Harvey, and I wondered about the strain Katie was under being a single mum with a child whose health was not good. So I suggested Amy might like to give up her job and spend her time helping Katie look after Harvey. I would be happy to fund the arrangement.

A new routine had begun which still saw me dashing away from Blackburn's training ground to catch the flight but instead of dashing to Katie's house, the Gatwick-based cabby, with whom by now I had struck up a friendship, would drive me to Amy's to collect Harvey. Still there was the difficulty of finding places to go and things to do for a few hours together. Amy would drive me to the parks or I would relax next door in the garden of the village pub while playing with my son. Compared with that house of Katie's, that was bliss.

But a new idea in this stressful first year of limited fatherhood was beginning to form. Harvey's best interests would only be served by Katie and me getting back together again. Why didn't I give it one more try? After everything that had passed between us, all the nastiness and bitterness of the past eighteen months or so, it seemed the longest of long shots. But maybe there was a chance. The least I could do was give it a try.

*

All of this unfolded while I was trying to make my way at Blackburn Rovers, which makes it all the more pleasing that our first season did not finish badly at all – we came in at sixth place and I was the top scorer with 13 goals. Coley and I even went on to enjoy a memorable victory over United, 1–0 at Ewood, earning a sporting handshake off our old manager and teammates. That is a rare good memory of this period. Coley and I terrorized our old pals that day, a real vintage reminder of what we had done not so long ago for United.

It was a new experience at Blackburn but at this stage an exciting one. But there was some adjustment after United. At United you expected every team to raise their game to do well against you and that would fire you up. But that was not the case now. Blackburn was a stable club, though, and still had ambitions. We qualified for European football that year which was no small achievement for a club of that size.

There were times when the old partnership got its magic back as well. It wasn't United but it was still good enough to stretch many a defence in the Premier League. With all the turmoil that was going on in my private life, I closed out that first season with a measure of satisfaction.

And there was more than Katie's erratic behaviour to cope with. I took a call from home telling me that my sister Verlaine had fallen ill. I loved all my family but there was always a special bond between Verlaine and me. Always. As the breadwinner of the Yorke clan, I always got the phone call when anything was wanted. Who wanted what now? I thought. A new car? Help with an apartment, some furnishings? But this news was altogether more serious.

Verlaine needed tests and specialist treatment and I immediately arranged for her to be taken to Trinidad's best hospital for this to be done. The news was worrying as the doctors confirmed cancer but, as the weeks rolled by and she appeared to make a full recovery, my concern eased. But it did make me even more enthusiastic to get out to see everyone that following summer, 2003, and I was particularly desperate for my family, and especially his grandmother, to see Harvey.

I never do things by halves. When I get an idea for something, it is full on. And with that in mind, I persuaded Katie to bring Harvey first for a luxury break in Barbados and then on to Tobago. I didn't put any agenda on the table other than the chance for the three of us to spend time together and for my family to meet Harvey as well. I had not seen enough of him in his first year and wanted to spend more time getting to grips with his health problems. My family, thousands of miles away, were naturally equally anxious. Would she come?

Happily she agreed and I booked a week's stay at the finest hotel in Barbados, Sandy Lane, arranged the hire of a four-bedroomed house in Tobago for the second phase and then contacted a friend of Coley's who was a jeweller my old pal had used in the past. I wanted something special, extra special, and we met up to discuss in minute detail what he could do for me. In the end, I took delivery of a pear-shaped ring which he assured me was a bargain – at £45,000. But money was no object for what I had in mind.

Maybe it was only right, right for Harvey certainly, for Katie and me to get back together; maybe, after all this time, I should propose. The last thing I said to Amy – who was all for the idea – before flying down to Gatwick to meet Katie was, 'You may have a nice surprise.' I knew she knew what that meant.

The trip didn't get off to a great start. When I did meet up with Katie and Harvey for the flight out of Gatwick she was accompanied by one of her boyfriends who had come with her to see her off. I don't know who he was. I didn't care really. I wanted him gone, though. That was very awkward, quite tense actually. He was holding on to her and kissing her as if to try to tell me something. He was wasting his time.

The press were on to us in an instant as well. Everybody knew what was going on and ours was, after all, a very bizarre relationship. As yet, there had been very little opportunity to catch Harvey and his parents together so they were all over us for a photograph.

Thankfully, when the stress of all that had passed, we settled on board the plane into our first-class seats and began to relax. Katie was clearly excited about going to Barbados and we had a long, long chat about everything that had gone on between us, a chat which helped us to talk through some things and ease a year of aggravation and nastiness. All the time, I sat there with this £45,000 ring in my pocket, still not sure what on earth I was going to do with it.

Sandy Lane is an unbelievable resort, guaranteed to take the breath away even when you see it for the tenth time never mind the first. The rooms, the view, the beach, the pampering facilities, everything is spectacular. Our room had a beautiful view of the beach and Caribbean and Katie was simply blown away by the location. She chilled out as at last we were able to spend time together without it ending in a row. We were even able to sleep on top of the same bed and as the days rolled by I began to think ever more seriously about going ahead with a full-on reconciliation. Sure, we had a couple of rows, when I stopped out later than she anticipated on nights she didn't want to go out – the same old point of dispute, I suppose – but we overcame it quickly enough. And it began to feel like we were a couple, enjoying romantic dinners, spending time with Harvey.

And then came the night that we joined my old mate Lara and his partner at the time for a dinner, a night that went brilliantly. Up until that point, there had been a couple of occasions when I had thought about taking out the ring only to stop myself, feeling the moment was not quite right. But as we stumbled back into our apartment from that beautiful night out, clearly knowing what was coming next, I was thinking: 'This is the time. This is it.'

That night I made love to Jordan, not Katie; the sex was wild, by mutual consent I must add, and I felt as if I was taking out on her a lot of the frustration and anger that had built up in the last year. It was fierce and passionate and after it was finished I moved to collect the ring from the safe in the room. I gave it to her . . . but I didn't say a word.

I thought about saying, 'Shall we try and make this

work?' but something held me back. I heard a voice inside my head asking me if I was really doing this for the right reasons. 'You may think you are doing the right thing for Harvey but are you?' it whispered. Katie knew what it was; it was clearly an engagement ring. But while obviously thrilled to be handed such a gift, she did not press for any explanation. Perhaps she loved the gift but not the man who had given it to her. Perhaps that moment flushed out our true feelings about this whole episode.

It was never the same after that. We still enjoyed ourselves on the beach and, for me, on the golf course. Stopping at the same hotel were Alan Shearer and Gary Speed with their wives and we arranged dinner with them one night. All remarked, out of Katie's earshot, how lovely they thought she was, how natural, not at all as they had imagined. And she was. I even mentioned to Shearer about the ring. But, for me, it never felt the same.

We had wallowed in such five-star luxury at this hotel that when it came to settling the bill it had reached £28,000, the bulk of which I reckon Katie must have run up having her nails and hair attended to. But it was time to move to Tobago where the luxurious rented house offered her and Harvey a beautiful pool and sea views.

My family home was fifteen minutes away but I called in to see my mum on the way from the airport with little Harvey in tow – and all the village seemed to know I was there. It was a heart-warming moment for everyone and especially for my dear old mum, finally getting to cuddle her new little grandson. Oh, that it could have stayed that way.

But the mood between Katie and me started to get a little sour again. I wanted to spend more time with Harvey and I wanted my family to spend more time with him. But now Katie was suddenly very uncomfortable about the whole idea. Her mood darkened. She came up with an excuse that really offended my intelligence, claiming that my mum and anyone else would not have the specialist knowledge to cope with Harvey's needs. I felt that she just wasn't very comfortable with the setting. We were away from her Brighton home ground now; we were in my back yard, in my home, everything there was going ahead on my terms. It seemed to me she was now experiencing a little taste of what I had been through on those desolate trips to Brighton. Now she was cut off from all her friends and family and she didn't like it. She wouldn't leave Harvey with my mum because she claimed the house did not have the right cot. And so on. Excuses, excuses, excuses.

In fact, she didn't acknowledge my family much at all. And she never stopped moaning about this not being right and that not being good enough. I couldn't believe what I was hearing. This was a woman who I knew had been happy to leave Harvey to the care of others back home in Brighton so she could go out clubbing – and now she wouldn't let him spend time with my family. She could not wait to grab Harvey and take him back with her whenever my family were around him.

It was deeply upsetting. I have only ever known my mum have one concern throughout her life – the care and well-being of her children. She raised nine, don't forget; she raised nine when we did not have two pennies to rub together. She's now got more grandchildren than I can count and looks after them as well. She had no issue with Kate. Of course, my mum was a woman of her time who stayed with the man she married through everything; she could not understand why Katie would want so much plastic surgery. But the last thing my mum would ever be is mean-spirited. She loves her family.

I had flown Katie and Harvey 5,000 miles and treated her to a fantastic holiday and everything. It would all have been worthwhile for my mum to have one night with her little grandson, one night when she could just cuddle him to sleep and be there for him. It would have meant the world to her, and this would not be the first time Katie had left Harvey in the care of someone else. The fact that Katie couldn't grant her that pissed me off like never before. While it is hard for me to hate anyone, I hated her at that moment. It was the final nail in the coffin of the reconciliation I had imagined, two weeks earlier, was possible. I wanted nothing more to do with her; I couldn't bear to be in her company after that. She probably didn't want to be in mine.

We flew home separately. Me alone, Katie with Harvey. And no, she never gave me back that fucking ring.

18

INTO THE DARKNESS

It was a beautiful, sunny August morning on the golf course at the start of my second season at Blackburn when I got the phone call that changed my world. It was my brother Gary phoning from home.

'It's Verlaine, Dwight, it's our sister. She's gone, man, she's died.'

I knew my beloved sister had been taken ill again but also knew she was in good hands. The last reports I had received were that she was feeling better. I was not overly concerned. The Yorke family has a strong, healthy lineage. Nobody gets ill in our family; we all live to ripe old age (and I'll probably still be paying for them, I would joke to myself). And yet here was Gary saying the words that cut me in two and left me numb with shock.

In any big family, you will always get siblings who have their favourite brother or sister. Verlaine was mine. We had a bond that was extra special and I loved her greatly. I always felt that she never got many breaks. She was a hard-working girl who never had much to show for it. In all the years that I had helped out all my brothers and sisters,

Verlaine always got that little bit extra. 'Don't tell them, Verlaine,' I would whisper to her, 'because they will all want some more if you do.'

And now she was gone. I had seen her on that disastrous trip home with Katie. She had seemed fine. It was impossible to take in. How could she have left us so suddenly?

The next ten minutes, half an hour, an hour . . . whatever it was, was blank. I know I actually said nothing to my companions; I know I completed the golf round, wiping a few tears away in the process. But I was numb with shock really. The next two years of my life were to bring some of the bleakest episodes in my life and I look back now and think it was that moment which plunged me into the darkness.

Graeme Souness was very understanding. I played a game that weekend because work is often the best way to keep your mind off something so painful. But he gave me all the time I needed to then fly home for my sister's funeral.

I expected to find my mum in a complete mess at the loss of her second-oldest child but was surprised by her incredible strength. I wish the same could have been said for the rest of the family. They were in pieces and so was I. It was a cruel reunion, the first time we had all been together for fifteen years or more. What an occasion to be brought back together.

I came back from Verlaine's funeral a changed man. The joy of football seemed nothing compared to seeing Verlaine's two young daughters, Keino and Latoya, now without a mum and me without my darling older sister.

Football paled into insignificance in comparison. It just didn't seem like a priority any more. For the first time in my life, I was playing the game without that famous smile on my face. And it showed.

I lost my way at Blackburn and this distressing episode, I now recognize, was a major factor in my slump. Another was my discovery that, despite his sensitivity over Verlaine's death, there was a side to Souness which ultimately ended my respect for him.

I felt I was spending too much time on the bench, that I needed more game time to get into my rhythm. He's the manager, he clearly felt otherwise. What I could not understand was the disrespect he showed me throughout this period. If he wasn't happy with me, then we needed to speak. Instead he ignored me. It was childish in my view.

I had played for the greatest club in the world and won the biggest trophies in the game. Souness, I'm sure, would have felt the same about his playing career. I thought that would build a mutual respect between us but instead I found myself being treated like a first-day apprentice. To be ignored, brushed aside when passing in the corridor, refusing to speak to me . . . it was terrible man management. What was he so frightened of? If you cannot communicate and get on with people, treat players straight and with respect, you cannot manage. Players much prefer to have gaffers who are upfront with them but Souness continually ignored me.

'He's nothing but a playboy who should get out of this club.' That was Souness's parting shot when I left Blackburn Rovers. Well, this 'playboy' was still able to play

Premier League football at the age of thirty-six, thirty-seven and you simply can't do that without working very hard and, ultimately, taking care of yourself.

I think Souness's comments say more about him than they do about me. As did his actions on the day my Blackburn career effectively came to a close. I was only grateful that it wasn't the end of my football career full stop.

By the time March of that 2003–2004 season came around, Coley and myself were not in the manager's favour. He had signed Jon Stead and you will find no quibbling from me about the impact he had in keeping the club in the Premier League that season. But there was still no need for Coley and myself to be discarded with the kind of contempt Souness now showed us. And it would erupt in a particularly nasty incident which ended whatever was left of the relationship I had with the manager.

It was a frequent policy of Souness to set up a five-a-side game between the players not in the team and his coaching staff. Including himself. This particular March morning found him in an especially obnoxious mood. Coley and I were already weary of his constant references to his glory days as a player with Liverpool. It was not that we disputed the manager had enjoyed a playing career he could be proud of. But we had won three titles in a row and the Treble to boot; it didn't impress us too much.

Souness spent the build-up to this session taunting us about what his old pros team were going to do to us. Not that it had any chance of becoming a reality. Souness, Tony Parkes and Dean Saunders had all had their day but they were never really going to beat our group. And they didn't.

We absolutely battered them and the atmosphere around the session darkened still further. Souness was still chipping away at me. 'It's all right doing it here but you won't do it for me on the pitch where it matters,' he was saying.

I wasn't the only player who was unhappy. In fact, there were quite a few who I suspect would have loved the opportunity to punch Souness's lights out at that time, Andy Todd, a tough central defender, perhaps one of them.

Anyway, the touchpaper to this ugly session was lit when I cleaned out the manager with a real, crunching challenge – perfectly fair I might add – which he clearly didn't like.

'You do that again and I'll break your leg,' Souness snarled at me.

The next thing I remember was running with the ball and seeing Souness's studs flying at my shin. Fortunately, at the last split second, I was able to just pull my leg back far enough so as to lessen the impact. He still caught me and raked his studs down my shin and the game came to an immediate halt.

Only he will know what was in his mind at that point but every time I have played back that challenge in my mind I always come to the same conclusion. Souness had wanted to teach me a lesson. Even if he had not intended it, the effect of his actions could easily have matched his threat to break my leg.

I just walked off, straight to the treatment room, to inspect the damage. When I saw the marks and realized how fortunate I had been not to have my shin snapped in two, my blood began to boil. I went looking for Souness and found him in the canteen. And I lost the plot.

'You prick,' I told him in front of everyone. 'You —! You are having a laugh. What the hell did you think you were trying to prove? I will never play for you again. You are a complete prick.' If he said anything in response, I didn't wait to hear it. I was not interested.

There's a theory that top-class players don't make top class managers and I have never subscribed to it. But Souness did not seem to know how to deal with players and I found his man management skills appalling. I have played at the top in England for twenty years and seen a huge range of changes in that time. I have adapted in order to survive. Souness had not and is much the poorer manager for it. I couldn't get away from his company and his control quick enough.

But that year continued to go downhill. It was at this time that I completely lost it when I was mugged in the Funky Buddha nightclub. The rage and the hurt inside me didn't go away after the thieves were carted off to the police station. It was just another low point in a terrible year that left me feeling even more down and depressed. Could football put the smile back on my face? Certainly not at Blackburn. I needed something fresh. It was a miserable time for me and football wasn't really top of my agenda. I was seeing life in a different way. I had lost form and the constant strife of the situation with Harvey and Katie was driving me into despair. My family were thousands of miles away and those halcyon days with United now seemed just as distant.

But then I got a call from Blackburn telling me I had been given permission to head for Glasgow and speak to

Celtic. This had its appeal. I enjoyed Glasgow, my old mate Russell was still playing there and maybe getting away from England to such a big club would be a good thing. Tony, having guided me through the bulk of my career, was now living the quiet life and I was accompanied north by my new agent, Simon Bayliff, for the talks with Celtic's then manager Martin O'Neill. A fine manager and an interesting guy.

Those talks went well, so well that the deal was pretty much done and I was at the point of signing on the dotted line in the Celtic boardroom when Simon took a call on his mobile and asked to be excused. After a few minutes, he indicated to me that we still had things to discuss and I remember walking down to the centre-circle of the deserted Parkhead pitch where I was made aware of a new development.

'That was Brucey – there's a chance for you to go to Birmingham,' said Simon. He was talking, of course, about Steve Bruce, then in charge at a Premier League-placed Birmingham City. This was eleventh-hour stuff. We were on deadline day, the clock was ticking and this information came with a lot of baggage. I was an ex-Aston Villa player possibly signing for Birmingham – that was not going to sit easy with some of the supporters. But it was the Premier League and that is where I had played all my football since coming to England. It was also my second home. So many friends still there from my Villa days; even Sheila and Bryn were still there. And, having begun to feel so isolated and cut off from my kith and kin, I needed to find a family again.

Simon had a checklist for occasions such as these. A way

to help you decide which club you really wanted to join. We would draw up marks for all the various key factors in deciding which offer to choose – the manager, team, city, personal impact, commercial impact, style of football. When we totted up the scores it was too close to call. Celtic 116, Birmingham 115.

'You've got about five or ten minutes to make up your mind,' said Simon and he was right. I couldn't keep Martin and his directors waiting and if I were going to sign for Steve Bruce, the Birmingham manager now waiting impatiently for an answer, I would have to get back south pretty sharpish.

Celtic is a huge, huge club, I reminded myself. With European football virtually guaranteed every season. But there again, Scotland was not the Premier League. We walked around the Parkhead pitch grappling with the dilemma before Simon looked me in the eye and said, 'Come on, what does your gut feeling say?'

'That I can still cut it in the Premier League,' I replied.

'Then you have your answer.'

I couldn't look Martin in the face, I really couldn't and I was grateful at times like that to have an adviser who can carry out such an unpleasant task. These are tough decisions that players have to make, especially when Celtic had gone out of their way to make me feel wanted and displayed such courtesy and respect. Simon took on the awful job of saying. 'Sorry, gentlemen, but we're going to have to pass . . .'

We dashed to the airport to charter a private plane to head back to Birmingham. We touched down at 11.00 p.m.

and signed the documents by 11.30 as the Birmingham officials met us at the airport.

Despite the obvious local sensitivities of my signing for Villa's arch rivals, it was one of the simplest transfers I ever completed. So simple, I didn't even do a medical. Time was pressing and my record spoke for itself. I didn't miss games, I didn't miss training. I was never injury-prone.

I knew throughout all of this period I was trying to find something and somewhere to get over losing Verlaine. It still haunted me. In quiet moments I would still find myself going over and over the tragedy. She was so young. I had only seen her six months ago. I thought she had beaten her illness. And then she was gone in the time it takes to listen to one short phone call.

And playing against that longing for some sense to be made of Verlaine's death was the constant sniping and nastiness of that girl in Brighton. That was how I regarded her by now. Why was she so angry? She kept chipping at me, either in private or in public, about my supposedly not caring for Harvey or contributing to his care. She was wrong on both counts but that did not seem to bother her. I could not work out why she was constantly on my case.

My close friends reckoned there were still some feelings there while Amy and the rest of her family continued to offer much more understanding of, and sympathy for, my position. I have nothing but gratitude for the way they treated me even when their daughter was firing off nasty, wounding comments that did nothing for Harvey's welfare and attacked my reputation.

After that attempt at a reconciliation with Katie had turned out so disastrously, the relationship with her went from bad to worse. I was now paying for Harvey's attendance at a special school where he immediately began to make progress. All of my contact over Harvey was now channelled through Katie's family. I could barely speak to his mother. Amy, I will always maintain, has played a huge role in Harvey's development.

My contact with Harvey was now reduced to second-party enquiries and visits through Amy and the rest of her family; Katie and I went through a long period of not being able to talk to each other. I would also avoid anything on the news or TV about her although it was pretty hard not to be aware that in early 2004 she entered that reality TV show set in a jungle, *I'm a Celebrity . . . Get Me Out of Here!*, where she struck up the relationship with Peter Andre. Let them get on with it, I thought; they are welcome to each other.

It was inevitable I would have to meet him, however, on one of my journeys to Brighton to see Harvey. The first time I met Andre I wanted to throttle him. I am not a violent man; in fact, I think I have got a very long fuse and that it takes an awful lot to rile me. But this man got under my skin at the outset. I'll never forget the first time I saw them together. They immediately put on this ostentatious display of affection, kissing and cuddling each other and calling one another 'babes' and 'precious' and such like. I felt it was like a show they put on for my benefit and thought it was somewhere between laughable and pathetic.

Anyway the usual rules applied that day. I had no transport, I clearly didn't want to stay around the house and
suffer any more of the Pete and Katie show, and they drove
me to a park, the pair of them in the front, me in the back
with Harvey. Andre in the passenger seat turned to me and
said, 'Listen, mate, it's got nothing to do with me' – that's
right pal so why don't you just keep your nose out of it –
'but Harvey needs his father.' And they had the gall to talk
about Andre adopting him.

I so, so wanted to lean forward and grab him around
the neck and throttle him for his insensitivity. So close.
I'm very proud of myself that I managed to restrain my
instincts. Having put up with everything his missus had
thrown at me, I now had to listen to this idiot lecturing
me on fatherhood? I don't think so.

I've never really changed my opinion of him since then.
I think the guy is a muppet. Sorry but there you are. No
way would I ever, EVER, allow Harvey to be adopted by
him. Over the years I have heard Katie saying how Andre
is Harvey's dad and what a terrible, uncaring father I have
been, all of which sticks in my throat. Maybe if she had
not made life so difficult for me, I might have been able to
take a far more proactive role.

But I had as little to do with them as possible after that.
I think the only other conversation we had was when he
offered to make me a coffee of his own recipe which 'when
you taste it, will make you never want to have alcohol
again'. I just looked at him gone-out. What is this bloke
going on about?

And I couldn't bear going to their home because they

had turned it into a shrine to their own vanity. How many pictures of yourselves is it possible to put up on the walls of your home? I don't know, but Katie and Andre surely held the world record. I found it creepy. I couldn't walk down a hallway without his preening mug staring back at me or the pair of them draped over each other. Eeeuugh! I'm Harvey's dad, now get me out of here, please.

But I did find an inspiration, on these arduous journeys south, in Harvey's school. If you are feeling sorry for yourself or if you are feeling pleased with yourself, it doesn't really matter – take a visit to such a place and I guarantee it will change the way you see the world. For me, it was never anything less than a humbling experience.

For all of my son's difficulties, they were nothing compared to some of the problems other children attending this school had to cope with. Nothing. Harvey can get up and run around and play, sings songs and be active. The children I saw with him could not leave their wheelchairs.

Sitting in the classroom playing with the children was just overwhelming. You cannot fail to be touched by it. And the staff are heroes, every single one of them. They look after and love the children as they would their own and I cannot speak too highly of them. I know what it is to have a tough start in life but I dread to think what these children and their parents are going through.

After a while we were able to send Harvey there free of charge. But it felt only right that I kept providing in order for one of the other children there to be sponsored, an arrangement I am still happy to fund to this day. These trips were a special time for me and always left me moved, and so grateful for the blessing of good health and a successful career. The benefits my son has shown from their care were and are immeasurable. I will never be able to thank enough the staff who make that all happen. I would leave and return Harvey to Amy's hoping that the outline of his dad's telltale baseball cap would stand me in good stead.

19

BIRMINGHAM BLUES

With all the upsets and frustrations of my life swirling around my head, it was not perhaps the best of times to be stepping into a new challenge such as that presented by Birmingham. The supporter resistance did not bother me. I came off the bench to score a winning goal on my debut, which was a big help, and Steve Bruce was someone I had known for a long time. In fact, I enjoyed settling in with the club and its players, who gave me the respect I cherished for my achievements in the game. But it wasn't long before I again felt like kicking football into touch once and for all.

A return to Blackburn's ground, Ewood Park, in November with my new club would, I knew, put me in the firing line for some stick after my very public bust-up with Souness earlier that year. It didn't concern me too much. As a footballer you soon realize you are never going to please everyone; some will love you, others will hate you. I had a bit of banter with the Blackburn fans during the warm-up, just smiling back at them as they had a pop at me. The usual stuff. Or so I thought.

But as I was among the substitutes, sitting there engrossed in the game, thinking about what I may be able to do if and when I got on, I became more and more aware of this guy seated near to the dugout racially abusing me. I'm not going to describe the abuse and give it a voice, but I will say that in all my years in England, I had never run into this behaviour before.

But it was that lack of respect again – and it got the same response as the thief who thought he could just steal from me. A rage swept over me and I found myself confronting this guy and telling him if he didn't shut up I would 'take him out' – thankfully a confrontation was avoided when the stewards arrived to march the moron away.

Unfortunately, that wasn't the end of it. I took great exception to one of the Birmingham owners, David Sullivan, claiming in interviews with the media that I had made too much of this incident. I had never met this guy but I could not believe that he had voiced such an ignorant and insensitive opinion. I was told that I should take no heed of it by Brucey, but I was disgusted by his attitude. What the hell did he know about it?

I was falling out of love with football and that episode tipped the scales. I wanted out. I wanted out so much that an ambitious new plan began to form in my mind. Footballers get a lot of time to kill relaxing away from the intensity of their ninety-minute combats and I had become increasingly fascinated by one of my favourite diversions – golf. It had improved a great deal over the years, even since that inspirational round with Ballesteros in Monaco. As anyone who knows me will tell you, when I get drawn into something, I give it everything I can, to the point of obsession. It was golf I loved now, not football. And people had always underestimated my dedication. What a way to show them, I thought. I found myself wondering if, at the age of thirty-two, I could do an about-turn, abandon football and become a golf professional?

I wasn't joking. I knew a few had tried. At that time, the old West Ham and Liverpool defender Julian Dicks was striving to make the same transition; over in America, another former Premier League footballer, Roy Wegerle, was attempting the same. I liked the independence of golf; the fact that it was you, and you alone, who faced the opposition. You were not reliant on anyone else.

At the Belfry golf hotel, where I was now spending more and more of my free time, I arranged a meeting with the senior pro Derek Simpson. I asked him out straight, 'From what you know of my game, with all the drills, all the practice, all the dedication that I know I can rely on, do you think I could make it to the professional ranks?'

Derek's view was, providing I displayed the right level of commitment, then 'yes'. It would take two years, perhaps a little longer, but 'yes'.

My Birmingham career was not working out as disillusionment with football spread to my game. I didn't feel Brucey was giving me enough opportunities and I told him so; clearly, he didn't feel I warranted them. But I didn't mind that. He was man enough to confront me over our difference of opinion, unlike Souness.

But it was in the early spring of 2005, as I seriously pondered whether I really could make something of this golfing ambition, that I took a call from Brucey saying, 'Look, mate, it's not really working out for you here and I've had a call from Sydney FC who are interested in taking you.'

There were other big decisions to be faced. During my early months back in Birmingham, I had been invited to the opening of a new club by an old pal and when I arrived with my friends, my eye was taken by a particularly attractive blonde. I got the gen on her – her name was Naomi, a local girl, and she was the bar's manageress. I was desperate to get to know her and so struck up a conversation. Actually, I should say I attempted to strike up a conversation with her. I got nowhere. It was the equivalent of watching a man huff and puff through a game without ever getting near the ball.

I tried everything I could think of to charm her but she wasn't having any of it. I did learn she was a Villa fan so, I reasoned, she probably knew about me and my reputation would have been enough to turn any sensible woman off by then. Ah well.

But she stayed on my mind and when I returned to the bar a few weeks later she was there again. Now I went into overdrive. When I wasn't pestering her for a date, I got my mates working on her. 'Why won't you go out with our pal?' and 'He's crazy about you, you know.' Poor girl. I think she ended up having to give in just to get some peace and quiet. Yes, she said, I could have my date. A quiet drink somewhere.

The speed at which our relationship blossomed after that was quite amazing. Naomi was very easy, very relaxed company. I could talk to her without a care in the world. We were on the run-up to Christmas, for which a significant chunk of my family were due to join me, and I invited her to Manchester to share the holidays with us. I was amazed when she agreed.

I don't know how many of my clan were there in the end but it must have been quite intimidating for her. And yet Naomi dealt with it all effortlessly. She was barely twenty-one when I met her and had never dated a black guy before but here she was meeting my mum and being confronted by this big splash of West Indian culture without a problem. My mum struggles to pick up English accents, be it Manc, Scouse or Brummie. She tends to go by people's moods and nods a lot! But I saw her smiling a lot around Naomi.

This girl was mightily impressive. She was fiercely independent and yet tidied and cleaned the house – quite a departure from my previous girlfriend – and was a wonderful cook. Wonderful. My mum hates me taking everyone out for dinner. It's not the Tobagonian way. 'Why do you want to waste all that money?' she would say. And having had years of experience making meals out of thin air to keep her children going, she could rustle up all manner of dishes from any variety of ingredients. But Naomi was a match. She really is an excellent chef. It had been a long time since I had met such a strong, independent and attractive woman.

Now came this potential move to Sydney. It was one of my favourite destinations but had never boasted any kind of domestic football of merit. But there were plans to launch a new league and Sydney FC had zeroed in on me as the one marquee signing – a player for whom the salary cap could be broken – that each club had permission to recruit. It was an intriguing prospect and certainly worth flying out there to see what they had to offer. It would prove to be the moment that my life turned back towards the sunshine.

At the time of my arrival, the cricket-mad Aussies were getting wound up for their forthcoming Ashes battle in England and so it was with some satisfaction that the arrival of a former Manchester United Treble winner for talks with Sydney was deemed big enough news to knock the Ashes chatter off the front pages. This was precisely what the club wanted me to do – to come and be a symbol of a new start for Aussie football, a figurehead even. Until then, its profile was so bad even netball was given more attention in their media.

I was very familiar with the city but still needed to be convinced the football was sufficiently credible. But I was told of ambitious plans to relaunch the game over there with a new A League; a kind of reheating of the Premier League rebranding that had done so much for football in England. Sydney were managed by the former German international Pierre Littbarski with Ian Crook, an ex-Norwich player, working as his coach. Littbarski had played for Germany in three World Cups and had managed in Japan before recently taking over at Sydney. He had big plans to transform the club and wanted me to be part of it. I had dinner with them and was excited by the challenge they were offering me.

I flew to that meeting not really sure what to expect but aware that with each passing mile I was getting further away from the continuous poison being directed at me from Brighton and my growing disenchantment with my career in England. Certainly it would be good to get out of range of the Katie–Andre show and her continual jibes.

But what about Naomi? She had her own life and her own plans but naturally the prospect of her joining me had its excitement for both of us. But hang on. The last thing I wanted to do was drag a girl halfway around the world without being able to fully commit to her. My role with Sydney was not just to play football. They expected me to be an ambassador for the new league and that would make a lot of demands on my spare time. And yes, Sydney is one of the most exciting capitals in the world, packed with beautiful women. Could I commit to asking Naomi to join me with those thoughts on my mind? I didn't think so. That was going to be awkward because she was a special girl in my life. What to do?

When I returned to my hotel room that night I was still in a quandary. The chance to get away from everything was appealing. It really had been a gloomy, miserable two years, the worst of my career. But was I ready to turn my back on English football? I would be a long, long way from everything. I turned it all over in my mind and just couldn't decide.

And then suddenly I heard Verlaine's voice as if it were inside my head. Clear as anything.

'Come on, little brother,' she whispered. 'I know how sad you have been but it is time to move on now.'

Who is that? Is that you, Verlaine?

'You need to fall back in love with football; you need to

fall back in love with life. Be the happy person I know you are. Bring some joy into your world again. Come on, it's time now . . .'

I knew for certain that she was telling me to go to Sydney. And it was the best advice she ever gave me.

20

THE FOUR-DAY PARTY

Sydney was beautiful. And from the moment I got there, I knew I was going to love it. Verlaine had been right. It was going to put the joy back into my professional life. The club had arranged for me to have a waterside apartment in Darling Harbour just a short distance from the famous opera house and offering panoramic views of the water line. And the interest my signing had stirred up in the media tickled my ego.

I knew I had to produce the goods on the pitch. In addition to my apartment, Sydney were paying me the equivalent of about £10,000 a week as their one marquee signing. They broke their wage structure for me. There was a lot of press coverage of my arrival and they amused themselves writing about my private life. Would I also produce the goods in the bedroom? 'All Night Dwight' they christened me, which was funny but was not my priority. They were expecting a playboy but I gave them a pro. Sydney were the Manchester United of the A League. The biggest club in the league and the one to beat. My arrival, even three years after leaving United and six years after the

Treble, only added to the scalp value. If I was All Night Dwight, the side was christened the Bling Team.

Conversations with Littbarski and Crooky reminded me that behind the glitzy headlines, there was a real determination to win the league. The standard was somewhere around Championship level and while the players were not of the level I had become accustomed to working with, they were a good bunch of boys who were willing to learn and improve. I liked them straight away.

Sydney welcomed me and so did Australia. The country, intrigued by this new launch of football – and possibly wanting a distraction from letting the Ashes slip away – gave me a tremendous reception. When I wasn't playing golf with the prime minister John Howard, I was hanging out with Jennifer Hawkins, Miss Australia. The actor Nicolas Cage apparently bought the apartment next to mine, although I never actually laid eyes on him, while my restaurant favourites were the regular haunts of some other Aussie A-listers such as Russell Crowe and Dannii Minogue. I got to know the Aussie cricket captain, Ricky Ponting, too as I found myself responding once more to the thrill of this adventure.

And the football challenge was reviving me as a player. One of the problems when you play up front is that you are obviously reliant on the players around you being on the same wavelength. When you've got Scholesy, Becks or Giggsy in that area, it clearly isn't a problem. But none of the lads at Sydney would claim to be in that class. As a result, I would find myself making runs without the ball reaching me.

It started off well enough – I scored on my debut – but as the first weeks passed by I became a little uneasy about what I was seeing. I began to drop deeper and deeper in search of influencing the games more until the prospect of my playing in midfield began to make sense.

I was on huge money compared to the rest of the lads and felt that, as the team leader, I should do something to help the team bond. So I threw a party, hiring a yacht big enough to accommodate a hundred people, and invited all the players. This night would prove to be one of the key moments of this team's eventual success, as the players relaxed together and had their say away from the pitch. Anyone who needed to get something of his chest could. I think it was a big success.

I was also helping to get the team publicity both on and off the pitch. In a traditionally non-football nation, there was a push to give the game a bigger profile. While my two diamond earrings and necklace serviced the Bling Team perception, a string of dinner dates with some beautiful girls kept up my reputation for living the single life. There were plenty of people out there waiting for me to fall on my face but they were disappointed. 'He's just a party boy, he's here for the girls and the money,' I heard and read. But on the pitch I felt I was fulfilling my commitments to the team's success, and it was on course and looked to me as its leader. I could get this team to play and, bonding well with new teammates Iain Fyfe and Justin Pasfield, I revelled in the responsibility.

And the game was booming. There is a big multi-national community in Sydney including Croatians, Italians,

Hungarians, Russians, who prefer their football to the Aussie sporting diet. There had been nothing for them to savour until now. Gate receipts were up for league games. The Socceroos were doing well in their World Cup qualifying campaign. And at the heart of all this excitement was a Dwight Yorke feeling good about himself again.

So good in fact that I came out of international retirement. I was back playing for my country in response to a personal plea from my original mentor Bertille. Yes, Bertille – who was still heavily involved in the team – was back in my life and I was back out of retirement.

Not that it was a straightforward decision. Leaving the national team had brought Russell and me a lot of grief in our homeland. Part of our reasoning had been that our national football team wasn't getting anywhere and the game in Trinidad and Tobago was in turmoil. People were pointing the finger at us and the home-based players were bitching at us behind our backs. We had had enough of the hassle. Our FA president, Jack Warner, a man who had played no small part in advancing my career in the early days, had turned viciously on us, accusing Russell and me of being more interested in the playboy lifestyle than helping their homeland. They were wounding attacks, and Russell especially found it difficult to forgive Warner. It was a tough decision but not one I regretted.

Bertille had always been special to me. And having been made our national coach, it was now his task to try to realize the dream, the national obsession of reaching the World Cup finals. The next, in Germany, were a little more than a year away and we had a chance of qualifying. Bertille had contacted me at the turn of 2005 to beg me to end my international retirement.

Did I now really want to step back into that? There was one other person to consult at that moment, another of my father figures, but someone who I felt, for the only time in our long relationship, had let me down. Graham Taylor. I was still miffed that the dream return to Villa, which at one time held out such hope, had never come to fruition; the fact that it was the headlines from my private life which played such a big part in that decision irritated me even more.

I went to see him at his home one night and we thrashed out a few of these problems, which was good, before I asked him about the offer from Bertille. 'Do you think I should go back, Graham?' I asked him. His reply was to the point.

'It's a short career, Dwight, and you may never get the chance to go down this road again,' said Graham. 'Don't have any regrets. And if there is the prospect of playing for your country at the World Cup finals . . . well, you have to take it.' It was good advice and confirmed what I had been thinking. I couldn't turn my back on Bertille. He had always been there for me. There was no one else I would have made this decision for. Thank God I did though. For it would take me to perhaps the proudest, most heart-thumping moments of my career.

We had some decent players with the striker Stern John and Shaka able to boast experience of top-flight football in England, a couple of promising youngsters in Kenwyne Jones and Cornell Glen and a raft of players of lower-division ability. But if you could harness that into a team then the whole could be greater than the sum of its parts.

My return was not received with unanimous approval. We have a pundit in our country named Alvin Corneal who I had little time for but who predictably delivered some negative sniping about my comeback, claiming it would take the team backwards. And he was fed further ammunition when my second qualifying game ended disastrously – a 5–1 defeat against Guatemala. I had been given the captain's armband and there were heated arguments in the dressing room afterwards when I lectured several players over their 'big-time' attitude. We lacked the mental toughness required. We were all too sloppy. It wasn't good enough and I told them so.

But if it was bad for us it was even worse for Bertille. The FA felt they had to make a change and it would ultimately cost him his job. When I found out who they wanted to replace Bertille there was only one reaction: 'You have got to be fucking mad! You are joking me. You will make us the laughing stock of world football. We cannot play for him.' My words were directed at the Trinidad and Tobagonian FA officials who had called a team meeting to tell us they had decided to appoint Ron Atkinson as our new national coach.

And the idea was crazy. Oh, don't get me wrong. This was no bitter hangover from our days together at Villa; or revenge for him leaving me out of his Wembley line-up. Not a bit of it. I always look back on my days under Big Ron as an invaluable stage in my development as a footballer. He gave me what I needed to survive in the

Premiership. And while I was there, I was never subjected to what I felt was racist behaviour. But in April 2004 he made some unguarded comments about the brilliant French player Marcel Desailly while working for TV. Believing the microphones were switched off, Ron had called him a 'lazy nigger'. And now they wanted him to be the national coach of a Caribbean team? That was too much.

So, yes, I own up to that. I was a leading voice of opposition which eventually forced our FA officials to scrap the idea and seek another candidate. As it turned out, it was one of the best moves we ever made.

We had one point from our first three games; whoever took on the task would have seven matches to pull the team around and take us to Germany. I had a little faith but it was clearly going to be a tall order. One thing I was sure about: I did not think the best way forward was to put the team under the control of a man who had made himself look so foolish in the global game.

Instead, the home FA appointed the Dutch coach Leo Beenhakker to replace Bertille in April 2005. He was not a man I was familiar with but his CV was impressive. Real Madrid, Ajax, his home nation's 1990 World Cup campaign . . . it was all there. His appointment was an absolute pivotal moment in an incredible story.

Having played one friendly and two qualifiers since my return, I already felt I knew some of the ingredients that were missing. The team lacked the kind of discipline and focus required and Beenhakker would set about bringing these much-needed qualities back to the squad. He quickly and correctly worked out we had some ability but we were a soft touch. That was a good start by a man who impressed me from the off. He knew what he wanted and he identified the problems swiftly and found solutions.

But there was something else missing. Or, I should say, somebody else. Russell. The Little Magician of our islands. I maintain that had my old friend been Brazilian or English everyone would still be talking about him today. But for some reason, and I have always suspected it was his modest international profile, that really big move never came off for him. He had more ability than me and if we could get Russell back, I was confident that the team could have a great chance of reaching Germany.

Unfortunately, the bad feeling between Russell and Jack Warner was much more entrenched than my own disagreements with our outspoken FA chief. I called Jack and put it to him straight. 'If you want this team to qualify for the World Cup, you must get Russell back,' I told him. 'And it has to be you. You have to call him and make your peace with him.'

On hearing this assessment – and credit to him here – Jack's response was instant. 'Done. I will call him.'

I had to send my own SOS to Russell too. 'I need you as a friend, buddy, I need you to help me do this, man,' I pleaded with him in one call. 'We need you. Save your retirement for later. Come and help us now.'

Thank God he did. Russell is regarded ahead of me as the best player our country has ever produced and I don't have a problem with that. He came back and scored on his debut.

Under Beenhakker and with Russell restored, our results

improved quickly. We were even good enough to turn that 5–1 defeat against Guatemala on its head and beat them 3–2 in the return fixture.

Ultimately, it took us to our final match of our group against Mexico needing a win against the major power of the section, to clinch a play-off showdown with Bahrain. We beat Mexico 2–1 and we were on course for our shot at glory. The team had been a puzzle waiting to be solved and Beenhakker had duly slotted all the pieces together. I still think Russell was absolutely vital.

And so we faced Bahrain. I knew little or nothing about the country let alone their team, but I was the most nervous I have ever been during any game as we faced them for the home leg. I can't explain how much this meant to me and my nation. A place at the World Cup was a dream that united everybody on the islands and now we were just two games away. We had been close before, in 1989 just before I came to Villa, when a defeat to the United States had sent the nation into mourning. But with an improved team came a renewed confidence that we could make it.

When I had been playing against some of the greatest teams in the world at Nou Camp or San Siro or Old Trafford or in Turin, I was not as nervous. I knew why. The players at United were of such quality that you knew they would do their job. You just had to concentrate on your own. But the lads in my national team did not have that same experience and this was a huge occasion for them. As a result, I found myself patrolling the pitch like a dad trying to make sure his kids are doing their homework. I didn't enjoy the match and we didn't do ourselves real justice. We drew 1–1 and with their home leg to come, you could see that Bahrain were delighted.

At home, our people were gobsmacked by the scoreline. They had perhaps been guilty of overconfidence. Now it was our opponents who were the confident ones. But our away form under Beenhakker had been impressive and steely. We were far from finished. The president of Trinidad and Tobago, Max Richards, chartered a private jet for us to make the journey all the way to the Persian Gulf. We knew we were going into hostile territory.

We ignored some gamesmanship from our hosts and wondered at the presence of the entire royal family in the executive seats. But the most striking feature I noticed was the way our opponents started the game. Whenever we got possession, they retreated. Never play football on the back foot. It is asking for trouble. I knew that and felt encouraged. We made chances and early in the second half, I provided the corner from which Dennis Lawrence would head the most important goal in his country's history.

The scenes, the emotions, at the finish were incredible. We, little Trinidad and Tobago, were going to the World Cup finals. I cried like a baby. Buckets of tears. The feelings eclipsed even the Treble. Such joy, such incredible satisfaction. Sharing this with my old comrades, Russell especially, was overwhelming. I knew back home the nation had been brought to a standstill. In fact, our president immediately declared a national holiday probably realizing no one would go to work anyway.

No one but me, that is. Naturally, everyone wanted me to go back to Trinidad and party, party, party to celebrate such a momentous achievement. But I couldn't. Instead I afforded myself a couple of drinks that night and that was all. And I was pleased, in a way. Of course I would have loved to have joined the party back home but I had duties with Sydney to get back to. You could say that I had matured since I purposefully missed the plane back to Manchester a few years before. I relished the fact that I did not invent any excuses or try any tricks to dodge my obligations. My club back in Australia were now my focus and I had to settle for a second-hand seat at the celebrations – ringing the boys to find out just how mad it had gone back home.

Legend has it that, after landing in Trinidad, it took them eight hours to complete what would normally be a forty-five minute journey to the capital city, such was the volume of people out on the streets. There are about 1.3 million people on the two main islands and I figure pretty much every single one of them must have been on that route. But do you know something? I didn't even have a drink on the plane. I called the players for regular updates. But I had moved my focus back to Sydney.

I don't think I have ever had a better time in my life. Even with all that success at United, all the high living, all the money and cars and girls. I don't think I have ever been happier than in the months that followed. We were in the World Cup finals and my Sydney team duly completed its mission to win the A League. On a memorable day in March 2006, we beat the newly created but already successful New South Wales team, the Central Coast Mariners, in the A League grand final. I was voted the man of the match and was delighted to see another of my new acquaintances in Oz, Ricky Ponting, with a Dwight Yorke souvenir shirt.

That final was played in our home stadium in front of a capacity crowd and the satisfaction I felt as captain of that team was immense. A lot of money had been invested in me and with that a lot of hope that I would give the game the shot in the arm it needed. I felt I had lived up to my end of the bargain.

And now I turned my attention to the World Cup just three months away. I was unbelievably excited and determined. As if the finals alone were not enough to spur me on, I had been awoken in the early hours of one morning in the previous December by a phone call from Marie at my management office back in England. 'Have you heard the news?' she was checking.

'Oh, it's the draw isn't it? What is it? Who have we got?'

'Paraguay . . .'

OK. Not bad.

'Sweden . . .'

Tough. Very tough. But not scary-tough.

'. . . and England.'

'England? England! I don't believe it. I just don't believe it. Bloody hell, England?!'

That probably went on for several minutes because I really could not take it in; this was unreal. Here I was, putting my life back together again, thankful for the reviving of my spirits which had come with both Sydney and my national team, and now another dazzling curve ball had arrived that I had not seen coming. When I left Birmingham after such a tame and unfulfilling experience, I honestly thought I was done with English football, that our paths would not cross again. But now this. England! I was buzzing. I had to take the phone off the hook for the next few hours because I didn't want to deal with all the calls I knew would be coming in about this news. I just wanted to sit quietly and take it all in.

England was my second home. But it is also one of the biggest – I think the biggest – football nations on earth. Maybe the English don't see it that way sometimes although they do put the most enormous pressures on their national team to achieve. But whenever you have a game against England, you are inspired beyond belief. When I took that call from Marie the game was still six months away but even then the excitement it generated was overwhelming. So many friends in the opposition camp. So much to anticipate. If I needed an incentive to continue my renewed love affair with the game, this was it.

From that moment I knew I had to put in place plans to fill the gap between ending my season with Sydney and joining up with my national squad to start our preparations for the finals. If I did nothing, rust would gather, my sharpness would dull still further, I would be starting too far behind in terms of fitness when we met up. I wanted to make sure that I would go to Germany as a player who could still cut it with world-class opponents.

I made a call to my old pal Albert at Old Trafford. And after we had exchanged a few pleasantries, I cut to the chase. 'Albert, do you think there is any way the gaffer will come and let me train with the guys?' I asked. Even after all this time, he was still the gaffer. 'I want to make sure I'm in the best possible shape for the World Cup but our season has finished over here.'

Albert did not think it would be much of a problem and said he would mention it to Fergie.

'OK,' I said, 'if you could just sound him out for me . . . I'll call you back in a couple of days.'

When I rang back Albert assured me it would be fine. 'But why don't you speak to him yourself, he's standing right here next to me.'

I suddenly felt a bit apprehensive. United were at the business end of their season and I was worried I was being a little too cheeky. I knew how intensely Fergie worked and knowing him as I do I was not sure he would have wanted to be distracted with a former player's training programme.

But on the final day I left United Fergie had called me into his office, looked me in the eye, shaken my hand and said, 'What you have done here will be forever part of this club's history. I hope you realize that.' It was a warm and genuine parting. But would he have time for me still now? Then I heard the familiar accent crackling down the line.

'Is that you, Yorkie?'

'Yeah, how's it going, gaffer?'

'Fine, fine. Listen, lad, no problem. Get yourself over here. We'll look after you. After what you did for this club, there will always be a welcome for you here. Just let me know when you are coming. Come in for a chat.'

It was wonderful to hear. Wonderful. I sometimes think that people might imagine that because we had our run-ins, there would be some kind of lingering animosity between us. Nothing could be further from the truth. This was the first of many times in which I would be reminded that, if you do your best for Sir Alex Ferguson, he will do his best for you.

I still get Christmas cards from him and invitations to his golf tournaments. Even now, whenever we meet, out go his arms for a warm embrace as he says with a big smile, 'Here he is – here's the boy who's given me all this grey hair!' We have some wonderful banter.

I realized at this stage of my life that his decisions years earlier were those a manager has to make. I know now what I didn't know then – that Fergie was trying to save me from myself. He saw the danger signs and tried to lead me from the road I was on. But I had to learn that for myself in my own way. I could only be me, couldn't I? And now, when I once more needed him, he was willing to help. Which is why I was grateful to him for extending the hand of cooperation. There would be a five- or six-week void in my programme and I was going to be able to fill it at probably the biggest club on the planet.

It was fantastic to hear and with that good news in my back pocket . . . well, there was time for one more slice of the old Yorke.

After reaching the World Cup finals and now winning the A League, I figured I had time for a fitting celebration before I headed back to England to take up Fergie on his invitation. I knew when this party was over, I had to get my head down again and I really wanted to give the lads a night to remember; I wanted to say a big thank you to them all for backing me for there had been many who had predicted I would flop.

I booked out my favourite bar, Ravesi's, on Bondi Beach and told the guys working that night that I would be picking up the tab. I sat there on what was a beautiful autumn day in Australia, 25 degrees or so, listening to people moan about it being cold while feeling a warm glow inside.

Thank God I had listened to Verlaine. I was captaining my country to its first ever World Cup, I had shown Sydney that there was a little more to me than All Night Dwight and one of the greatest managers in the history of the game had extended to me the hand of respect. A respect that I felt had been missing from Souness, from Birmingham, from Katie and Andre, from that little creep who felt he could steal my watch. God, life is good again. The cheeky smile was back: the one that had become my trademark; the one that had won a dollar or two from the local crooks in Canaan all those years ago.

I had invited all the boys and they would soon be arriving along with girls, girls, girls. Hey, I think I'll nip outside and ask those three if they want to come and join us. They seem very lovely. 'Excuse me, girls, do you fancy having a party?'

Let's get this party started. We did, and we were still going four days later.

21

'EVEN GOD MUST HAVE BEEN DANCING'

Eight years after joining Manchester United, I was back. And I was probably more nervous than the first day I walked into the training ground. Not because of any kind of resentment or annoyance from the players that I had bolted myself on to their training. Far from it. A lot of my old teammates and friends were still there – Giggsy, Scholesy, Ruud, Rio Ferdinand. They were brilliant to me. But I knew it was going to be a challenge just to train with them. I was thirty-four. I had been away from the Premier League for a year. To stand still at that level is to go backwards. To move away from it to a lesser standard of football on the other side of the world . . . well. It was going to be tough.

Fergie was absolutely brilliant to me. Brilliant. I don't know if I will ever be able to thank him enough. I'll always remember an echo of our old days together when we met up.

'. . . and if you're late, Yorkie, I'll bloody fine you, don't you worry about that!' he said, part in jest, part in warning. He had no need to worry. While I wouldn't have minded the wages from which he could take a fine, to be honest, there was no way I was going to take any liberties.

When I arrived, I half expected to be eased into their schedule with a week or so perhaps training with the youngsters or reserves, or even on my own. But not a bit of it. They made me feel as if I was part of the main team again. Albert even showed me to my old spot in the dressing room as I was kitted out with all the trappings of a first-team player. Wonderful.

And what a reminder of how good these players are; it was a refresher course in the demands of playing for Manchester United. That ball zipped around the training pitches like a meteorite; such quick feet, everywhere I turned. In moving away from this level of play I had not noticed the dip in standard and I could not catch my breath for a few days. In fact, it took me more than a week to get up to speed with them. I seemed to spend most of the first week 'in the box'. You will have all seen that in pre-match routines, when a couple of players are circled by the rest of the group and have to try to win back the ball as they ping passes around. If you give it away then into the box you go. It was exhausting.

There was one new guy in the pack who caught my eye, a player who was attracting a lot of interest. I was impressed by Cristiano Ronaldo's physical strength as well as his ball skills. But what I like to see more than anything in these gifted footballers is a determination to put in the time and effort to improve. It's one of the qualities which separate the greats from the also-rans. Watching Cristiano working on his ball skills reminded me of the sort of drills I used to do. Technique in football is advancing at an incredible speed and there is an art and feel for a football which doesn't just come from natural ability. It also comes from hours and hours of extra practice and I saw in Cristiano this determination to improve.

I was also intrigued by some of the new coaching methods Fergie's new assistant manager, Carlos Queiroz, had introduced, especially the long-range shooting. It is no fluke that United were scoring so many spectacular, long-range goals – and still do. The sessions where they were urged to strike for goal from twenty-five, thirty yards or more, developing the technique to hit the ball with frightening force and yet control its direction, were new to me. Arrogant? Most players at that level have to have a certain type of arrogance to do what they do. But I didn't see anything different in Cristiano. He knew me by reputation and showed me respect; there was no resentment over my presence. When you play for United, and especially when you enjoy the great success the club demands, you join an exclusive family. It was nice to be reminded that I was part of it.

And Sir Alex made me feel like I was in his squad again. There were certain meetings I was invited to attend; I was afforded all the fitness tests, from my eyes down to my toes, that the rest of the boys went through. I did everything short of playing for them again – what a thrill that would have been – and it proved a beautiful experience for me. I sometimes wonder if Fergie has a little soft spot for me despite all those grey hairs he reckons I gave him. At the end of it all, I bought him half a dozen bottles of fine wine to show my appreciation but my gratitude extended way, way beyond that gift.

And, of course, throughout this month or more with my

old comrades, the banter had been flying around. Led by Rio, the English boys were soon taking the mickey about what they were going to do to us when the big day came in Germany; I took it all with a smile and told them they might just have a surprise in store.

But would they? Was it really possible that my tiny home-land's national team could stop England tearing us to pieces in the heat of a World Cup battle?

It was good to be back in England and good to resume a relationship with Naomi that went beyond telephone calls and text messages. She was certainly a special girl and ready to give me the space to pursue this once-in-a-lifetime challenge to play in the World Cup; she did not want to burden me with demands.

There was one aspect of my life that wasn't perfect. That was my relationship with my son. I had missed him so much when I was in Sydney and was hoping for a thaw in the frosty impasse with Katie. But it was not to be. We were caught in the same old weary stand-off. Still she would not consider bringing Harvey to Manchester; but I found those trips down to Brighton unbearable and pretty point-less. My time with him was so limited under such difficult conditions it was of little value to either of us. I stayed in touch with my son only through my updates from Amy, who I know would have loved for her daughter and me to be on better terms, if only for Harvey's sake. But it wasn't to be.

My love life had got a little more complicated. In the February of that year, Trinidad and Tobago had played

Iceland at Loftus Road in a friendly, a match we won with two goals from myself. It was also the night that I met and was immediately attracted to the TV sports presenter Charlotte Jackson. We got along famously and after that first meeting stayed in touch. I found myself caught between two girls. I had not planned it or imagined it; it just happened that way. I would later wish I had handled it differently but I overcame the feelings of guilt and opted for the easy life. I didn't tell either about the other.

Football, though, was the big focus for me again. The excitement and pride felt back home in reaching the finals meant, quite rightly, that the squad congregated in Trinidad for a tour of our nation where good-luck receptions were planned. I had not seen the players since that night in Bahrain but it was immediately clear to me that the group's spirit had not been thinned by time apart. And the enthusiasm of our public in this quest was made clear to us as we said our farewells on tour.

Still the texts kept flying between myself and my friends back at United led by Rio, Wes Brown and Gary Neville. It continued to be great fun and I was feeling a little more confident about my responses: 'watch this space' . . . 'it's going to be historic' . . . 'prepare for english football's saddest day' . . . those were the kind of messages I was sending back to the regular taunts from Old Trafford of how badly they were going to beat us up.

My growing confidence at my team's ability to compete well in Germany was not just based on the tremendous spirit running through the camp. We had another ace up our sleeve. Beenhakker. With every step our Dutch coach

was making, he was reminding me more and more of Fergie
– and to my mind there could be no higher comparison.
He came up with a little masterstroke, for example, when
we flew over to England to base ourselves at a training
camp in Chester to get down to the serious work.

Bicycles.

Yes, I know it doesn't sound much but believe me it
worked. Beenhakker arranged for every member of the
squad to be equipped with a bicycle, map book, puncture
repair kit and lock and key and made it the players' responsibility to find their way to training a ten-minute cycle ride
down the road. It didn't matter what happened – if you
got a puncture or the chain came off – that bike was your
responsibility. As was getting to training at the designated
time. It may have seemed like a surprising and insignifi-
cant task, but it began to become a source of pride and
independence for the players.

Beenhakker also knew training camps could be drudgery;
players locked away, day after day, for training, training
and more training. So his message to us all came with the
hint of the occasional break from the routine: 'Don't forget
your dancing shoes.'

My role was important. I was captain and the most experienced player, and I had to lead by example. If down
the years there had been tensions and arguments about my
contribution to my national team, this was a time for ban-
ishing them. I knew that there were certain players who
would be able to handle the pressures, the media, the expec-
tation – Stern John, Shaka, Russell, myself. We knew what
they were like. But some of the more inexperienced lads

would need to be kept in check. I refused to consider any of my old indulgencies. It was now my turn to set the right example and I figured if the guys saw me applying myself correctly, they would surely do likewise.

I had had a taste of leadership in Sydney and now I relished this responsibility. I felt as if I had the weight of our nation on my shoulders but Beenhakker's outstanding preparations made me believe we could surprise folk.

The countdown to the World Cup continued with a constant drip feed in the media of how easily Sweden and England would take care of us. What they could not know was that within our group, there was a rising determination not to be the whipping boys or be embarrassed by the games. I saw excitement in the eyes of my teammates and not fear.

I had not experienced this level of anticipation for a long, long time. By the time the opening match against Sweden came around, my senses were electric – the hair on the back of my neck stood up, I felt goose pimples all down my back. It was just the most amazing feeling, walking out, leading my team into our nation's first ever World Cup finals game.

But if it was making me feel this way, what on earth were the guys behind me experiencing? They had not played at Old Trafford or Nou Camp; nobody had done anything at that level. So I was conscious that I had to calm them down, remind the guys to stay cool and yet play with the pride I knew they were feeling. At the same time, I knew what I had to do. 'You have got to play well today,' I was telling myself. 'If you go missing, they will crumble. You must put a performance in. They need to see that.'

I did. I was in the best condition possible – yet again, I gave a little nod of appreciation to Fergie for helping me do that.

I think Sweden underestimated us, underestimated our physical condition, our willpower and our ability. We knew facing England in the following game – the match that screamed out to every one of us – would be all the more difficult if we crumbled at the first hurdle. We wanted to send out a message to England, who themselves never seemed able to beat the Swedes, about what we could do. In the end, we shocked the whole tournament.

Shaka was out of this world saving us on many occasions. We went down to ten men in the second half when we had defender Avery John sent off. But we hung in there like men possessed and when we reached that final whistle, unbowed and unbroken, I knew our task for that day was complete. Against all predictions, little Trinidad and Tobago held Sweden to a goalless draw nobody expected. I was named Man of the Match. But at the end of the game I was incapable of thinking. I had never experienced fatigue like that after any other game. I was so exhausted, mentally and physically, I could barely walk. It was the hardest game of football I had ever played. The physical effort had been one thing, but the concentration had been another. Talking to everyone throughout the game, reminding them of their jobs . . . absolutely shattering.

Reports came back of the impact in our homeland. Thousands upon thousands had poured on to the streets and started impromptu, horn-beeping, flag-waving motorcades. They should have been in our dressing room. Crazy, man;

the boys just went crazy although, for once, I was too tired for dancing.

What was approaching next was going to make even greater demands of me.

In the days that separated the games against Sweden and England, there was one thought that overrode all others. I would be leading out my country against my second home, the biggest football nation in the world, the country that had given me the opportunity and the stage to enjoy such an eventful career.

I doubted I would get this opportunity again and so I began talking to Jack Warner about something I was longing to do. Would it be a problem, I asked him, if I could choose my own mascot to walk out with at the England game?

'I don't see why not. Who do you have in mind?' he asked.

I was wearing boots at that World Cup specially embroidered with the name of the mascot I wanted to have at my side. 'My son, Harvey.'

I had set up all the arrangements. I offered to fly his mother and her family out to Germany and had sorted out accommodation for them. I had got an executive box at the stadium set aside. I spoke to Amy, who thought it was a wonderful idea while Katie's stepfather, Paul, a huge sports fan, was just thrilled at the chance of watching England at the World Cup.

For me, it was all about having Harvey there. Our contact had been minimal but, I will always maintain, not because I wanted it to be. His father was about to step up for one of the defining experiences of his life and was desperate for his son to share it with him. If it could be the start of a new beginning in our relationship, then so much the better.

The plan was put to Katie. And immediately kicked into touch.

'Why?' I asked. 'What is the problem?'

The noise would frighten him, she argued. I tried to bring her round. I knew Harvey was sensitive to noise and so I told Katie that she could remain at the mouth of the players' tunnel if there were any problems; that he need only walk a few steps with me; that if there were any chance of distress of course I would get Harvey out of harm's way.

'Come on, woman,' I pleaded with her. 'This is once-in-a-lifetime stuff.' All I cared about was sharing at least part of one of the biggest days of my life with my son. I thought she, and especially her PR team, would go for it to be honest, what with all the publicity that this would undoubtedly bring her. But she would not relent. With a heavy heart, I had to accept the fact it wasn't going to happen. What a shame that he cannot say he was there when he grows older. It is a memory of a lifetime and I wanted my little boy to share it.

Seven minutes. We were just seven minutes away from a defining moment that would be talked about for ever. England, mighty England, held by the minnows of Trinidad and Tobago. And we were seven minutes from making it a reality. Seven minutes that will probably gnaw at me for the rest of my life.

From the moment that the draw was made, Nuremberg on 15 June was circled in red on my calendar. What was probably one of those annoying contests for England, a match where they had everything to lose and nothing to gain, was the biggest moment in the history of Trinidad and Tobago.

Having played such an epic game against Sweden, our spirits were high. But closer examination of the England–Paraguay match on the same day made us even more optimistic. Becks won the match with a free kick but it had not gone well for England and the familiar sound of knives being sharpened around their training camp and back home could be heard.

I was surprised they had opened themselves up to more criticism with the whole WAGs thing – the decision to accommodate the players' partners around the team base. Was it a World Cup campaign or a shopping trip, the critics were saying. I knew only too well the pressure Becks and his teammates would be feeling. And it did us no harm to have their camp uneasy.

We knew our players were nowhere near as good as England's but as a team? Well, we would soon find out. Beenhakker began working up a Plan B if we needed it, which involved me retreating into a sweeper role. We had already tried it out in a pre-tournament friendly against Slovenia. If we came under the cosh, that would be the plan.

The texts kept coming, from Becks, Rio, Gary Neville.

More banter, more taunting but all in good fun. But I was confident that we had the game to trouble them. We knew if they did not take control early, frustration would build up in the players and their supporters, one feeding off the other. And with frustration comes a loss of discipline. And more anxiety. Sure, they would dominate possession; we had to plan for that. But if we could pick away at their anxieties, anything was possible.

Our coach set about constructing the framework to choke England. For Beenhakker, shape is everything. He calls it his 'house'.

'Give me my house!' he would shout when players strayed from their positions. 'Whatever you do, you have to give me my house.'

For Beenhakker, losing or changing the shape was the worst sin possible. And I'm talking about positions on the pitch worked out to metres of precision, which had to be taken up during different stages of a game. It was a proven Dutch method that had been successful against England down the years and now Beenhakker intended to snare them again in the same trap. It was just a case of whether our players would be good enough to achieve the same outcome.

We conducted our preparations against the constant party music of our islands – steal drums, calypso, the sounds of carnival. An open training session was arranged as a thank-you to our supporters who had made their way to Germany to back the team and it was good to see my brother Clint among them. We had been determined to make this adventure a celebration of Trinidad and Tobago culture, distinct from the rest of the Caribbean. Our music

was a constant companion in the run-up to this momentous occasion.

Game-day brought the greatest buzz around our camp.
Our FA sprang a great morale-booster by flying in all of
the old squad who had come so close to qualifying in 1989.
It was probably the first time I had seen my old teammates
since then and it was a joyous reunion for me.

Our journey to the stadium was accompanied by tremendous local support. The Germans, enjoying the prospect of
an uncomfortable afternoon for their old rivals, waved and
cheered to us as they mingled with our fans.

Back home, my brother Gary had taken out a £3,000
loan to host the biggest party my village had ever known
at the Yorke family home. There were about eighty to a
hundred people tucking into food and downing rum and
Coke. It's a good job I didn't know about it until after the
event. It would be another bill I would have to pick up.
But I suppose I could not be too harsh as the whole village crowded round a giant TV screen; in front of it sat
my mum who, I knew, would feel the excitement in a different way. She would be worried for her boy, worried that
everything was going to be OK.

I didn't see any of my text-mates before the game. I did
encounter Sven-Göran Eriksson and my old United coach
Steve McClaren after arriving at the stadium. McClaren
was particularly pleased to see me but I was probably the
more relaxed. They were already under fire. I knew it and
they knew it. This day had to go well for them and what
can you say to someone who is going to do everything he
can to stop that happening?

And I bet the England dressing room was dull in comparison with ours. The music, the colour, the excitement of the players . . . it was exactly what was wanted. Before it became time to bring it to order.

Ten or fifteen minutes before we went out for the warm-up. I called the dressing room to order. 'OK, OK . . . let's get focused now. Shut the music down. Who needs a massage? Who needs to take in fluids? Whatever it is, get it done. It's time now. When we walk out of here, we go out as one.'

This was something I had picked up from Keano. I had been with teams where players just wander out to do their pre-match stuff but my old United captain would have none of that. No one would dare run out on to the pitch in front of him, not even for the warm-up. He would lead us out and every one of us would be behind him. That's what I had adopted and when we emerged from the tunnel for the first time, the reception was ecstatic.

I glanced over, occasionally, to my old pals doing their own thing in the other half of the pitch. A little nod of recognition here, an eyebrow raised there. I didn't expect anything else.

Win, lose or draw, this group of players always said prayers before and after a match. We had some very Christian team members such as Marvin Andrews, Anthony Wolfe and Silvio Spann; one would always bring the group together for a moment in prayer. And then Beenhakker took the floor with his final instructions – stick to what we have worked on and remember this is the day your home has craved for ever. Do not waste it. Go out and make history.

Before naturally adding, 'And don't forget . . . no matter what happens, give me my house!' We left the dressing room to shouts of 'C'mon, c'mon' as we geed each other up knowing what was about to unfold could change our lives.

I knew where I stood in the next phase of this drama as the two teams converged alongside each other in the tunnel. I knew the England boys would pay me the courtesy of respect; I was the one member of the opposition who had achieved things that even some of their group had not managed. I could and would be able to look them in the eye without flinching. I didn't want the England players looking down on us. This was important for the boys now glancing at some heavyweight names. Ferdinand, Gerrard, Lampard, Owen and Becks. They had to detect that their captain was standing his ground and take strength from that.

My blood was pumping as I reminded myself: 'This is what life is about. Moments such as this.' I realized I had no nerves inside of me. I was calm, calculating. I was going to enjoy it. I knew I was going to be up against Lampard and Gerrard. Their legs had less miles in them than mine but experience was now my weapon of choice. And ability? I never *ever* doubted my ability.

When our national anthem played there wasn't a happier man in the stadium. Had little Harvey been there with me, they might have struggled to stop me floating away. And then the greeting, marching down the England line shaking hands, looking for signs of anxiety. I got a cheeky smile and nice firm handshake off Rio, a little nod off Frank, but no words were exchanged.

And then the toss-up with Becks, and a strange place to run into your old neighbour! We had a brief word, wishing each other 'all the best, mate', feeling a little weird that after experiencing so much together as teammates we were now locked in a duel which would leave one of us broken. But it was kinda fun, that moment. I reckon Becks knew what I was thinking – 'Yorkie reckons his lot are going to do us.' And that's exactly what I was thinking.

I called the huddle just before the start and gave the boys one final reminder. 'This is it, the point of no return. Believe in what you are doing, fight for each other, fight for our country . . .' They were up for it.

Well, you all probably know what happened next. We reached the end of phase one in good shape. Shut them down and don't let them score for the first twenty minutes. That was our focus. In fact thirty minutes passed and they still hadn't. What's more they were not really penetrating us and those telltale signs of frustration began to bubble to the surface. A little bit of moaning started while I was growing and growing in confidence. Even more so when John Terry pulled off an incredible goal-line clearance to stop Stern John scoring from a setpiece. I've watched that many times on playback and it is an amazing piece of defending.

I was in the zone that day. I knew, almost through a mind's eye, everything that was going on around me. I was seeing and picking passes beautifully; I could hear our fans becoming more boisterous while England's grew more anxious; I could sense the unease in the technical area from McClaren. I could visualize everything. When the half-time whistle sounded, I ran off straight away, knowing the job was only half done. The key thing was to not waste this opportunity now because of the excitement of getting this far.

Much to Beenhakker's delight, we had stayed in the 'house' and he again took the floor, pressing all the right buttons, saying all the right things. It was manic at first when we got back but as we calmed the players down they began to take in his words. Again, we needed to hold them off for another fifteen minutes but do not doubt – you will get another chance. England were already getting frustrated and would soon start changing personnel, said Beenhakker. And that's when you know you have got them in trouble.

At home, I knew the people would be going crazy. Around England, I knew the criticism would be piling up and even in that dressing room they would be feeling it. I knew they would already be fretting about the Sweden game ahead if they could not beat us.

Before the second half, one more huddle.

'Do not waste that first half,' I told them. 'No cheap goals. When we walk off this pitch, it must be with heads held high and nothing left to give.'

England did come at us ever harder and I must give credit to our two central defenders from the lower divisions of English football, Dennis Lawrence and Brent Sancho, for their incredible efforts throughout the pressure.

Owen got substituted and on came Wazza – Wayne Rooney, who I had got to know during my training stint at Old Trafford just a few weeks earlier. His fitness had been in doubt but now England needed him to pull this game out of the fire for them – and it would lead to one of my most satisfying moments.

Suddenly, we were one-on-one with each other and Wazza knocked it past me confident he could just blow past me. But I had read the script and anticipated, earning myself that vital extra split second and cleaned him out. That was my favourite moment and I still rib him about it now. I know he has subsequently told Kona, 'I can't believe Yorkie ran me.'

But we got pushed deeper and deeper and now we were spending less time on the ball and just holding them. We were into the final ten minutes and we were so close, so very, very close.

It's a cruel game at times and never more so for me than that day. I never saw the now infamous hair-pull by Peter Crouch on Brent's dreadlocks but, to be honest, I have never spent a lot of time wasting energy on it. The goal Crouch scored with seven minutes to go killed us. It would not have been so bad had England scored in the first ten minutes and gone on to win easily. But for us to get that close . . . it was agonizing. The Gerrard goal which quickly followed was a kick in the shins to a man who had already had his heart ripped out.

I didn't move for up to forty-five minutes after reaching the dressing room. I was drained. Seven minutes. Seven bloody minutes. That's all I could think. By then, I heard the growing whispers in our dressing room from the lads who had seen the replays and realized Crouch's goal may have been a foul but I didn't want to get involved. I was in a world of my own. The boys had given everything,

absolutely everything. I don't like players asking for mem-
orabilia from the opposition if they have been beaten but
I couldn't begrudge my team now going off in search of
the England shirts they wanted for souvenirs.

Once again, we said prayers before leaving the dressing
room and the words were good. We were thankful for no
injuries, prayed for a safe journey home for all and were
grateful for our opportunity to play at this great, great
tournament. But if only He had been able to grant us
another seven minutes.

It was mixing with friends and supporters, both English
and from my homeland, which began to bring me round.
Beenhakker gave us the chance to let off some steam after
that game; we still had Paraguay to play but that was effectively a dead rubber. But at a hotel where our families and
friends were gathered the following day I began to realize
that, despite the result, we had clearly brought a sense of
the extraordinary to the World Cup. The English guys I
met were so relieved to have got through; the Germans
were telling us how great our display had been, how unfor-
tunate that first goal was for us.

And back home, the impact had been nothing short of
phenomenal. The games had brought everything on our
islands, even crime, to a stop. The roads had been empty,
the bars packed. It was clear our people were still proud
of us and slowly but surely I began to climb out of the
depths of despair I had fallen into almost from the moment
Crouch scored.

A private jet was sent to take us home and, even though

defeat by Paraguay had followed the England game, it could not douse the spirit of that journey. Nine hours I think it took us to get home and in that time nobody slept. We may not have the strongest team in the world but if ever they add partying to the list of Olympic sports, you can put Trinidad and Tobago down for the gold medal. Absolutely guaranteed. It is in our culture; that plane did not need jet engines to power it across the world. The spirits of the passengers were fuel enough.

We drank and sang our favourite calypso songs amazed that, when we should have been exhausted or wrecked, we found the energy to enjoy what I would guess must be the greatest party ever hosted in the skies. It was a bouncing plane which took us home. In fact, more than that. Even God must have been dancing.

22

ORLANDO

Another phone call, another familiar voice and another unexpected surprise.

'Hello, how ya' doing, Yorkie?' said the distinctive tones at the other end of the line. It was Keano, or skipper as I still called him, ringing me late one night as I gazed through the glass panels of my Sydney apartment. I remember it so well, partly because of the caller and partly because, for once, rain was falling on my panoramic harbour view.

The World Cup was over. August was upon us. A new season in Sydney beckoned. Or did it? I knew he had just been appointed manager of Sunderland, now playing in the second tier of English football, the Championship. It had been big news that day in Australia, such is Keano's profile in the game.

'Skip, what are you doing calling me? What can I do for you? I haven't heard from you since I left United.'

He had clearly lost track of me, too, because he was convinced I was playing in America and was surprised when I told him no, he had located me in Sydney, where I was about to start my second year in the A League.

'I want you to come and play for us,' he said. 'I'll look after you. I won't mess you around. No bullshit. I'm not going to bring you back and not play you.'

This was a serious proposition. For a start, deep down I was flattered. To have a man of my old captain's standing wanting me back was heartening. The World Cup was more than a month gone now but I had played well, I knew I had. I had also enjoyed pitting my wits again against top-class European footballers. And now the great Roy Keane wanted me. Not bad for a thirty-four-year-old supposed playboy.

But I didn't want to go back. Not at first.

'I'm in Australia,' I reminded him, 'and I'm having a great time over here. It's just not on, skip. I'm not coming back.'

He persisted in the call, stressing that my help was needed to 'sort out the dressing room' and get some old United qualities in there. Again, I enjoyed the compliment that of all the players, great players, this man could have turned to at that moment, he had sought me out.

'I'm not sure, skip, I'll have to think about it.'

That was how we left that first conversation but Keano would prove to be persistent – and, although he could not have known it, he had chosen the perfect moment to lure me away from my Sydney paradise.

The weeks after the World Cup had been almost as exciting as the tournament itself. The homecoming we received was overwhelming while I was further honoured by being made a Sporting Ambassador. I have not had a chance to embrace this status because I have been so busy but rest assured it is a role I intend exploring fully when I do finally get the opportunity.

And there had been some other significant developments, especially in my love life, still torn, as it was, between my attachment to Naomi and interest in Charlotte. In my more recent conversations with Naomi, I had found myself talking about the prospect of becoming a father again. I can see where this would have come from – the absence of Harvey from those momentous days in Germany had left an ache inside of me. That wasn't right. But I felt more frozen out of his life than ever. My relationship with his mother now was so poor I could not imagine that outlook was going to change in the near future.

Naomi was still in Birmingham and maintaining our long-distance relationship was going to be tough. She, not unnaturally, wanted a little more permanence. I certainly didn't want to lose her. I was secure about our relationship but I felt I needed something else. And during our time together in Germany, I had found myself asking Naomi what her reaction would be if we had a baby. I was just feeling for a response, I suppose. But she kind of hinted that she was not against the idea. It might secure our relationship even more and it would be a commitment. Having missed out so much on Harvey, that commitment was not going to be a problem.

But while I was wondering about all of this, things were changing in Sydney. For reasons best known to the owners but never made clear to me, they had changed coaches and brought in Terry Butcher for the second season. All of football knows Terry – a formidable player and a hero of the

England team throughout the Bobby Robson era. But I was getting calls from other players on the team saying that they weren't enjoying training. 'Come back and help, Yorkie,' they were saying. After a week or two of training with him, I could see what they meant – I thought the sessions were boring. I also felt that the brand of football played under Littbarski was loved by the fans and I was not sure that Terry would deliver the same entertainment. And the rumours were going around that I might be the next departure. Now, against this slightly unsettling backdrop, came this call from Keano.

He kept calling too, saying, 'Yorkie, come on, I really need you here,' and dangling the bait of a two-year contract at me. But still I was reluctant to tear myself away from Sydney. The moment, however, I heard that the club was negotiating a £200,000 compensation fee for my services, I knew they didn't want me around. I had been expecting a little more enthusiasm from them to keep me.

Roy's offer was £15,000 a week for a two-year deal, £5,000 a week more than my Sydney wages. But the apartment, the lifestyle, the weather ... could I really say goodbye to it? I didn't have much choice. By negotiating with Sunderland, it was clear that Sydney no longer wanted me. And you don't stay where you are not welcome.

In the end, I had to be all but dragged down the tarmac and on to the plane. My exit caused a bit of a stir and even ended up with my having nowhere to train for a few days while the deal was being done. On one occasion I went down to the park next to my apartment and joined in with some lads having a kickabout. The TV crews were there in a flash.

I had also only just arranged for my favourite white Lamborghini to be shipped over from England and it was due to arrive at the docks any time now. But the deal was done and there was time only for one more big night out at Ravesi's on Bondi. It was, if I say so myself, the latest in a long line of outstanding Yorke parties. I stuck 20,000 Australian dollars behind the bar and invited only girls to join my teammates and the staff at Sydney to whom I wanted to say farewell and thanks. At one stage it looked as if I had gone over the top in weighting the invitations too heavily towards the girls. For a time there was only Ozzie, my security guy, and myself surrounded by fifty absolutely stunning-looking women in the bar. We felt like a couple of pimps. It got so ridiculous I had to go out into the street and just grab some passing lads to come in and even up the balance of the sexes.

I nearly missed my flight two days later so reluctant was I to leave. Players were turning up at the airport to say some emotional goodbyes and I really did say farewell to Australian soil with mixed feelings. Still, at least I had stood on it. The Lamborghini pitched up in time to see its owner flying back to England. It never made it on to the docks but remained in the hold until the ship turned round and headed back.

I must admit my first impressions of Sunderland were better than I ever expected. I had never played in the Championship before; I didn't even know many of the places and grounds we would be visiting. I was so uneducated about it I thought when I got to Sunderland's training ground I would find some dressing rooms, a gym and burger van outside to grab a bite to eat! What I found was totally the opposite. An absolutely top class training complex with all the facilities I had become used to. And I happened upon what I soon called my 'mini-Sydney' Gateshead apartment, overlooking the Tyne. But I was miles behind on fitness and whatever influence Keano was hoping I could bring to the team would be delayed by my lack of suitable pre-season training.

Keano and I had been great teammates and had socialized. But we were never buddy-buddy. When you were out for a beer with Keano you knew that he didn't want to be approached for an autograph or picture and the supporters picked up the vibe fairly quickly. It never bothered me; I was always happy to oblige. But that famously brooding look of Keano's warned souvenir hunters they approached at their peril.

But that's how it is with Keano. He is very much his own man and I don't have a problem with that. His aura and personality are what make him such a big force in the game; they provoked a kind of fear in playing for him, a fear of feeling the lash of his tongue if you did not come up to scratch.

He had taken the job because there had been a disastrous start made by his old Irish teammate Niall Quinn, who now focused solely on matters 'upstairs'. But Keano was taking over a team languishing at the foot of the Championship.

Championship football, however, was a bit of a culture shock. Although not as technically good as the Premier League, it was frantic and demanding physically and my first months there were hard. I was missing Sydney and struggling to adjust to playing with players who would be just that split second behind with the pass that Scholesy or Giggsy would make.

In the end, a chance sending off saw me drop into midfield when we went down to ten men and suddenly I found a position from which I could influence games much more effectively. I did not play every match in that first year when we won promotion but I played a good role and, just as in Sydney, was pleased that I had justified the faith shown in me.

I like to think that Keano knew he could rely on me to bring a good positive personality to the dressing room, one of the reasons I was recruited. He even invited me to call him Roy but I declined. He was the 'gaffer' – I had too much respect for the office as well as him to take liberties. And, anyway, it would not have been good for the dressing room if one player was given such special privileges.

Our previous relationship did not cut me any other slack. On one famous occasion when I recall the clocks were going back an hour, I didn't bother to adjust my bedside timepiece the night before, reminding myself that when I woke up the time would be showing an hour later than it actually was. Trouble was I did not realize that my digital display clock actually adjusted to the hour change itself. So when I woke up at 7.30 a.m., I thought it was 6.30 a.m. . . . . well, you get my drift. I drove into training – I remember we had had a good result at the weekend – only to be alarmed as I got out of my car to hear the familiar sounds of practice already in session coming from the pitches. I had to face the music and I'm sure Keano thought I was taking the mickey with my explanation. But that's truthfully how it happened. A few days training and then playing in the reserves was my punishment.

But it was Keano I came back for. It was only my old skipper who could drag me out of Sydney and our success over the first two years, winning promotion and then keeping the team in the Premier League, were of great credit to him. The intensity which drove the team to those successes, however, never let up and, I think, ultimately doomed Keano's managership.

On the first day of 2007, I saw a rare text message on my phone when I switched it back on after a 2–0 Sunderland victory at Leicester. It was from Katie and for me it would be the trigger to one more deeply distressing experience at her hands. Sadly the circumstances were even more painful for my son.

The text told me that Harvey had suffered a burn – but that he was in hospital and it was not too bad.

I was naturally alarmed. I rang Amy immediately to find out some more information. She could only repeat the same story. It had happened the previous day and yet only now was I being told about it. What was going on? Amy could tell me no more.

I left immediately for the hospital only to be confronted by a security operation that would have done justice to the secret police not a British hospital. I was a fairly high-profile father who just wanted to find out what had happened to his son. But Katie had left specific instructions with the hospital staff that no one, but no one, was allowed in to see Harvey. I could understand that she might want to keep out any prying eyes from the media but you would have had to have lived on Mars for the previous few years not to know this was Harvey's dad in reception.

I rang Katie to find out what the hell was going on. He's not that bad, she again tried to assure me, telling me how he had climbed up the stairs and into the bath and switched on the hot water tap. I was trying to digest everything but the secrecy and security were raising alarm bells.

But the resistance from the hospital staff towards letting me in to see Harvey did not surprise me. Katie must have her own way and she would have issued her instructions in no uncertain terms. She can control Andre in the same way. But she can't control me.

I had to kick up an almighty fuss to get in, but when I did was shocked at what I discovered. Harvey was bandaged from his right foot all the way up to the top of his leg. That didn't look like something that could be described as 'not bad'. I didn't know where his mother was. Becky, his nanny, was sitting with him.

She looked like a frightened rabbit when I walked through the door. She anticipated what I was going to ask and gave me her answer before I had had chance to say anything.

'Dwight, I'm not allowed to say . . .' she said.

I said, 'Becky, come on.'

She replied, 'I can't say any more.'

I was furious. I was furious because it had been nearly forty-eight hours before I had been informed about Harvey's bad injury. Furious that I had been prevented from seeing my son on first arriving at the hospital. Furious that I had been told that the injury was 'not bad', and yet I was looking at a boy whose leg was bandaged from thigh to toe.

The nurses assured me Harvey would be all right and would make a full recovery, so maybe it did look worse than it was but to me it looked terrible with all those bandages. They would not say any more. But it sounded like they were reading a script somebody else had written. I wasn't convinced.

And I saw it. I asked Becky to leave the room as Harvey said, 'Daddy, it itches.' As a sportsman who knows his way around the inside of treatment rooms, I know how to bandage. And I had a look at the burn that I was told was 'not bad'. It was the most horrible thing I have ever seen – especially as it was a child and my child at that. It is a good job I am not a hot-tempered man. Because what I saw that day would have had other parents smashing up the ward in fury. Poor Harvey. He will only feel comfortable in long pants now, I am sure.

I don't know what happened that day. I know Katie and her husband have given their account of how a four-year-old boy suffered such injuries. I was not there; I cannot say. But for everything that she hurled at me about my parenting skills, it is fair to say I felt that theirs were not particularly impressive that day.

I was sick of it all after that. Sick of her and her limp husband. I kept it very simple. I didn't want to have anything to do with her any more and knew that Harvey and I would never be allowed to build any kind of bond. Amy keeps me informed of his progress. I send cards and presents for birthdays and Christmas without ever receiving a reply to suggest he has got them.

It is of no interest to me whatsoever that there seems to be more upheaval in Katie's life ahead now that she and Andre have split. I know the break-up will come as no surprise to Katie's family because they had a turbulent realtionship. I have been asked if I want to comment on it. I was immediately offered £25,000 to give my view on their relationship for a newspaper; at times, I have been offered £50,000 by media companies to give my side of the story when Katie has been firing her bullets at me. I have always declined.

I am not, by nature, a bitter person but no one has driven me quite so close to that negative emotion than Katie but still, I maintain, I do not have a bitter bone in me. But the woman is infuriating at times. You do end up losing your cool with her because she cannot have it any other way but her way. She likes her men to roll over and accept she's in charge and cannot handle people who are as forceful as she is.

But I do want what's best for Harvey. I love him and I hate the fact that I haven't been able to be more involved in his life. In the last two years, I have seen far too little of him. Far too little. I know that. Partly because the entire experience has been so negative and unpleasant I had no enthusiasm to take it on; but, yes, partly because I have not been the best dad in the world.

It is not what I would have chosen. His health problems are well documented but he is not the disabled child stuck in a wheelchair I keep hearing about from Katie's TV shows. Not at all. Harvey has disabilities but, as the correspondence I have from doctors confirms, there are no reasons why he cannot enjoy a normal adult life. In November 2004, I went to the Great Ormond Street Hospital to receive training from a clinical nurse specialist on the care of Harvey, training intended to ensure there could be no objections to my having him spend a weekend with me, perhaps, and not just a couple of hours. It never materialized for many of the reasons I have outlined. Perhaps it can in the future. I truly hope so.

I hate the fact that Harvey is a stranger to me and I want it to change. I hate the fact that he will never get the chance to follow his father's sporting footsteps. He doesn't want to know how to kick a football. You have no idea how much that saddens me. An enthusiasm for sport, with all its obvious benefits, would have been good for Harvey's health. I could have given him that and I feel guilty I have not been there to lead by example. And, sadly, all I've ever seen his mum and Andre do whenever I visited was to sit in front of the television, probably waiting to watch programmes about themselves!

No, I have not had the input I wanted from the day Katie decided what his name would be. I can only trust that one day Harvey will be old enough to think for himself and make up his own mind. He will be able to come to speak to me and we will be able to discuss all this. Not even the control freak in Katie can stop that happening.

And, Harvey, I want you to know that I look forward to that day.

I really do.

It wasn't too long after this that the idea Naomi and I had spoken about became a reality. She was pregnant. I was thrilled and it was time to grow up and deal with an uncomfortable situation honestly.

I had known Naomi now for three years and knew her to be a fine young lady. She was such a capable person who was sympathetic to everything I had gone through with Katie. In those previous conversations when we had discussed the prospect of having a baby together, she had been at pains to say that if it didn't work out between us, she would never deprive me of access or make it as unpleasant and difficult as I had found with Harvey.

She also took a strong interest in the Harvey situation. She was of the generation that pored over those celebrity magazines I had come to detest. I didn't even want to see them in the house when we were together. But she seemed to know more than me about what was being said and what they were up to. She was becoming involved in that part of my life just as I was beginning to banish it from my mind.

It had been and would be tough to find time together. There are so many more games in the Championship and we were still separated by the miles between Sunderland

and Birmingham. But when she told me, early in 2007, that she was pregnant it was time for me to face up to an uncomfortable truth I had been avoiding for some time.

Naomi knew that I had been seeing someone else but it was time to come clean. I told her about Charlotte and I told Charlotte about Naomi and her pregnancy. Charlotte was not best pleased; she was a very sharp, confident woman and she was never going to take this news well. It wasn't the best conversation I've ever had in my life but I am pleased I summoned up the nerve to do it. And I am happy to say that since then we have become good mates. She lectures me from time to time if she feels I have behaved badly but we will, I hope, always be good friends. But that is where it will stay.

I was excited about becoming a father again and a day didn't go by without my talking to Naomi, checking how she was. Although I had said I did not want to know the sex of our child, she was the opposite. And one or two conversational slips in the months leading up to his birth let me know we were expecting a son. I was going to have a major say in the upbringing of this one. He was going to be *my* son, the way that I would have liked Harvey to be.

And little Orlando came to us on 1 August 2007, an absolute gift from the heavens. I had been away on a pre-season tour with Sunderland when the main excitement had been the £45,000 I would have collected on the winner of the British Open had Sergio García not blown his lead in the final round and lost to Pádraig Harrington in a play-off. When I got back to Sunderland I got the message that

Naomi was in labour. But she had not had time to call me and although she had told me which hospital she would be at, I'm afraid it had not really sunk in. I could not remember where she was going.

Unfortunately, there are issues with Naomi's parents, which meant I could not call them for guidance and I missed the birth. But at the next opportunity, and on getting a text from Naomi that I was now the father of another boy, I jumped on a plane from Sunderland and a short while later got my first look at little Orlando.

It was absolutely amazing. Mind-blowing really. This is happening again, I thought, only this time without all the nastiness and fighting. It was a special, special day. I leaned over to kiss Naomi and thank her for bringing me such a gift, a beautiful, healthy baby boy. And then I watched the pair of them fall asleep. Beautiful.

And since that day, Orlando has been my man. He can get anything he wants out of me can that boy. He is at the front of the queue. Am I compensating for my regret over Harvey? Probably. But you will have to forgive me. My deepest wish is that all three of us can one day be good together.

Naomi? We're fine. We always have been. I know everyone would like us to do the conventional thing. Right now, I still have ambitions in football. But she's cool. Naomi is smart, independent, a wonderful mother. She's got her own life and goals. But she knows we will always be together in some way. And who knows? We will have to wait and see.

*

I've still got on my phone the text Keano sent me hours after he had walked out on Sunderland. I keep it because ... well, because to this day it shocks me and yet at the same time doesn't.

Keano had, of course, learned from the master himself and even when we had secured promotion at the end of my first season, he wasn't satisfied. He wanted the title. He warned players he would not settle for anyone taking their foot off the pedal. Any player who dropped off in training would drop out of the team. It was leadership by inspiring fear.

Keano had days when he would join in with the five-a-sides – and let me tell you that even at this stage, without regular playing, he was still a phenomenal footballer. And ferociously competitive. So much so that any player on his team who misplaced a pass or miscontrolled the ball would be subjected to a stream of vicious lecturing or even abuse from the manager. It reached the stage where nobody wanted to be on the same side as him. He terrified them. I recall my Trinidad and Tobago teammate Stern John joining us, getting bawled out for one such error, and spending the next five minutes hiding from receiving the ball.

'Gaffer,' I said to Keano at the end of one of these sessions, 'you're scaring the shit out of the players.'

I hoped he would take it as it was meant; someone trying to offer a little constructive advice. But he looked at me as if to say: 'Am I so wrong to demand that they pass it and trap it right?' A general can only lead his troops this way for so long, however. The players began moaning about him in the dressing room, not that this would have bothered Keano. It's not about being popular with him. Just the results.

To reach the Premier League and play there at the age of thirty-six was, as you might imagine, a subject of fantastic personal satisfaction. I enjoyed our promotion with a couple of drinks but nothing excessive; these were different days now. I didn't drink for three months leading up to that campaign because I wanted to be super fit.

And it was thrilling to go back to my favourite old clubs at Old Trafford and Villa Park to trade blows again. As I recall, we played a terrific match at United and only got beaten by a late winner from Louis Saha. The reaction I got at Old Trafford was heart-warming; unfortunately at Villa they still feel the need to deride me. This both saddens and mystifies me. I did well for the club but the club did well out of me – bought for £10,000 and sold for £12.6 million. And it wasn't as if when I left I was signing for Tottenham or Everton, clubs of similar stature. I was pulled away by the biggest club in the world and there isn't a single professional footballer out there who would not have done the same. I hope one day that changes at Villa.

So all credit to Keano for getting us through that first year back in the top flight. But it was difficult for him to accept that he was now in a top-flight team that did not win the majority of its games – all that he had known at United. And when a wave of big signings last summer including Anton Ferdinand, Teemu Tainio, Pascal Chimbonda, Steed Malbranque, El Hadji Diouf, David Healy and Djibril Cissé didn't provide an immediate improvement in results, then the tensions began to rise.

The manager's darkening mood was made only too clear on an ominous night for his regime, on 24 September 2008, when we struggled to get past the League One side Northampton, managed by my old Villa teammate Stuart Gray, in a Carling Cup tie. We eventually got through on penalties 4–3, but only after launching an unexpected comeback to retrieve a 2–0 deficit in the last five minutes of normal time.

It was a night made memorable for the first signs of tension between Keano and the Sunderland supporters. That was nothing compared to the eruption we witnessed at half-time, as we trooped in a goal down, booed off by a discontented public. We knew we were in for a tongue-lashing. We waited for the fireworks. Keano emerged from the washroom, quietly, calmly. He washed his hands, dried them and asks our kit manager if he can get the tactics board.

'Sure, boss, it's over here.'

The board goes up. And Keano's aura of calm completely disappears. He takes a running jump at the tactics board and smashes it over with a kung-fu kick. He screamed at Danny Collins, 'Never come to me and ask for a contract again.' And then the captain, Dean Whitehead, is next.

'Captain? Captain? Some fuckin' captain you are,' he rages, slapping Dean about the head in the process, before turning on us all. 'I can't trust any of you ——. None of you. I'll rephrase that. The staff I can trust. But you lot? None of you.'

No one knew Keano's moods better than me and I sensed that his regime was heading for a point of no return. It would not be too long before I became enmeshed in his brooding demeanour.

I was brought back into the team for an improved sequence of results including a victory over Newcastle and a draw at Arsenal before we headed to Stoke in late October for a match that, by now, everyone was aware presented a physical challenge as much as a footballing one. Keano doesn't like Tony Pulis's style of football and was therefore particularly keen for us to do well there. But it was a game every bit as brutal as we might have imagined. Stoke bombarded us and we could not get any respite – although we still reached half-time with the score 0–0.

That didn't prevent a furious reaction from the manager in the dressing room. Keano once again delivered a kung-fu kick on the tactics board which sent it crashing. He launched into a tirade at the team that began with his telling me that I was being substituted. I took the decision on the chin. With the ball flying over midfield in an aerial bombardment, it wasn't really that surprising.

We lost 1–0, which did nothing to improve his temper, and I later learned that he was unhappy with me because I had not reacted to his decision to substitute me. Managers sometimes like to see their players have a pop back as if it is a display of how wounded and disappointed they are. When I got the chance to speak to him, I told him my view.

'We still had forty-five minutes to play and I didn't want to bring the dressing room down any more than it already was,' I argued. 'That game was still 0–0. They needed encouraging not slaughtering. And me getting into a row over that would have done nothing for us.' I stick by that; ranting at the players made no sense when there was still half a game to go.

Two days later I got a call from Tony Loughlan, Keano's assistant, to say the manager wanted to see me.

'Listen, Yorkie,' he told me when I got there, 'you've been great for me. But I think I've had enough of you. And as a manager I've got to make a decision. I no longer want you to train with us.' I was to be banished to the reserves.

Again, it made no sense to me. 'Gaffer, a couple of games ago you were praising me for the way I played against Newcastle and Arsenal and now I'm going to get the blame for what happened at Stoke?' I said.

But he had made up his mind. Five minutes before that showdown, a first-team meeting had been arranged downstairs and, gloomily, I headed down the steps to make my way there. Arriving at the same door from the opposite direction was Keano. He stopped me in the corridor as we both converged on the entrance at the same time. 'No no, Yorkie, you're not in this meeting. You're outside with the reserves.' I have no doubt that, had I actually got to the meeting before him, he would have frogmarched me out in front of the whole squad.

After that, the atmosphere around the club plummeted still further. For three, sometimes four days a week, we would see no sign of Keano and I have to say that not too many players were disappointed when there was no sign of his car in the mornings. The dressing room started to get really disconnected, splitting into little cliques and groups of self-interest. Keano's assistant did not help. I always think that a manager's number two should be a middleman, a bridge between the dressing room and the manager, especially when things were rocky. Someone to find compromise. But Tony seemed to share his gaffer's moods.

I was the outcast and so that meant I had to be an outcast to Tony as well.

Meanwhile paranoia rampaged through the club. Even the smallest of details, about whether or not we were having a day off or were going go-karting or paintballing, were treated like top-secret information. 'Can't tell you,' Keano's staff would say frightened, I suspect, to put one word out of line. Players were at each other's throats and fighting one another; they could not wait to get in to training so they could get out again. It was all disintegrating before our very eyes.

For the next five weeks it was like this and the results inevitably crumbled still further. And then, suddenly, I got a call from our elusive manager, who had not spoken to me since I was banished from the meeting. 'Yorkie, I know things haven't been great between us but I just want to know if you're on board with me.'

I was so stunned to receive the call, never mind the question, that I couldn't think of an answer. Instead I said I would pop in and discuss it with him the following day. Twenty minutes later I got a text from him: 'Don't bother – I think I've got my answer.'

It would have been easy for me to tell him I was on board. I guess that was what he wanted. I'm sorry I couldn't

do that. I'm not saying I would not have thrown my sup-
port behind Keano eventually; such is the immense respect
I had for him as my leader then I probably would have.
But we needed to talk first.

By now I was convinced that club management was not
for Keano. I think he is an impact manager, which is why
I believe he could be ideal for the international stage. I do
not think the 24/7 care of a club manager is suited to his
temperament. I do not think he can deal with everything
that lands in the tray of a club man. But his standing in
the game is such that he could still take a group of players
and get a positive reaction from them for a couple of games
a time – and then march off and walk his dogs for a month
or two.

Anyway, there would be one more text exchange with
Roy. Two days later, he was gone. The rumours of it had
been flying around for a while by then but when it happened, it was still a surprise.

I bore no grudges. I just felt Keano was being Keano and
I happened to get caught in the firing line. So I sent him a
text, saying how sorry I was how things had turned out
but thanking him for the chance at Sunderland and wishing
him all the best for the future.

Ten minutes later, I got my reply. The text I still keep.
'Go fuck yourself.'

It was close, too close for comfort, but we eventually
survived the threat of relegation in the wake of Keano's
abrupt exit. Ricky Sbragia was promoted from the coaching
staff to bring a measure of calm back to the club and to

a degree it worked. Nice guy Ricky, a guy who gets on with everybody, which was one of the things Keano didn't like about his style. He felt he got on too well with the players. But we have to do things how we see them and Ricky always had a cheery 'good morning' for everyone.

There was a sense of relief that Keano had gone and I was more than happy to help out with a little coaching behind Ricky and Neil Bailey, one of the club's faithful backroom staff men who some felt was roughly treated when he was demoted to reserve team coach despite our successful year. It was the same players but hearing a different, calmer voice and to be fair to Ricky, he tried to improve the areas Roy had neglected – team shape and the players' focus on their role within that.

It brought the team a short-term lift in results although the last couple of months were not pleasant for anyone. The confidence ebbed as we got sucked into the relegation fight and Ricky felt the strain. I guess he knew long before the finish that management was not for him.

Once the novelty of Ricky's initial input had worn off, we slipped back into trouble. Ricky is such a nice man and there are players who let him down and let the club down. One or two started taking the piss; one or two told him to 'fuck off'. Things got heated and Ricky was undermined, I guess, by the fact that he arrived in the job via a back-door route.

We survived on the last day of the season not through our own merits but the failures of others, notably Middlesbrough and Newcastle, the club's two big north-east rivals, but the toll it had taken on Ricky was enormous.

He had had to make some tough decisions in the end because he knew he could no longer be the nice guy. I saw him at the end of the last match of the season, a 3–2 defeat by Chelsea, and the poor man was in tears at the release of it all. I saw some of our players celebrating Sunderland's survival that day as if we had won something and could not share their excitement. They were happy and joyful. I couldn't relate to it. I could understand it but not really relate to it. Those players should not have been in that position in the first place. Escaping relegation by the skin of their teeth, losing 3–2 at home, was hardly a cause for joy and laughter. But that's what our dressing room was like.

Something is not right – and they are fooling themselves if they think otherwise. I look around my dressing room and see players who only talk about the Champions League in terms of awe and wonder. 'Did you see United?' or 'Did you see that goal from Barça?' If they had anything about them that is where they should want to be. But the rewards are too good for a much poorer service these days.

I had wanted to play more and felt that my experience would have been a help to him and the players and Ricky, in hindsight, agreed. None of which has lessened my appetite for a crack at management. I think I can do it. I think I have seen the changes and can relate to the modern-day players, the demands made of them, how to get the best out of them. That is now arguably the most important part of management.

Everyone sees the smiling Dwight but I think my playing career has shown that there is a steel inside as well that you would be wrong to underestimate. I am into my coaching badges; I think I have what it takes to make it in management. As things stand, I have now been released by Sunderland and am free to seek an opportunity elsewhere. But there is still a World Cup qualifying campaign being waged by Trinidad and Tobago in which I wish to remain involved as a player.

That means finding a club for one more season. I still feel as if I can play on. In fact, I feel in extremely good condition. And my homeland wants me to continue playing. Maybe these legs can carry me through one more drama. We shall see.

EPILOGUE

The 16th of May 2009. Just like old times. The Living Room club in Manchester and United players dancing on tables, celebrating yet another championship. At the invitation of Sky TV, I was at the game which they drew with Arsenal to claim the point required for the title. It brought it all back to me to be invited to join Giggsy and the boys for their celebrations that night. In fact, I don't think I've ever seen Giggsy enjoy one more. He reminded me of the white Dwight Yorke the way he was dancing on the tables!

But you join a special club when you play for United and achieve great things. Very special. I remembered being back at Old Trafford in March, the night my old club played Inter Milan in the Champions League, to invite Fergie to my golf tournament back in Tobago.

I was hanging around waiting to grab a moment with my old gaffer – and even now, such is the presence of the man, that can be an unnerving experience. I was half expecting Albert to come strolling up to me and say the sentence I used to dread: 'Yorkie, the gaffer wants to see you.' I probably even started working out what I was going to say before snapping out of it and remembering this was ten years later.

Anyway, after the game I caught up with the great man and he greeted me as warmly as ever and took me into the inner sanctum of his office where two bottles of wine were uncorked. One, of course, was for the rest of us; one for José Mourinho.

When one of Fergie's staff picked up José's bottle by mistake – God knows how much that wine had cost – the gaffer barked out in alarm, 'Hey – what do you think you're doing? The other one. The other one.'

We all burst out laughing. It was nice not to be on the end of that whiplash tongue. But it was even nicer to be given a ringside seat at such a privileged location. I would guess that, at that moment, just about every football fan in Europe would have loved to have been inside Fergie's office to watch his great adversary Mourinho bounce in, shake hands and begin the unmistakable banter between two great generals who fight and respect each other with equal force. The camaraderie between them was magical. It was my privilege to be there to witness it. One of the many rewards I like to think, of my career.

There is nothing that I cherish more than the respect of my teammates and the opposition. The fact that I was a welcome guest to such A-List conversation told me I had my old gaffer's respect. And that means everything.

At the end of May this year, I was on the main street in Alderley Edge with Naomi and little Orlando, holding my son's hand as I tried to reach into the car to retrieve some money. Orlando took this to be a sign that I was getting ready to leave, snatched his hand clear of mine and ran around the other side of the car – the road side. My heart leapt into my mouth and a shiver went through me.

Had a car been coming at that moment . . . well, it makes me shudder. I rushed around and swept up Orlando as quickly as I could. In that moment, I got a real sense of what Verlaine and Clint must have felt when they saw me flying under a car all those years ago, how my dear old mum must have fretted when someone rushed to tell her little Dwight had just been knocked over and was feared dead. A second later, a second earlier with Orlando . . . I have to stop myself from thinking of the consequences. But it was a reminder of just how precious and fragile our time here is.

Far too precious to be lost to bitterness and fighting.

I think we all should remember that, don't you?

CAREER ACHIEVEMENTS

31/08/2006 – 28/05/09
Sunderland   62 App   6 Goals

01/07/2005 – 31/08/2006
Sydney   21 App   7 Goals

31/08/2004 – 01/07/2005
Birmingham City   16 App   2 Goals

26/07/2002 – 31/08/2004
Blackburn Rovers   69 App   19 Goals

20/08/1998 – 26/07/2002
Manchester United   151 App   64   Goals

19/12/1989 – 20/08/1998
Aston Villa   288 App   97 Goals

01/08/1988 – 19/12/1989
Signal Hill (Tobago)

Honours

League Cup (1996)

FA Premier League (1998/1999, 1999/2000 and 2000/2001)

FA Cup (1999)

European Cup (1999)

International Level

Trinidad and Tobago   72 Caps   19 Goals

To date Dwight has been capped 72 official times for Trinidad and Tobago, but he has in fact played over 100 matches for Trinidad and Tobago that were not recognized as International friendlies.

Awards

Carling Player of the Year (1999)

Runner-up Professional Footballers' Association
    Player of the Year (1999)

ACKNOWLEDGEMENTS

Mine has been an incredible and eventful journey, and one I could never have travelled without the help of so many. Firstly, my family – you have made me who I am today. Words cannot express what that means to me.

To my 'Team of Life' in the UK – Tony Stephens, Simon Bayliff and Marie Priest – who have guided and advised me, and handled and nurtured my career. Tony, whose wisdom, knowledge and guidance have been life-changing. Simon, who carried the baton after Tony, you have advised me with confidence and reassurance through difficult times. The rest of the team at WMG who are there for me at the end of the phone, and of course, Marie, my invaluable PA and dear friend. I simply could not live without you.

Goodness knows what my finances would look like without the expert guidance of Suzanne Wallace.

I must also thank my housekeeper, Norma, and my gardener, Graham, for making sense of the Yorke household in England and for making sure I have always had a home to come back to, and not just a house.

From my earliest days in Tobago, I will always be indebted

to Bertille Sinclair, the father figure who saw and believed from early on and without whom I might never have started my journey. To my business advisors back home, Neil Wilson and Tim Nafiziger, for their continued support and advice.

Great friendships last forever and with that in mind, I am grateful to have had constantly by my side Kona Hislop, Russell Lapaty (the most talented footballer my homeland has ever produced), and Brian Lara, in my eyes the greatest batsman ever. Brian, thanks for a treasured friendship and for being an inspiration.

In football, I must mention my first manager in England, Graham Taylor, who decided to back a hunch all those years ago, and two figures at Manchester United who assumed a massive significance in my life. Sir Alex Ferguson gave me the opportunity of playing for one of the greatest teams in the world. I know at times you thought I wasn't listening to a word you said, but, honest, gaffer! I was! It just sometimes took a while to get through. I am grateful for all that you did and I will continue to respect you and look up to you for the rest of my life. Another debt is owed to Albert Morgan, who is to everyone at Old Trafford so much more than his 'kit-man' title suggests.

And the Birmingham crew of course. What adventures we shared! Bal, Yoga, Smally, Ugo, & Ritchie – the memories live on.

Finally, a big thank you goes to Martin Swain, who helped me with this project. He first interviewed me when I had just stepped off the plane to join Villa all those years ago, and I doubt he could have imagined the story that would follow. He has done me proud shaping the book at such short notice.